CRITICAL METHODS IN TERRORISM STUDIES

Edited by Priya Dixit and Jacob L. Stump

Routledge
Taylor & Francis Group

LONDON AND NEW YORK

First published 2016
by Routledge
2 Park Square, Milton Park, Abingdon, Oxon OX14 4RN

and by Routledge
711 Third Avenue, New York, NY 10017

Routledge is an imprint of the Taylor & Francis Group, an informa business

© 2016 selection and editorial material, Priya Dixit and Jacob L. Stump; individual chapters, the contributors

British Library Cataloguing-in-Publication Data
A catalogue record for this book is available from the British Library

Library of Congress Cataloging-in-Publication Data
Critical methods in terrorism studies / edited by Priya Dixit and Jacob L. Stump
pages cm
Includes bibliographical references and index.
1. Terrorism–Research–Methodology. 2. Terrorism–Study and teaching. I. Dixit, Priya. II. Stump, Jacob L.
HV6431.C7625 2015
363.325–dc23
2015000982

ISBN: 978-1-138-01871-6 (hbk)
ISBN: 978-1-138-01872-3 (pbk)
ISBN: 978-1-315-77726-9 (ebk)

Typeset in Bembo
by Cenveo Publishers Services

Printed and bound in the United States of America by Publishers Graphics, LLC on sustainably sourced paper.

CRITICAL METHODS IN TERRORISM STUDIES

Critical Methods in Terrorism Studies shows how to use a range of critical approaches to conduct research on terrorism.

Featuring the work of researchers who have already utilized these methods to study terrorism, it includes a diverse range of critical methodological approaches including discourse analysis, feminist, postcolonial, ethnographic, critical theory, and visual analysis of terrorism. The main objectives of the book are to assist researchers in adopting and applying various critical approaches to the study of terrorism. This goal is achieved by bringing together a number of different scholars working on the topic of terrorism from a range of non-variables-based approaches. Their individual chapters discuss explicitly the research methods used and methodological commitments made by the authors, while also illustrating the application of their particular critical perspective to the topic of terrorism. The authors of each chapter will discuss (1) why they chose their specific critical method; (2) how they justified their methodological stance; (3) how they conduct their research; and, finally, (4) an example of the research.

This book will be essential reading for students of terrorism studies and critical terrorism studies, and highly recommended for students of political violence, security studies and IR.

Priya Dixit is assistant professor at the Department of Political Science, Virginia Tech, USA.

Jacob L. Stump is assistant professor of political science at Shepherd University, USA.

CONTENTS

CONTRIBUTORS

Katherine E. Brown is a Lecturer in Defence Studies at King's College London. Her research is focused on counter-radicalization efforts, political Islam and gendered human security concerns from a critical feminist position. She has published widely on these issues, more details of which can be found at: http://www.kcl.ac.uk/sspp/departments/dsd/people/dsd-a-to-z/brown.aspx.

François Debrix is Director of the ASPECT programme and Professor of Political Science at Virginia Tech. He is the author, among other books, of *Tabloid Terror: War, Culture, and Geopolitics* (2008) and *Beyond Biopolitics: Theory, Violence, and Horror in World Politics* (2011).

Priya Dixit is an Assistant Professor of Political Science at Virginia Tech. Her research interests are critical security studies (especially terrorism), qualitative research methodologies (especially discourse analysis and ethnography) and critical theory in international relations. Currently, Priya is researching the role played by Gurkhas in global security, taking a historical and comparative approach.

Verena Erlenbusch is Assistant Professor of Philosophy at the University of Memphis. Her research lies at the intersection of political philosophy, the philosophy of law and continental philosophy. She is interested in Foucault's genealogical method, especially as it relates to phenomena like terrorism, race, power and violence.

Charlotte Heath-Kelly is a postdoctoral fellow at the Institute of Advanced Study, University of Warwick. Her monograph, *Politics of Violence: Militancy, International Politics, Killing in the Name* (2013), was shortlisted for the BISA Susan Strange book award. Recently, she has held a British Academy small grant and Warwick Research Fellowship to investigate the reconstruction of post-terrorist space and is preparing her second monograph.

Richard Jackson is Professor of Peace Studies at the University of Otago, New Zealand. He is the editor-in-chief of the journal *Critical Studies on Terrorism*. His research focuses on critical terrorism studies, the causes of war and pacifism. His latest book is a novel entitled *Confessions of a Terrorist* (2014).

Jonathan Joseph is Professor of International Relations at the University of Sheffield, UK. His publications include *The Social in the Global* (2012) and *Hegemony: A Realist Analysis* (2002). He has also edited a number of books, including *Scientific Realism and International Relations* (with Colin Wight, 2010). His current work is on resilience and the intersection of hegemony and governmentality.

David Maher is Lecturer in International Relations at the University of Salford, UK. His research investigates the links between political violence and economic development, particularly in the context of civil war and terrorism. David also analyses how processes of economic globalisation and US foreign policy affect armed conflict.

Caitlin Ryan is a Visiting Assistant Professor of International Relations at Ohio University. Her research interests are the relationships between power and resistance, and in how security and insecurity are experienced. She has conducted research in the West Bank of the Palestinian Territories and Liberia.

Yamuna Sangarasivam is an Associate Professor of Anthropology at Nazareth College. She engages her interdisciplinary training in musicology (University of Minnesota, Minneapolis), dance ethnology (University of California, Los Angeles) and cultural/political anthropology (Syracuse University) to inform her studies of terrorism, nationalism, resistance and the politics of race.

Alexander Spencer is an Assistant Professor at the Ludwig-Maximilians-University in Munich, Germany. He has published a book entitled *The Tabloid Terrorist: The Predictive Construction of New Terrorism in the Media* (2010), as well as articles in *Security Dialogue, International Studies Perspectives, Critical Studies on Terrorism* and *Critical Studies on Security*.

Jacob L. Stump is an Assistant Professor of Political Science at Shepherd University. He studies the social construction of danger, especially as it relates to terrorism.

Andrew Thomson is a lecturer at Queen's University Belfast, where he teaches on security and terrorism studies. His most recent publications focus on pro-government militias as well as paramilitary state terror in Colombia.

Harmonie Toros is Lecturer in International Conflict Analysis at the University of Kent, UK. She researches conflict transformation and terrorism studies. She has published extensively on critical approaches to terrorism, based on her fieldwork experiences. She has also written about legitimacy in terrorist conflicts. Her research focuses partly on talking as a conflict resolution approach, specifically when dealing with actors labelled as 'terrorists.'

ACKNOWLEDGEMENTS

This project follows on from our previous one and, like that one, couldn't have been conceptualised and completed without assistance from a great deal of people. We have both been fortunate over the years for the extremely supportive group of friends, family, colleagues and professional and social networks that have been invaluable for this project and in our lives.

These friends and colleagues are too many to name here but Priya would like to thank the Department of Political Science at Virginia Tech, especially her colleagues who have been supportive and helpful over this process. Gratitude, too, to the very helpful staff at the department. Jacob would also like to give a very special thanks to his daughters, Dora and Maomi, and their giggles and hugs. Shiera Malik has also been a constant source of support.

Of course, we are both grateful to the many authors who gave up their time and wrote chapters for this book – through their work and their writings, we can see the diversity and the growth of Critical Terrorism Studies. Without them, this book would not be possible.

LIST OF ABBREVIATIONS

AAA	American Anthropological Association
ACLU	American Civil Liberties Union
ASPECT	Alliance of Social, Political, Ethical, and Cultural Thought
BBC	British Broadcasting Corporation
CCR	Center for Constitutional Rights
CDA	critical discourse analysis
CIA	Central Intelligence Agency
CTS	critical terrorism studies
ELN	National Liberation Army (of Colombia)
FARC	Revolutionary Armed Forces of Colombia
FBI	Federal Bureau of Investigation
FDI	foreign direct investment
GDP	gross domestic product
HM	historical materialist
HTS	Human Terrain System
IDMC	Internal Displacement Monitoring Centre
IDP	internal displaced person
IMF	International Monetary Fund
IR	international relations
ITUC	International Trade Union Confederation
LTTE	Liberation Tigers of Tamil Eelam
NGO	non-governmental organization
oPt	occupied Palestinian territories
UNCTAD	UN Conference on Trade and Development
UNRWA	UN Refugee Works Agency

PART 1
Introduction

1

STUDYING TERRORISM AND PRACTICING CRITICISM

Jacob L. Stump and Priya Dixit

This introductory chapter accomplishes three basic tasks. The first is to locate this book in the context of the literature on terrorism, particularly what we call dissident literature that later became Critical Terrorism Studies. The second accomplishment of this introductory chapter is to briefly describe the contents of the book, focusing on the various ways that the chapters approach the topic of terrorism, what they argue, and the perspective they adopt. Third, this introductory chapter sketches out some of the implications of a number of themes raised by our authors for the production and dissemination of knowledge about terrorism.

The emergence of a dissident literature in the study of terrorism

The study of terrorism is one of the fastest growing areas of research with thousands of dissertations, reports, books, and articles published annually (Gordon 2004: 109). Yet the study of terrorism has been disparagingly called 'counterinsurgency masquerading as political science' (Schmid and Jongman, quoted by Jackson 2007b: 245). As a field of study, basic and largely unquestioned knowledge about terrorism is 'highly contestable and open to debate' and, Richard Jackson says, knowledge about terrorism 'functions ideologically to reinforce and reify existing structures of power in society' – such as the state (2009: 67).

Much of the knowledge about terrorism has been generated by a comparatively small group of scholars mostly in Western Europe and the United States. Ranstorp referred to this cluster of disciplinarily diverse researchers as an 'invisible college' of 'experts.' Since the mid-1970s, they have been pivotal in circulating information about terrorism, advising government officials and policy-makers, and speaking in the media. '[I]t is not surprising,' Ranstorp says, 'that there has been a relative absence of core debates and critical challenges of assumptions necessary to intellectually push the field forward with new waves of innovative research' (Ranstorp 2009: 19).

The invisible college, which has constituted the defining boundaries of the study of terrorism, has effectively limited the possibility for more critically inclined research to develop (Stump and Dixit 2013: 18).

At the same time, even as the field of terrorism studies as a whole has remained less than innovative when it comes to theoretical development, we argue that a theoretically, methodologically, and empirically diverse array of dissident literature began to emerge in the 1980s. This dissident literature in the study of terrorism mirrors other developments in other related disciplines such as international relations (IR) (see, for example, the 1990 special issue of *International Studies Quarterly*, 'Speaking the Language of Exile: Dissidence in International Studies'). While IR and the study of terrorism have largely remained estranged from each other, which can 'probably be attributed to the fact that many non-specialists are turned off by the political bias and analytical shallowness on offer' (Ranstorp 2009: 24), a dissident literature did arise nonetheless. It was far less formally institutionalized than in IR. Just the opposite – alternative voices in the study of terrorism mirrored the dispersed and multi-disciplinary background of the invisible college. While the invisible college limited the knowledge about terrorism – both what counted as important for research and how to go about doing the research – this emerging dissident scholarship diversified research concerns and methods. However, dissident studies of terrorism were peripheral to significant debates taking place within the study of terrorism defined by the invisible college and peripheral to debates taking place in IR, the social sciences, or humanities more generally. Unlike the invisible college, which became increasingly institutionalized in think tanks, academic positions, and peer reviewed and professional journals, the various dissident studies on terrorism remained atomized and exiled.

Despite this, a series of publications began to appear. These studies primarily focused on various aspects of state-based terrorism – that is, a focus on state violence targeting certain non-state groups and populations. This refocusing effectively challenged the predominant focus on non-state acts of violence carried out against sovereign states. Take Herman's book, *The Real Terror Network* (1982), as one early and important example of a dissident voice. Herman shifted his focus to state violence against populations. In empirically rich detail, he depicted a US foreign policy called Operation Condor: a set of military and economic linkages between the US and various National Security States in Latin America – such as Argentina, Bolivia, Brazil, Chile, Paraguay, and Uruguay. The state terrorism that Herman discusses consists of a coordinated system of surveillance and assassination carried out by domestic security services against groups deemed dissident and dangerous, especially domestic groups advocating Marxist, socialist, and democratic agendas.

Along similar lines, Lopez and Stohl's (1984: i) analysis of *The State as Terrorist* focused on the 'causes, consequences, and dynamics of that style of governance by force that has come to be known as state terror,' especially as it related to Latin America, the Philippines, and South Africa. A few years later, Herman and O'Sullivan (1989) analyzed the linkages between the US government, media corporations, and the growing number of 'terrorism experts.' They argued that this configuration of government agencies, individuals and media sites effectively shaped public opinion and knowledge related to terrorism, creating and sustaining a propagandistic cover or mask for US state terrorism. Around the same time, Perdue (1989) located state terrorism in a global political-economic-media context of domination and subjugation. He focused on a number of different modes of state terror: the terror of nuclear weapon states, racial terror in apartheid South Africa, settler terrorism in Israel and the Palestinian occupied territories, US supported state terrorism in Nicaragua, and so on.

Our point here is to highlight the burgeoning dissident literature taking shape in the 1980s, especially work focused on state-based terror targeting domestic and international populations. This vein of research remains rich and diverse, still focusing on a range of contexts, people, groups, and governmental institutions and policies (see, for example, George 1991; Sluka 1999; McSherry 2002; Selden and So 2004; Blakeley 2009; Jackson and Murphy 2011). In this book, one particularly fine example is Maher and Thomson's investigation of class antagonisms in Colombia, particularly the role of state terrorism in making possible and sustaining economic development that marginalizes the poor and working classes. Other chapters in this book that in different ways focus on state policies that terrorize certain populations of people include Joseph and Jackson's respective chapters illustrating Critical Discourse Analysis and Caitlin Ryan's chapter on women in the occupied Palestinian Territories.

During the 1980s, dissident voices developed in a variety of ways beyond the focus on state-based terrorism. Take for instance Wagner-Pacifici's (1986) book. She examines a wide range of public texts surrounding the kidnapping and murder of Aldo Moro (the former prime minister of Italy) by the Red Brigades in 1978. Notably, Wagner-Pacifici studies a non-state group's act of violence against former political leaders of a prominent Western state, which is a hallmark of the invisible college, but, alternatively, her study approaches the topic from an interesting new, theoretically and methodologically sophisticated angle. She conducts a dramaturgical analysis. To do this, Wagner-Pacifici drew from disciplines largely outside the regular repertoire of methods and methodological commitments sustained by the invisible college. Wagner-Pacifici cited work in sociology, symbolic anthropology, and literary criticism and she conceptualized terrorism – the actions depicted in the media, by political leaders, by members of the Red Brigades – as a social drama produced through the various public texts and their performance in social contexts.

Following in this interpretivist and effectively critical vein of analysis of terrorism were texts like Michael Taussig's (1991) seminal work on the terror associated with colonialism, shamanism and the violence connected with the use of indigenous labor to extract rubber from South America in the 1800s. Or books like Feldman's *Formations of Violence* (1991), which closely examined the relationship between political terror and the body in the context of Northern Ireland by drawing from political theorists like Lacan, Foucault, and Nietzsche. Similarly in the vein of dissident literature emerging in the 1990s were books like Oliverio's *The State of Terror* (1998). In it, she examines the mutually constitutive relationship between the state and terrorism, and how the discourse of terrorism can be deployed by political leaders and media sources to mask state-based violence and to highlight non-state violence.

Other significant interpretive pieces that appeared in this vein include Sangarasivam's (2001) excellent discussion of her experiences as an ethnographer in Sri Lanka, both in relation to her colleagues and to the state; Aretxaga's (2002) insightful analysis of terror as a militarily and discursively constructed national thrill that resolves domestic instability and doubt about US identity and purpose; and Gunning's (2004) analysis of the transformative and emancipatory possibilities of peace with Hamas.

In other words, along with the developing focus on state-based violence, there was also another strain of dissident literature. This strain drew from Continental social and political philosophy, postcolonialism, symbolic interactionism, and materialism, as well as ethnographic field work and interpretive reading approaches. By the late 1990s and early 2000s, dissident voices deployed a rich field of methodological commitments, theoretical lenses, and methods of analysis to study the topic of terrorism.

The world political events that collectively came to be known as '9/11' or 'September 11' marked an important shift in the development of the dissident study of terrorism. The topic of terrorism became a 'growth industry' (Smyth *et al.* 2008: 1) for writers, researchers, and university teachers; this includes the more critically inclined approaches to the topic. By 2008, it was clear to several analysts studying the topic of terrorism that it had

> become one of the most powerful signifiers in contemporary discourse. It is a term that generates vast amounts of social and political activity, induces powerful emotions and, though a vast array of social practices, constitutes a legal and political subject, a cultural taboo, a myth and an object of fear, hatred, surprise, administration, 'entertainment' and identity. (Smyth *et al.* 2008: 1)

It was out of this post-'September 11' context that Jackson (2005) published his book, *Writing the War on Terrorism*. In it, he closely examines the public language deployed by the Bush administration to justify the 'war on terrorism' to an American audience. He convincingly explains how rhetoric worked to normalize and institutionalize a violent and militaristic foreign policy – entailing multiple wars, military interventions, and torture.

Shortly thereafter, by 2006, the first gestures toward a more defined and reflexively aware *critical* study of terrorism became institutionally sedimented – especially with the establishment of a Critical Studies on Terrorism Working Group within the British International Studies Association, the organization of a conference ('Is It Time For a Critical Terrorism Studies?') and a published symposium in the journal *European Political Science*. This symposium made the case for a critical approach to terrorism (Jackson 2007a: 225–7), emphasized the role of state terror (Blakeley 2007: 228–35), identified the core commitments of such a research project (Jackson 2007a: 244–51), sketched out a critical research agenda (Smyth 2007: 260–7), highlighted the significance of emancipatory politics (McDonald 2007: 252–9), and reflected on the limits and problems associated with a critical approach (2007: 236–43). A new peer review academic journal, *Critical Studies on Terrorism*, came online in 2007. Richard Jackson, a founding editor of the journal, also published a short online piece that further justified the need for a critical approach to terrorism (2008) and he was also the lead editor of *Critical Terrorism Studies: A New Research Agenda* (Jackson *et al.* 2009), which outlines and critiques the predominant and orthodox approaches to terrorism and begins to sketch out what research in this new critical vein could look like.

Since then, a number of books, articles, and debates have been published that expand on various areas of the rather new and quickly developing area of study. Critical Terrorism Studies (CTS), a Routledge press series, for instance, started in 2009 and by the end of 2014 will have published nearly 20 books. These texts have primarily focused on introducing the field, conceptual and theoretical development, and empirical investigations of terrorism and terrorism-related issues in a variety of different contexts.

With all of this activity, comparatively little ink has focused on the methods of CTS, or how to systematically do this kind of research. Stump and Dixit (2013), seeing this gap in the literature, introduced students to the nuts and bolts of methods for studying terrorism from a more critical persuasion. This volume connects in with that endeavor: to have accomplished researchers describe how they came to adopt a critical mode of inquiry into terrorism, to describe their particular method and perspective, and to illustrate their approach with empirical examples. Our initial attempt was to provide a review of critical methodologies and outline critical tools that exist in the study of terrorism; this volume gives space to a diverse range of scholars who have used critical tools and outlines their ways of studying terrorism critically.

This book is about doing critical terrorism studies, about researchers putting methodologies and methods to work, applying them to some set of texts, some bits of data, some field site or field of inquiry. In this vein, there is a wide spectrum of approaches that, in a variety of ways, critically study terrorism. These authors' works are informed by different places, different histories, different experiences, and different ways of relating to and making sense of the world. As such, the chapters in this volume draw on different logics and they use different methods to gather up information and to analyze, explain, understand, critique, and interpret that information – and perhaps aligning with others to emancipate some person or group, or intervene in some way in some political matter relating to their study of terrorism. This book gestures toward a plurality of critical approaches studying terrorism and, moreover, it creates a space for the authors to explicitly reflect on their methodologies and methods.

Doing critical terrorism studies

In different ways, these chapters each reflect on their research tradition and methods and how they are applied to concrete examples. They illustrate the diversity and transdisciplinarity of dissident modes of terrorism studies. Subsequently, this section is organized to highlight the variety of methodologies and methods used to study the topic of terrorism that are illustrated in this book.

Take Chapter 3 by Maher and Thomson who focus on state terrorism in Colombia. Drawing from Marx's materialist conception of history and closely examining a single case study, Maher and Thomson do a detailed process-tracing that provides a class-based explanation of violent attempts to contest and stabilize political and economic structures. Maher and Thomson argue that the state's perpetration of violence against poor and working-class people has created opportunities for both domestic and foreign capital to expand. The Colombian state has forcibly displaced poor people, cleared and developed spaces that the poor once inhabited, and systematically targeted armed and unarmed groups that oppose state intervention and capitalistic development. They conceptualize terroristic violence as a specific kind of tactic used by state and non-state actors; it is dialectically entwined with capitalistic development and neoliberal globalization. As their chapter shows, historical materialism is particularly useful at explaining and critiquing state terrorism and elite domination of the poor and working classes and detailing the interconnections between terrorism and capitalism.

In contrast to the class-based analyses of Maher and Thomson, Jonathan Joseph and Richard Jackson reflect on Critical Discourse Analysis in their respective Chapters 2 and 6. CDA entails a focus on the relationship between discursive representations and social processes and practices. The critical aim of such a research perspective is to closely investigate how representations are socially consequential and how powerful social practices can warp discursive representations and have negative consequences for people's lives.

While both Joseph's and Jackson's respective chapters employ CDA and focus their analyses on the relationship between discursive representations and social processes, there are also some important differences between their approaches. Most clearly, perhaps, are their differences in methodological positioning, or the philosophical foundations that inform their perspective. Jackson, for instance, has made the case for a 'minimal foundationalist' perspective, which conceptualizes the label 'terrorism' as a social construct that is historically contingent and relevant to understanding and responding to certain kinds of violence associated with the present historical moment (2011). Joseph, however, works from a comparatively different methodology, one that adopts a more maximal foundationalist perspective. Such an approach emphasizes the extra-discursive over the discursive and thus works to critique how certain extra-discursive processes produce and interact with discursive representations of terrorism and counter-terrorism (Joseph 2009). Because Maher and Thomson's chapter works from a historical materialist perspective that also emphasizes the extra-discursive almost exclusively over the discursive, Joseph's particular discussion and application of CDA seemed to fit less well under the heading of discourse analysis. Nonetheless, Jackson and Joseph's respective chapters use the same method of analysis (CDA), but approach the method from a comparatively different angle, which we discuss here.

Take Jackson's chapter first. In his particular approach to CDA, Jackson emphasizes the discursivity of terrorism 'as an empty signifier' constructed through 'language usage and social practice.' Extra-discursive features of the social world can have causal impact, but Jackson 'takes reasons as causes,' where 'norms and rules structure or constitute – that is, "cause" –' interpersonal and institutional doings.

After laying out his approach, Jackson discusses the key findings of his wide body of research related to the war on terror – especially during the Bush administration. Among other politically significant topics, Jackson investigated the rhetorical processes through which the Iraq war and the torture of prisoners were justified by political leaders. In his chapter, Jackson reflexively sketches out how he came to use CDA, the specific methods and conceptual tools he employs, and the challenges of this approach in the critical study of terrorism. With CDA, Jackson has worked to 'deconstruct and challenge the core narratives of the war on terror, especially those that have directly resulted in human rights abuses' by Britain and the United States.

Similarly, Joseph focuses on UK anti-terrorism policy, particularly the implementation of the *CONTEST: The United Kingdom's Strategy for Countering Terrorism* document. Combining CDA with Foucault and Gramsci, Joseph describes the types of texts that he searches for, his process for selecting texts, and the analytical tools that he employs to examine them – looking for 'convergences of position, consistency of message, conflicts among statements and so on.' In the example Joseph depicts, he argues that the policy document 'constructs subjectivity in a certain way while promoting strategies that attempt to govern people from a distance.' This means that social cohesion is sustained through representations of 'us' positioned in a relation of risk and vulnerability to a 'radicalized other' who is 'Muslim' and threatening, and sustained through strategically implemented social practices that have negative consequences on Muslims in the UK. In particular, these anti-terrorist policies limit the availability of public subjectivities of Muslims (either as moderate or extremist), frame Muslims as of instrumental value to government security operations, and increase a sense of local suspicion among Muslim communities of the government's anti-terrorism strategy. The strategy governance represented in the CONTEST document, Joseph says, 'works through the pretense of being helpful and solving problems, while containing an underlying authoritarianism which leaves little choice as to whether this is really necessary or whether alternative options are available.' Such state strategies also normalize relations between the state and (majority) society against others, often minorities and those depicted as different.

While conceptualizing terrorism as a social construction constituted through discourse, Alexander Spencer in Chapter 7 moves away from CDA and the historical materialism of Maher and Thomson. After describing the history and political significance of metaphors and their analysis, Spencer sketches out an approach to the study of terrorism that treats terrorism as a metaphor linked to other metaphors in popular discourse. That is, Spencer examines how terrorism has been described in various ways (as '"war," "crime," "uncivilized evil," and "disease" respectively') between 2001 and 2005 in the German newspaper, *Bild*. This ongoing linking of metaphors in public discourse is the process through which terrorism (and other going concerns) is constituted as a threat to security. Critically, Spencer shows how this constitutive process functions to authorize certain modes of security and counter-terrorist policy as commonsensical – such as constituting military means as the only intelligible response to actions and individuals described as 'terrorists' while foreclosing alternative responses.

Still in terms of discourse, in Chapter 8 Erlenbusch approaches the topic of terrorism from a different angle. Focusing on the historical conditions surrounding the emergence and use of the word terrorism, she draws on Foucault's and Wittgenstein's insights. For Erlenbusch, the meaning of terrorism is entirely contextual, or part of a 'historical-political rationality'; it is a label 'given to variable discursive and non-discursive practices whose meaning is determined within a network of concepts, ideologies, interests, and rationalities.' Instead of popular newspapers or contemporary political elite discourse, her focus of analysis is on the words and actions of revolutionary French political leaders and how they deployed the label of terror. She argues that in revolutionary France, there were four different meanings associated with terrorism and each meaning constituted certain institutionally situated subjectivities. The critical aim of her approach is to illustrate the historically contingent and variable meaning of terrorism, which, critically, helps 'to undercut the determinism of ahistorical and essentialist accounts of terrorism and develop more productive ways of thinking about violence' in the present.

All of the approaches discussed thus far have primarily focused on gathering and analyzing textual-based data, such as governmental and non-governmental organization documents, political speeches, and newspapers. Other chapters in this book illustrate the value of fieldwork and the ethnographic sensibility in particular. These chapters, by focusing on the experiences and meanings generated by terrorists and other politically marginalized actors, also resurrect subaltern and subjugated knowledges but do so in slightly different ways to those which analyze textual representations.

Take Chapter 5 by Yamuna Sangarasivam as an example. She conceptualizes terrorism as a site or place defined by local and global histories, but also set within the broader cultural context of US imperialism. She looks closely at the relationship between Tamil nationalism (as embodied by the Liberation Tigers of Tamil Eelam) and the Sri Lankan government's construction of the nationalist group as a terrorist organization. Drawing on documents, participant observation, and interviews, Sangarasivam puts together a set of vignettes that illustrate the production of transnational and transcultural subjectivities, like Tamil national identity and the terrorist. Found in the place of terrorism, she argues, are enduring racial and religious inequalities. Sangarasivam reflects on the implications of the embeddedness of the researcher in these inequalities and how the production of knowledge about terrorists and terrorism are constitutive of the global war on terror.

In Chapter 4, Harmonie Toros also adopts an ethnographic sensibility, but instead of anthropology she combines it with a psychological orientation toward person-centered therapy and the Frankfurt School's Critical Theory. The result is an 'empathetic ethnographic approach' that adopts an 'unconditional positive regard' toward the research co-participants who are labeled as terrorists – accepting them as whole individuals composed of violent and non-violent potentials, negative and positive emotions. There are emotional and research-based issues to navigate. Toros discusses a 'fieldwork crisis' or the difficulty of developing an empathetic connection with someone who has killed other people in conflict. Her research goal, nonetheless, is to investigate the role of conversation in triggering empathetic and humanized relations toward those labeled terrorist. To illustrate her approach, Toros depicts fieldwork conducted in Northern Ireland where she interviewed and held meetings involving participant observation between loyalists and republican former and current paramilitaries. Critically, Toros argues that such an approach 'may produce knowledge that challenges established "truths" about terrorism and political violence, about actors engaged in such violence, and how it may be transformed.' The fieldwork experiences of Toros and others in the book explicate how resistance is often part of everyday actions and daily life, a point made clear by Ryan in Chapter 9 as well.

Caitlin Ryan conducted field work and interviews with Palestinian women in the occupied West Bank, with an emphasis on the women's lives and experiences and the ongoing conflict. Moved by an 'inherent discomfort with the prevailing international perception that the Palestinian "other" is not to be trusted, taken seriously, or valued, because she/he is a "terrorist,"' Ryan draws on Edward Said and Frantz Fanon. The reflexive postcolonial methodology that she discusses in the chapter critiques conventional ways of studying terrorism and highlights a myriad of ways in which Israeli 'counter-terrorism' has been experienced in daily life. She directs the reader's attention to the relationship between the processes of policy categorization – e.g. Palestinians as dangerous 'others' – and people's lives. In critical response to the asymmetric power relations, confusions, and insecurities, Ryan presents a subaltern narrative of resistance in Palestine that is accented by depictions of the daily insecurity experienced and represented by Palestinian people.

In Chapter 11 on 'Talking about Revolution: Ex-Militant Testimony and Conditions of "Tellability,"' Charlotte Heath-Kelly uses interviews with Italian and Cypriot persons who had waged armed campaigns to overturn British colonial rule, and she reflects on her own experiences and choices to pursue a critical approach. Heath-Kelly sketches out a poststructuralist feminist methodology. Her focus is on the relationship between what can and cannot be said and when. In particular, Heath-Kelly depicts how storytellers compose in the present a sensible story of their past 'militant' actions. Reflecting on the changing meanings of words in the interviewees' stories, such as 'victory,' 'defeat,' and 'war,' Heath-Kelly argues that a 'close inspection of militant violence and its subsequent tell-ability can help us to expose the constitution of illusory foundations for political authority, and the other histories which are silenced to give the appearance of coherence to the dominant narrative.'

Another chapter that sketches out a feminist perspective is Chapter 10 by Katherine E. Brown, 'Marginality as a Feminist Research Method in Terrorism and Counter-Terrorism Studies.' She first traces out the history of marginality and its application in research, noting: 'By considering women's position in terrorism and counter-terrorism, it is possible to see more on the page of international relations.' By drawing from an extensive set of examples from a diverse range of sources, Brown foregrounds work that explicitly focuses on women's experiences and (generally) notes how woman are marginalized in traditional research on terrorism.

Further, she illustrates how (and when) women refuse to acknowledge their marginal positioning and the implications of such a refusal. Critically, Brown argues that marginality is a feminist research position that can be used to understand and explain the meanings of terrorism in varying contexts, and from this feminist position she critiques the sociopolitical structures and institutions that compose orthodox Terrorism Studies and ignore the marginal and the everyday.

The last two chapters shift their focus away from written texts and ethnographic experiences. In Chapters 12 and 13 respectively Cynthia Weber and François Debrix engage with visual culture in the context of the US war on terror. Debrix's chapter reflects on the iconography of terror. The visual is conceptualized as both a site for analysis and a tool for illustrating questions about modernity and ethics, questions which are often made invisible in the practices of terrorism and counter-terrorism. The chapter does not analyze a series of images in order to note their political or ideological underpinnings. Rather, Debrix uses visual depictions of events commonly labeled terrorism to interrogate contemporary American under-standings of the 'war on terror.' In particular, he directs the reader's attention to the practices that underlie visual illustrations of dead, injured, and dying bodies, or what he calls: 'Falling Bodies.' Debrix critically argues that these icons serve to constitute specific meanings of the sovereign state and the terrorist and their relationships to society – the state that 'rescues' people and the terrorists who have no respect for human lives. These visuals of bodies and the war on terror served to legitimate state practices that violently and coercively target those labeled terrorists and other threats deemed significant.

Finally, a conversation between Priya Dixit and Cynthia Weber on film and terrorism rounds out the section on visual culture. They talk about Weber's use of visuals in response to the 'war on terror,' especially her thoughts on the practice of filming and her 13 short films, *I Am an American*. By allowing for different modes of depiction, including motion and color, Weber says that research questions can be answered filmically. In contrast to textual representations, film creates more possi-bilities by enabling the film-maker different and often more affective depictions of emotions and images. The practice of filming other persons raises a number of issues, which Weber reflects on. In particular, she says that filming prioritizes the question of 'whose point of view' is being visualized, and it highlights the question of 'the ethics of looking.' These two points are important because the act of filming constitutes certain kinds of subjects and positions them within the context of the 'war on terror.' It is an act that gives voice and agency to the film-maker and the participants beyond the possibilities of written text. Critically, Weber says, a film or novel 'can move you to feel something,' they can 'implant a question in you, implant a doubt. It can move you emotionally and move you to action.'

So, the chapters in this book illustrate a variety of ways to study terrorism critically, from different methodological perspectives to different sources of information and different methods of analysis. CTS has historically been and, we argue, should con-tinue to be an undertaking composed of multifarious possibilities – all of which offer interesting, theoretically and methodologically sophisticated analyses of terrorism.

Knowing terrorism

> Knowledge of the social world, as opposed to knowledge of nature, is at the bottom of what I have been calling interpretation: it acquires the status of knowledge by various means, some of them intellectual, many of them social and even political. Interpretation is first of all a form of making: that is, it depends on the willed intentional activity of the human mind, molding and forming the objects of its attention with care and study. Such an activity takes place perforce in a specific time and place and is engaged in by a specifically located individual, with a specific background, in a specific situation, for a particular series of ends … it will be evident that such unscientific nuisances as feelings, habits, conventions, associations, and values are an intrinsic part of any interpretation. (Said 1981: 155–6)

Said's words here succinctly summarize the aims and goals of an interpretive project such as ours: the social constructionist ethos, taking social practices and texts as foundational to meaning-making, and the reflexive orientation of the critical terrorism researcher. Said also directs attention to context and emphasizes knowledge-production and formation is a situated action. It is situated in the sense of being within particular cultures, whether this is the governmental culture that produced official texts, the media that frames 'terrorists' in particular ways or 'the field' where daily lives of people play out. The knowledge produced by the various chapters here are also 'situated' in the sense that they are part of the researcher's own actions and subjectivity and their own interests in asking particular questions in the first place.

But the implications of Said's words go beyond this – just before the paragraph quoted here, he describes how knowledge about the Middle East in the West has always been filtered through the lens of colonialism, wherein one party (those doing the representing, writing, and communicating) exerts power over those being depicted (people, actions, spaces in the Middle East). This is paralleled by scholarship on terrorism wherein the 'invisible college' set the terms for what counted as terrorism research and who would be appropriate subjects of such scholarship. As we discussed earlier, there has been a long history of dissident scholarship that challenges this practice but the institutional and government links, especially in the United States, remain dense in the post-9/11 era as well. In other words, many terrorism scholars enjoy close relationships with power – the power of the state in the United States for many. This can be problematic in terms of producing knowl-edge about terrorism, especially in terms of determining what knowledge counts as knowledge in the first place. It can also be problematic as the questions asked and the research then conducted is filtered through the interests of the state. Similar to Said's claim about imperialism and colonialism framing particular modes of knowledge production, the ways in which knowledge of terrorism becomes such are themselves situated within specific cultural, economic, class, and racial contexts. However, when the knowledge becomes popularized, such situatedness is unac-knowledged and silenced.

How do we produce knowledge of terrorism? None of the chapters in this text purport to test hypotheses, measure variables or make necessary and sufficient causal claims about terror, terrorists, or terrorism. Rather, the knowledges produced by the methodologies and methods displayed in this book's chapters are informed by a variety of different epistemologies. The chapters illustrate historical materialism's emphasis on class antagonism and dialectics, discursive epistemologies that focus on the construction of meaning and its interaction with social processes and institutions, experiential knowledge of postcolonial and nationalistic politics and social processes, knowledge of postcolonial and nationalistic politics and social processes, feminist standpoint epistemology of the marginalized, de-colonial knowledges of subjugated populations, and filmically depicted stories of ordinary people. We hope to show that knowledge of terrorism can be produced through a number of methodological perspectives and by using a number of methods of information-gathering and analysis.

Similarly, this book does not attempt to provide a definitive definition of terror, terrorists, or terrorism, even though attempting to define terrorism and debate its ultimate and/or contingent features is a rather common practice. Just the opposite – each of the chapters conceptualizes terror, terrorists, and terrorism differently: conceptualizations range from a state and non-state tactic of violence bound up with capitalistic development, to terrorism as a metaphor or empty signifier, to an ethnographic site of colonial encounters, racial inequality, and violence. These respective conceptualizations of terrorism, we argue, should be thought of as analytical tools that are more or less useful at explaining, critiquing, or changing the social and political world in which we live. Following Stump and Dixit (2013: 8), 'a single, unified definition that claims to capture the total substance of terrorism or even the minimum foundation of terrorism is not required to study the practice of terrorism from a critical perspective.'

Returning to Said at the end of this introduction, it is worthwhile pointing out his caution that knowledge can and has been used as a tool for influence and domination, that particular 'regimes of truth' are produced and become entrenched over time, thus categorizing 'terrorism' as a non-state activity (for example) while states remain exempt from being defined as 'terrorist.' The task of critical scholarship, especially interpretivist methods and methodologies, is to expose these regimes of truth, to outline the ways in which the dominant modes of knowledge-production remain so and to centralize resistance. But, as the chapters that follow indicate, this dismantling of regimes of truth is not an easy task. For many of the authors in the pages that follow, their journey to a critical ethos began with realizing that the question they were asking was (a) often not deemed a legitimate or a researchable question in International Relations/terrorism studies and (b) that the available methods were unable to help them answer their specific research question. This, of course, exposes the hegemonic ways in which research on terrorism is conducted – the questions that are allowed (and others that are disallowed) and the methods that are deemed appropriate. Our book and the authors who have contributed their works here challenge this hegemony and begin dismantling the existing 'regime of truth.' As such, they (and we) see this volume as an ongoing step towards transforming the terrorism studies research project.

References

Aretxaga, B. (2002) 'Terror as thrill: first thoughts on the "war on terrorism,"' *Anthropological Quarterly*, 75 (1): 139–50.

Blakeley, R. (2007) 'Bringing the state back into terrorism studies,' *European Political Science*, 6 (3): 228–35

Blakeley, R. (2009) *State Terrorism and Neoliberalism: The North in the South*. New York: Routledge.

Feldman, A. (1991) *Formations of Violence: The Narrative of the Body and Political Terror in Northern Ireland*. Chicago: University of Chicago Press.

George, A. L. (1991) *Western State Terrorism*. Hoboken, NJ: Blackwell.

Gordon, A. (2004) *The Status of Terrorism in the Academy: Comparative Aspects and the Role of Periodicals*. PhD thesis, University of Haifa.

Gunning, J. (2004) 'Peace with Hamas? The transforming potential of political participation,' *International Affairs*, 80 (2): 233–55.

Herman, E. S. (1982) *The Real Terror Network: Terrorism in Fact and Propaganda*. Boston: South End Press.

Herman, E. and O'Sullivan, G. (1989) *The 'Terrorism' Industry: The Experts and Institutions That Shape Our View of Terrorism*. New York: Pantheon.

Jackson, R. (2005) *Writing the War on Terrorism: Language, Politics and Counterterrorism*. Manchester and New York: Manchester University Press.

Jackson, R. (2007a) 'Introduction: the case for critical terrorism studies,' *European Political Science*, 6: 225–7.

Jackson, R. (2007b) 'The core commitments of critical terrorism studies,' *European Political Science*, 6 (3): 244–51.

Jackson, R. (2008) 'Why we need critical terrorism studies,' *E-International Relations*. Online at: http://www.e-ir.info/2008/04/08/why-we-need-critical-terrorism-studies/ (accessed 24 May 2014).

Jackson, R. (2009) 'Knowledge, power and politics in the study of political terrorism', in R. Jackson, M. B. Smyth, and J. Gunning (eds), *Critical Terrorism Studies: A New Research Agenda*. New York: Routledge.

Jackson, R. (2011) 'In defense of "terrorism": finding a way through a forest of misconceptions,' *Behavioral Science of Terrorism and Political Aggression*, 3: 116–30.

Jackson, R., Murphy, E., and Poynting, S. (eds) (2010) *Contemporary State Terrorism: Theory and Practice*. New York: Routledge.

Jackson, R., Smyth, M. B., and Gunning, J. (eds) (2009) *Critical Terrorism Studies: A New Research Agenda*. New York: Routledge.

Jackson, R., Jarvis, L., Gunning, J., and Smyth, M. B. (2012) *Terrorism: A Critical Introduction*. New York: Palgrave Macmillan.

Joseph, J. (2009) 'Critical of what? Terrorism and its study,' *International Relations*, 23: 93–8.

Lopez, G. and Stohl, M. (1984) *The State as Terrorist: The Dynamics of Governmental Violence and Repression*. Westport, CT: Praeger.

McDonald, M. (2007) 'Emancipation and critical terrorism studies,' *European Political Science*, 6: 252–9.

McSherry, J. P. (2002) 'Tracking the origins of a state terror network,' *Latin American Perspectives*, 29 (1): 38–60.

Oliverio, A. (1998) *The State of Terror*. Albany, NY: State University of New York.

Purdue, W. D. (1989) *Terrorism and the State: A Critique of Domination Through Fear*. Westport, CT: Praeger.

Ranstorp, M. (2009) 'Mapping terrorism studies after 9/11: an academic field of old problems and new prospects,' in R. Jackson, M. B. Smyth, and J. Gunning (eds),

Critical Terrorism Studies: A New Research Agenda. New York and Oxford: Routledge, pp. 13–34.

Said, E. W. (1981) *Covering Islam: How the Media and the Experts Determine How We See the Rest of the World.* New York: Pantheon.

Sangarasivam, Y. (2001) 'Researcher, informant, "assassin," me', *Geographical Review*, 91: 95–104.

Selden, M. and So, A. Y. (2003) *War and State Terrorism: The United States, Japan, and the Asia-Pacific in the Long Twentieth Century.* New York: Rowman & Littlefield.

Sluka, J. (1999) *Death Squad: The Anthropology of State Terror.* Philadelphia: University of Pennsylvania Press.

Smyth, M. B. (2007) 'A critical research agenda for the study of political terror,' *European Political Science*, 6: 260–7.

Smyth, M. B., Gunning, J., Jackson, R., Kassimeris, G., and Robinson, P. (2008) 'Symposium: critical terrorism studies – an introduction,' *Critical Terrorism Studies*, 1 (1): 1–4.

Stump, J. L. and Dixit, P. (2013) *Critical Terrorism Studies: An Introduction to Research Methods.* New York: Routledge.

Taussig, M. T. (1991) *Shamanism, Colonialism and the Wild Man: A Study in Terror and Healing.* Chicago: University of Chicago.

Wagner-Pacifici, R. E. (1986) *The Moro Morality Play: Terrorism as Social Drama.* Chicago: University of Chicago Press.

PART 2

Critical Realism/ Materialism

2

READING DOCUMENTS IN THEIR WIDER CONTEXT

Foucauldian and realist approaches to terrorism discourse

Jonathan Joseph

I came to critical realism when thinking about a PhD and considering the best way to approach Gramsci's work. In the end I came to the conclusion that critical realism offered the best explanation of the relationship between structure and agency, something that is obviously central to Gramsci's work, but which is often confused with philosophical arguments for and against objectivity. I wrote a PhD in a philosophy department, focusing on the concept of hegemony while drawing out the distinction between objective, subjective, and intersubjective accounts of social interaction. This work later came out as Hegemony: A Realist Analysis *(London: Routledge, 2002).*

Critical realism was important in my thinking about the 'real' world and its independence from human understanding. It was also useful as a tool for shaping my consideration of different theoretical accounts of the social world. This helped me when I switched to international relations and it was relatively easy to negotiate my way around the theoretical field that is IR. However, I because increasingly frustrated at being seen by others as a meta-theorist. When looking at how the concept of hegemony applies to IR, I found myself criticising the philosophical assumptions of neo-Gramscian theory rather than looking at real social practices. Consequently, I turned to the question of how international governance actually happens.

At this point I found that Foucauldian work provided a better account of the fine detail of governance than did the overly general Gramscian approaches. It also offered a block to the overly subjective tendencies in Gramscian work. Hegemony was better at accounting for the general social conditions, while governmentality better described the outcomes. The Foucauldians in IR were not happy with this combination, but my challenge to them is to account for the conditions of possibility for governmentality and why it should come to prominence in the first place. In The Social in the Global: Social Theory, Governmentality and Global Politics *(Cambridge: Cambridge University, Press 2012) I combined the two approaches while looking at a range of documents produced by the World Bank and European Union.*

I continue this approach in the piece below. Of course relying on the study of documents is not always reliable which is why I use realist, Gramscian and Foucauldian arguments about the social conditions of their production. The crucial point then is that the question of how to read documents is intimately connected to the question of how to conceptualise the wider social context.

This chapter will explore the relationship between the method of discourse analysis, the Foucauldian approach to governance and critical realist arguments about metatheory. It does so through application to UK anti-terrorism policy and will focus on the document *CONTEST: The United Kingdom's Strategy for Countering Terrorism* which was presented to Parliament in 2011. It analyses some of the main ideas in the document, and in particular it is concerned with the way the document constructs subjectivity in a certain way while promoting strategies that attempt to govern people from a distance. It does not attempt to employ a sophisticated discursive or linguistic analysis of the text. But by briefly exploring the method of critical discourse analysis (CDA) it does attempt to look at discursive devices which frame the discussion of counter-terrorism in their wider social context. In keeping with this approach, the analysis is more concerned with *why* such framing devices are in operation. This pushes the analysis outwards rather than inwards, looking at the relationship between discourse and the wider political context. Although I employ Foucault's governmentality approach to do this, I conclude by emphasising the need to go beyond the poststructuralist focus on discourses and practices in order to better explain how and why they come about.

The UK government approach to terrorism is divided into four strategies – pursue, prevent, protect and prepare. In particular we are concerned with the 'prepare' component of the strategy. Elsewhere I have noted the promotion of preparedness through the idea of resilience in the UK's National Security Strategy (Joseph 2013). Looking for similarities across strategy and policy documents is a useful way to build up a picture of dominant discourses and strategies. There are different ways of doing this. One fundamental distinction is between using CDA and its underpinning critical realist philosophy versus taking a more poststructuralist or constructivist stance. Critical realism maintains that there is a real world 'out there' that is independent but open to investigation. Therefore it distinguishes between knowledge or discourse and the reality that this discourse is about. It charges poststructuralism and constructivism with the error of conflating knowledge and the real world or denying the distinction between them. Furthermore, critical realism and CDA, unlike some poststructuralist and constructivist approaches, go beyond the 'how' to look at 'why' things happen and suggests that the 'why' involves strategies that cannot be reduced to what is imminent in the texts or practices, but resides in the relation between discursive practices and underlying social relations, something that I will explore in conclusion. Nevertheless, it is worth highlighting now that I believe that is it possible to draw on a governmentality approach to explain counter-terrorism strategy without accepting the poststructuralist assumptions that usually accompany it. Indeed, I argue that while governmentality helps us understand counter-terrorism *strategy*, a realist approach that highlights underlying social relations helps us better understand governmentality.

Looking beyond the text also better reveals its contradictions by showing how the ideas contained in certain documents are undermined in practice. The promotion of resilience in counter-terrorism discourse is in keeping with other areas of policy. But in actuality, it is undermined by a values-based strategy of community intervention as well as heavy-handed policing and practices of surveillance. In highlighting these contradictions, a realist-informed CDA can potentially show how such policies might be challenged.

Method: critical discourse analysis

Discourse analysis focuses on such things as the production of meaning and the constitution of subjects, objects and identities. Critical discourse analysis (CDA) is most closely associated with the work of Norman Fairclough (1992, 1995) while in critical terrorism studies (CTS) it is most associated with Richard Jackson (2005). CDA, as the name implies, is critical of the processes by which meaning and identities are produced. This means, for example, criticising the normalising role of discourse in that it presents things in certain ways, neutralises certain meanings, excludes possible alternatives or claims things to be commonsensible and widely accepted.

CDA is also distinguishable in the sense that it attempts to locate discourse in a wider social and historical context. In other words, unlike certain poststructuralist approaches to the study of language and meaning, CDA does not believe that our experience of the world is limited to the realm of discourse and that there is nothing, so to speak, outside of the text. In one of his earlier works Fairclough outlines how he see texts and discourses as instances of socio-cultural practice. Adapting Foucault, he defines discourse as an ordered set of discursive practices associated with a particular social domain or institution (Fairclough 1995: 12). But drawing on Gramsci, he highlights how power relations control and constrain productivity and creativity in discursive practices and he raises the issue of how a stable configuration of discursive practice (an order of discourse) might be produced (Fairclough 1995: 2).

CDA is distinctive, therefore, in its linking of the production of meaning to a wider context beyond the discourse itself, and how it highlights such issues as the social reproduction of power relations. This gives CDA a realist character insofar as it points to a real world beyond our discursive understanding of it. Such a position is seen in contrast to poststructuralist approaches that draw on Foucault (see, for example, Stump and Dixit 2013: 109). This is, however, somewhat unfair to Foucault. Unlike Derrida, Foucault places more emphasis on practices rather than discourse. And he argues that the task of archaeology is to reveal the relations between discursive formations and non-discursive domains such as institutions, political events and economic processes (Foucault 1989: 162; see also Joseph 2004). So with both approaches claiming to be studying an array of discursive and non-discursive practices, the issue is probably more connected to the question of focus and critique. In this respect, CDA is certainly more explicit about its critical component and does not shy away from a focus on forms of domination and ideological distortion in the way that more poststructuralist approaches might. CDA is realist in the sense that it draws a distinction between actual social relations and the representations and understandings we have of them, and is critical in the sense that it suggests these representations and understandings may be distorted by power relations within society. For example, deep-rooted class relations within a society produce particular forms of class consciousness. In recent years there has been a decline in such consciousness which does not mean the end of class relations but in fact helps to reinforce these deeper class relations. A critique of discourse is therefore also a critique of the social institutions and practices that produce it. This should lead to an uncovering of deeper social structures and mechanisms as well as questioning of the role of institutions and practices. We will draw out this broader realist project when we look at documents in their wider context.

The next step is the practical step of choosing which texts to analyse. For CDA this can be very wide-ranging and includes speeches, documents, government legislation, media and newspaper reports, interviews, advertisements, films and TV shows, books and memoirs. Making the right choices affects the type of research we do and the conclusions that we might draw. So I run a risk in this piece insofar as I look at just one document. Certainly a longer, more thorough analysis of government policy would look at a wider range of documents as well as other forms of text or discourse. This would be interested in convergences of position, consistency of message, conflicts among statements and so on. It might be looking to highlight something particular, such as differences between departments or branches of policy. And it would likely follow this up with the study of other texts like speeches or press releases and conduct interviews such as has been done by Richard Jackson in his work on terrorism.

In this much shorter investigation I take for granted that the CONTEST document is representative of government policy. This can be justified on a number of grounds, most notably its status as the main such document in this area. And despite not drawing on a wider literature, we can still go some way to point to a significant range of policy inconsistencies and conflicts when we move to the wider context as I do when discussing community resilience and cohesion.

An examination of 'CONTEST: the United Kingdom's Strategy for Countering Terrorism'

A discourse analysis approach to the study of documents would look at the type of language used in the CONTEST document to see how it works to portray things in a certain way. In particular, I start off with how discourse defines subject positions. As Fairclough notes, texts set up positions by which subjects can make sense of themselves and others by constituting or interpellating[1] them in particular ways (Fairclough 1992: 84–7). In doing so the language sets up a number of positions based around constructing a 'them' and 'us' dichotomy which in this case constructs 'us' as reasonable, tolerant and law abiding and 'them' as fundamentalist, radicalised and Muslim. One notable feature of the new discourse on terrorism is the way that the 'them' and 'us' positioning gets run through the notion of social cohesion. This section will look at how this and other issues can be drawn out through discourse analysis, while the next section will look at the need for a wider societal overview to fully understand the UK government's strategy.

Some discourse analysis has already been done on the UK's current anti-terrorism strategy. For example, MacDonald *et al.* (2013) analysed 110 documents related to the CONTEST and *Prevent* strategies. So as well as looking at the main documents, they examined the output of various connected ministries such as the Department of Education and the Department for Communities and Local Government. While they do not make a particularly convincing case for their theoretical approach – using Foucault's concept of governmentality (see more on this below) – they do provide detailed insight into the way the discourse shapes our understanding of terrorist threats and challenges. In particular, they have picked up on the new discourse of responsibility that identifies 'us' with local communities, with normal, law-abiding and reasonable people who have similar values and shared responsibilities. For example, across the documents that they studied, the term 'local' appears on a regular basis (indeed I counted nearly a hundred occurrences in the CONTEST document alone) as do terms like 'community' and 'partnership'. The terms 'shared' and 'sharing' are frequently used in relation to such things as 'practice', 'information' and 'values'. This works to give a sense of cohesion while also suggesting an undercurrent of threat and discord. The discourse tries to solidify the notion of who we are while also revealing our position to be under threat. And while emphasising cohesion, it also emphasises increasing social complexity with multiple agents and actors and a myriad of duties and responsibilities. For example, a summary of the *Protect* strategy states:

> The purpose of *Protect* is to strengthen our protection against a terrorist attack in the UK or against our interests overseas and so reduce our vulnerability. Our priorities are informed by an annual National Risk Assessment, a version of which we publish, which assesses the threats we face and the vulnerabilities we have … We recognise that in all these areas our *Protect* work is becoming more complex. In many areas our own protective security depends on effective security measures in third countries. (Home Office 2011: 12–13)

While the discourse repeatedly uses the terms 'our' and 'we' to emphasise inclusion, it also plays up the idea of risks, vulnerabilities and greater complexities. We are made to feel worried by the fact that in a more complex world, we depend on security measures in third countries, while at the same time we are reassured by the fact our own government is carrying out an annual National Risk Assessment. This justifies the next stage of the UK government's strategy, *Prepare*, which, I will suggest in the next section, is all about governmentalising the population through greater use of monitoring, surveillance and normative regulation.

In order to justify this, a 'them' has to be created which in this case consists of a 'radicalised other'. The term 'radicalization' is liberally used throughout the document. No definition is offered apart from the bland claim that radicalization refers to the process by which people become terrorists (Home Office 2011: 36). It is not made clear why radicalization is taking place – indeed the document makes a virtue out of the fact that it will not jump to any conclusions: 'The grievances upon which propagandists can draw may be real or perceived, although clearly none of them justify terrorism' (Home Office 2011: 36). As well as radicalism, the term 'extremism' is frequently used in relation to groups, individuals, ideas and material. Interestingly the term 'fundamental' is not used in relation to extremism but only in relation to 'our values'. Instead, the document makes explicit use of the terms 'Islam' and 'Muslims' to identify where the threat is coming from. As far as the strategy is concerned, the main danger is from 'Al Qa'ida inspired' extremists, a claim that simultaneously identifies and then blurs the exact nature of the threat but which is blatant in its identification of Muslims as the main danger. We will look at criticisms of this identification shortly.

Returning to the 'us', the strategy is to draw on our strong values, our common ground, our cohesion:

> In all our *Prevent* work we must be clear about our purpose and our methods. The great majority of people in this country find terrorism repugnant and will never support it. Work to challenge ideology should not try to change majority opinion because it does not need changing. Our purpose is to reach the much smaller number of people who are vulnerable to radicalization. We must mobilise and empower communities not give the impression that they need to be convinced terrorism is wrong. (Home Office 2011: 60)

While solidifying the notion of ourselves, this passage identifies a small number of people who might be vulnerable to Islamic radicalism. As MacDonald *et al.* (2013) note, 'radicalization' is portrayed as a kind of disease that affects the weak and vulnerable. As part of the resilience strategy outlined in the next section, this contagion must be dealt with within the community through raised awareness and caution towards those who might exhibit worrying symptoms. So we are simultaneously reassured that we are normal and healthy while also made aware of possible threats and dangers in our midst.

In dealing with this issue, CONTEST is presented as an entirely reasonable and measured response. Indeed, the new government's strategy is portrayed as far more balanced than that of its predecessor: in limiting such things as stop and search powers. These 'reasonable' modifications should ensure that counter-terrorism work is 'effective, proportionate and consistent with our commitment to human rights' (Home Office 2011: 11). But there is a hint of menace behind all this reasonableness along the lines of 'we are tolerant of others, but we won't be taken advantage of ...' A following paragraph goes on to state: 'We will not change the law – we remain committed to protecting the freedom of speech which many of those same extremists set out to undermine. But preventing radicalization must mean challenging extremist ideas that are conducive to terrorism and also part of a terrorist narrative' (Home Office 2011: 12). Discursive strategies like 'we will not change the law' reinforce a sense of 'our' values versus 'theirs', suggesting 'they' will not defeat 'us' or make 'us' change our practices. But in actuality this is usually just what happens.

At this point we need to move from the study of discourse to the wider social context. While I do not have the scope to carry out my own investigation here, I can draw on the links others have made, in this case taking up pieces by Arun Kundnani (2009) and Paul Thomas (2010) to examine the way the British government intervenes in the Muslim community. As we have seen, the aim of government strategy is to focus on community cohesion, address community grievances, identify vulnerable individuals and engage in resilience building through education, welfare and community organisations. The reality has been somewhat more problematic and at least three negative consequences can be identified.

First, as we have already suggested, the Muslim community is addressed in a broad, monocultural way. The 'values-based approach' is described by Thomas as having an inherently judgemental and interventionist nature (Thomas 2010: 446). British Muslims are forced into subject positions of either moderate or extremist which bears very little relation to the actual values and identities of the communities themselves and does not treat Muslims as citizens with their own ideas (for a range of views on this see Kundnani 2009: 35–41). The clumsier these efforts are at social engineering, the less likely it is that the strategy will identify the real underlying issues.

Secondly, rather than building social cohesion the strategy is seen by most local community workers as an exercise in intelligence gathering. Kundnani says there is strong evidence that the *Prevent* programme has been used to establish the most elaborate system of surveillance that, among other things, embeds police officers within the delivery of local services and identifies areas where intervention should take place (Kundnani 2009: 8, 6). Strong pressure is put on community organisations to accommodate police needs while there is little movement in the other direction.

Thirdly, the implementation of the strategy has led to tensions between government departments and local authorities as well as community organisations. Rather than building social cohesion, the strategy creates local suspicion given the heavy-handed and top-down approach to community intervention. We will explore this issue in more detail in the next section on resilience-building. But as Thomas notes (2010: 444), in the face of strong scepticism, considerable pressure has been put on local authorities to adopt 'National Indicator 35' around developing 'resilience to violent extremism' and reporting to government offices.

Our conclusions from this brief summary can be that the strategy is riddled with contradictions *between discourse and practice*, notably creating suspicion among the very communities the programme claims to be trying to build cohesion among, forcing people into pre-defined subject positions that only fosters further social, political and religious divisions among British Muslims, and taking a top-down approach that is the very opposite of what the government claims community resilience to be. This latter issue will be explored in the next section.

The wider context and the need for theory

As the above analysis shows, it is important to move from the construction of meanings within texts to a study of the broader social and cultural context in which textual production takes place. While the last section showed how discourse can be given meaning by looking at its relation to various practices, this section shows the value of approaching discourse and practice through a theoretical lens. In this case, we apply Michel Foucault's concept of governmentality to the counter-terrorism strategy to argue that the main aim of the government's intervention has less to do with making Britain safer than with developing new ways of governing populations.

A very brief summary of what governmentality is would emphasise how it aims to govern from a distance by use of an array of liberal techniques. A number of key features that are relevant to this study include ideas such as (1) a concern not to govern too much and to minimise government intervention; (2) to govern instead by encouraging the free conduct of others; (3) to encourage the 'natural' processes of the market and civil society; (4) to apply the values of political economy to human conduct (Foucault 2008: 10, 42, 63–4, 319). A more specifically neoliberal discourse can be identified with recent governmentalising strategies that emphasises such things as enterprise, risk-taking and risk-awareness, and the responsibilisation of human conduct in line with a private and individualistic model of society (Foucault 2008: 147).[2] We will now look at what light these themes might shed on the study of the CONTEST document.

Carrying on from where we left off, we can look at the cohesion and intervention strategy as an exercise in governmentality that aims principally to develop knowledge and tactics for better regulating populations. Such an intervention into further and higher education is presented as a reasonable management of the public interest:

> Universities and colleges promote and facilitate the exchange of opinion and ideas, and enable debate as well as learning. The Government has no wish to limit or otherwise interfere with this free flow of ideas, and as we made clear in our review and new strategy on *Prevent* we must be careful to balance the need to preserve national security with protecting our civil liberties. But universities and colleges also have a legal and moral obligation to staff and students to ensure the place of work and study is a welcoming and safe environment. Universities and colleges have a clear and unambiguous role to play in helping to safeguard vulnerable young people from radicalization and recruitment by terrorist organisations. (Home Office 2011: 67)

The governmentality aspect of this paragraph works by emphasising the notion that the free exchange of ideas is not only a right but a responsibility. While any reasonable government would wish to preserve civil liberties, universities and colleges must realise that they have a duty to prevent certain ideas (never defined) from being circulated or face the consequences. It is not at all clear what the legal, never mind the moral, obligation to staff and students actually is, but the overwhelming sense is one of a normative agenda that works by getting us to regulate our conduct in a particular way.

As an exercise in governmentality, this approach is presented as if it was devolving responsibility to local institutions and groups who can make their own decisions about what is good practice. But as we also saw in the last section, this is in a reality a top-down approach whereby government tells people what to do and forces them to agree to a particular agenda and way of seeing things. In the words of the document: 'The department of Business, Innovation and Skills will lead the delivery of *Prevent* in these sectors by helping universities and colleges better understand the risk of radicalization on and off campus', while later this is even presented as something enabling: 'We will fund the National Union of Students (NUS) to undertake a programme of work to ensure that their sabbatical officers and full-time staff are fully trained and equipped to manage their responsibilities.' Then finally, 'As with schools, we look to universities and colleges of further education to develop constructive dialogue with local *Prevent* groups and community organisations' (Home Office 2011: 67).

By now, this sort of language should be familiar to many readers. It works through the pretence of being helpful and solving problems, while containing an underlying authoritarianism which leaves little choice as to whether this is really necessary or whether alternative options are available. This governmentality works by claiming to be devolving powers to local bodies so they can take responsibility for their own decisions, but in reality these bodies have little choice about the wider strategy. It is a top-down form of government that operates through devolved techniques of governance and has little to do with the specific issue of terrorism. Rather, this is a pervasive discourse present across a range of different fields of governance. Indeed if readers are detecting something familiar in the counter-terrorism discourse, they might consider how terms like 'terrorism' and 'radicalism' could easily be substituted with terms taken from health and safety manuals to see how it is not specific fields but practices and techniques that are of most significance.

As we now know from our daily lives, governmentality constructs an artificial game of competitive conduct in areas like health and education that should not be subjected to such neoliberal values. Part of this is an obsession with performance indicators and the CONTEST document is no exception:

> We will assess the progress of CONTEST against a set of performance indicators, complemented by deeper evaluation of specific programmes. Evaluation will be supported by wider research and horizon scanning, vital if we are to remain ahead of new or changing threats and vulnerabilities. We are committed to publishing data where security classification allows. We will publish an annual report on our counter-terrorism work. (Home Office 2011: 15)

Anyone familiar with British public services will know that an obsession with performance indicators does not necessarily mean the same thing as getting the things to run properly and indeed meeting targets can become an obsession in itself that undermines efforts to address underlying problems. But the *rationality* of governmentality has this obsessive logic, concerned to monitor things, to assess, to measure and indeed to reflect on its exercise and effectiveness. This element of governmentality is evident as in the following passage:

> But we are also determined to have a strategy that is not only more effective but also more proportionate, that is better focused and more precise, which

uses powers selectively, carefully and in a way that is as sparing as possible. These themes and this language also runs through this strategy – in *Pursue*, *Prevent* and in *Protect* and *Prepare* – and are reflected in its founding principles. (Home Office 2011: 15)

Alongside a concern for having the right measures is a concern with the right procedures. The document talks of the vital importance of testing and exercising and of learning and absorbing the lessons from these exercises (Home Office 2011: 14). This is written in relation to CONTEST's programme for resilience and preparedness and we will spend the rest of this section outlining why this too is a form of governmentality.

The notion behind resilience is that it enables communities to withstand and 'bounce back' from disasters such as terrorist attacks. The concept comes from systems theory, but its policy use is particularly concerned with how people, organisations and institutions cope and adapt to risk and unexpected shocks. Indeed there is an element of fatalism to this approach since external shocks are seen as inevitable thereby making preparedness and adaptability the only course of action. As the document says:

> The purpose of our *Prepare* work is to mitigate the impact of a terrorist attack where that attack cannot be stopped. This includes work to bring a terrorist attack to an end and to increase our resilience so we can recover from its aftermath.

The resilience agenda is being promoted across a range of areas from local communities to development aid and therefore has a rather generic character. The document itself suggests that a generic approach to resilience capabilities makes best use of resources and avoids duplication (p. 93). I would go a step further and suggest that because resilience has very little specifically to do with disaster response and is really more about finding new ways of managing populations through installing a state of mind that emphasises preparedness, self-awareness and willingness to learn and adapt, then a generic approach will do just as well as one which claims to be related to terrorist attacks.

Resilience is a key feature of recent National Security Strategy (Cabinet Office 2010) and the *Prepare* strategy has evolved to reflect these priorities. These include informing the public of the risks they face, supporting business continuity, helping businesses prepare for disruption and enhancing cooperation between public and private sector providers of national infrastructure (p. 94). Again all this is presented as a form of governance from a distance that encourages 'partnerships' and works through appeals to local ownership of the process:

> *Prevent* is primarily a local strategy and while the Home Office will retain overall responsibility for the strategy, it will largely be implemented in prisons, colleges, and universities by our partners in the Devolved Administrations, local authorities, the police and community organisations. This local work

will be coordinated by a network of local managers, within local authorities and docked with existing safeguarding and crime reduction partnerships. (Home Office 2011: 112)

The reality is that that these partners have been forced into a certain way of acting. The 2004 UK Civil Contingencies Act compels them to make risk assessments, draw up contingency plans and run training exercises. It forces them to participate in Regional Resilience Forums and Regional Civil Contingencies Committees. It does represent a form of devolution, but rather than a genuine devolution of power, what this clearly indicates is devolution of responsibilities. The resilience approach reflects the reality of the new neoliberal order with the state's responsibilities shifted onto individuals, communities and the private sector. Rather than directly helping us face up to dangers and threats, the new form of governance operates by informing us how to help ourselves, how to familiarise ourselves with possible threats, how to adapt our behaviour to respond to them. What at first appears to be an innocent term in one document is actually part of a joined up strategy of governance. It is promoted as the type of governance needed in an increasingly complex and uncertain world. In reality, this notion functions to naturalise the neoliberal condition and to install a greater sense of individual responsibility and self-discipline in the context of the state retreating from many of its basic obligations.

Realist conclusions

By this point the chapter is in danger of turning into a piece about anti-terrorist strategy as a form of governmentality. This is not really the intention. Rather, the aim of the last section was to show the effect of reading a document through a theoretical lens. It might be said that this is unnecessary and that reading a document in such a way distorts its meaning or implies a particular reading of a text. But we will conclude by defending this strategy as not only legitimate, but indeed as necessary and unavoidable once we recognise that there is more to reality than what is in a text. While we might limit our analysis to what is actually written in the document, we have tried to show that more can be learned by bringing in the actual practices that the document is related to, thus giving a better picture not only of what the document is saying, but also what it is *doing*. By going a step further, we are obliged to make assumptions about various connections between the text and the wider context. Indeed, we also need to go beyond observable practices and look at what might explain these. Hence a governmentality approach, despite its poststructuralist theoretical origins, does imply a realist attitude insofar as it suggests the reality of something underlying and unobservable. The various connections we have made suggest something like an underlying rationality or strategic vision that informs practices of governance. Whether it is limited to underlying rationality or strategies of governance as in Foucault's case, or to hegemonic projects and processes of capitalist reproduction, these are all things that are only observable through their effects and so necessarily require a conceptual element as part of their explanation.

Working out what this theoretical element should be is no easy task. But it is a necessary task for someone taking the CDA approach. As Jackson argues, if discourses are 'broader than just language being constituted in definite institutional and organisational practices', then we need to examine the way they create or maintain power relations and are how they are themselves able to become dominant or hegemonic (Jackson 2005: 19). To address not just what is happening but the wider conditions that make these things happen requires the identification of suitable theoretical explanations. For example, Herring and Stokes have suggested historical materialism as the best means to analyse the relationship between dominant discourses, counter-terrorism practices and the class and social interests within capitalist society (Herring and Stokes 2011: 13; see also Maher and Thompson this volume). My analysis here has not gone as far as to make this suggestion, but clearly a choice like this would be necessary if I were to elaborate upon and defend my main arguments. In particular, I have suggested that anti-terrorism strategy can be explained in relation to changing forms of UK governance and I have hinted in turn that these changes can be described as neoliberal in character. To elaborate on this requires going beyond poststructuralism and discourse analysis to provide an explanation of why it is that forms of governance are changing.

A historical materialist approach to governmentality, in contrast to a poststructuralist one, would therefore seek to explain these changes in forms of governance in terms of changes in hegemonic projects, the reconfiguration of class forces and deeper contradictions within the capitalist economy and the institutional forms of its regulation (see Joseph 2012). And in doing so, it invites the possibility of challenging governmentality by highlighting the tensions across the different processes. While critical realism does not do this directly, it points to the need for theories that seek to explain such conditions of possibility for the emergence, reproduction and possible transformation of discourses and practices. There is no guarantee that a particular theory will prove capable of providing such an explanation but there are means of assessing degrees of suitability and compatibility. As a meta-theory, critical realism can act as an aid both to the methodological stance (use of CDA) and theoretical stance (such as historical materialism) by interrogating the types of claims that are made and what kind of social ontology these presuppose. To summarise the critical realism (CR) approach to these questions, it assumes a deeper nature of reality that makes both material and discursive practices possible. As Fairclough *et al.* write:

> A CR approach to the explanation of concrete phenomena such as semiosis, analyses them as conjunctions of structures and causal powers co-producing specific effects. To do this it abstracts these structures, identifying them and considering their respective causal powers and liabilities. Having done this, it then moves back towards the concrete, combining the abstracted constituent elements, noting how they combine, with what consequences. (Fairclough *et al.* 2003: 33)

This then is the final stage on the journey from textual analysis to wider context. The critical realist method moves from the concrete to the conditions of possibility and back again. This is a necessary meta-theoretical move in order to better understand which theories might provide better explanations of complex social contexts. Critics – empiricists and Foucauldians alike – will complain that this is a speculative move. A realist retort is that it is the nature of reality itself to have these deeper layers that cannot be explained merely through empirical investigation but necessitate a conceptual approach that makes reasonable and informed judgements about what these deeper layers might be like. Clearly we could limit ourselves to a study of these documents as representative of new forms of governance. But to explain why these new forms of governance have emerged, to account for their prevalence in places like the UK and to connect them to the changing role of the state and the restructuring of capitalist social relations, we need the kind of depth ontology proposed by critical realism. This is not at all to belittle the important work that discourse theory and Foucauldian poststructuralism can do in revealing the *workings* of different strategies of governance. Rather, it is a matter of putting these discourses and strategies in their proper social context in order to better explain such things as their emergence, reproduction and, hopefully, the potentiality for counter-strategies that challenge them.

Notes

1. Interpellation is Louis Althusser's term for how subjects are 'hailed' in the sense that they think 'that's me who is being addressed'.
2. Of course this is far too brief a summary; for more elaboration see Joseph (2012).

References

Cabinet Office (2010) *A Strong Britain in an Age of Uncertainty: The National Security Strategy*. London: Cabinet Office. Online at: http://www.direct.gov.uk/prod_consum_dg/groups/dg_digitalassets/@dg/@en/documents/digitalasset/dg_191639.pdf?CID=PDF&PLA=fur l&CRE=nationalsecuritystrategy (accessed 29 July 2012).

Fairclough, N. (1992) *Discourse and Social Change*. Cambridge: Polity.

Fairclough, N. (1995) *Critical Discourse Analysis: The Critical Study of Language*. Harlow: Longman.

Fairclough, N., Jessop, B. and Sayer, A. (2004) 'Critical realism and semiosis', in J. Joseph and J. M. Roberts (eds), *Realism, Discourse and Deconstruction*. London: Routledge, pp. 23–42.

Foucault, M. (1989) *The Archaeology of Knowledge*. London: Routledge.

Foucault, M. (2008) *The Birth of Biopolitics*. Basingstoke: Palgrave Macmillan.

Herring, E. and Stokes, D. (2011) 'Critical realism and historical materialism as resources for critical terrorism studies', *Critical Studies on Terrorism*, 4 (1): 5–21.

Home Office (2011) *CONTEST: The United Kingdom's Strategy for Countering Terrorism*. London: Home Office. Online at: https://www.gov.uk/government/uploads/system/uploads/attachment_data/file/97995/strategy-contest.pdf (accessed 1 April 2013).

Jackson, R. (2005) *Writing the War on Terrorism: Language, Politics and Counter-Terrorism*. Manchester: Manchester University Press.

Joseph, J. (2004) 'Foucault and reality', *Capital and Class*, 82: 141–63.

Joseph, J. (2012) *The Social in the Global: Social Theory, Governmentality and Global Politics*. Cambridge: Cambridge University Press.

Joseph, J. (2013) 'Resilience in UK and French security strategy: an Anglo-Saxon bias', *Politics*, 33 (4): 253–64.

Kundnani, A. (2009) *Spooked: How Not to Prevent Violent Extremism.* London: Institute of Race Relations.

MacDonald, M., Hunter, D. and O'Regan, J. (2013) 'Citizenship, community, and counter-terrorism: UK security discourse, 2001–2011', *Journal of Language and Politics*, 12 (3): 445–73.

Stump, J. L. and Dixit, P. (2013) *Critical Terrorism Studies: An Introduction to Research Methods.* Abingdon: Routledge.

Thomas, P. (2010) 'Failed and friendless: the UK's "Preventing Violent Extremism" programme', *British Journal of Politics and International Relations*, 12 (3): 442–58.

3

APPLYING MARXISM TO CRITICAL TERRORISM STUDIES

Analysis through a historical materialist lens

David Maher and Andrew Thomson

Introduction

Extrapolating from Marx's articulation of a materialist conception of history, we argue that a historical materialist (HM) approach provides scholars of critical terrorism studies (CTS) with a useful framework to research terroristic violence. This involves an analysis of the political and economic contexts of terrorism and ancillary social relations within capitalist development, including class inequalities, modes of exploitation and imperialist domination, among others. Moreover, we believe that elucidating how CTS can apply an HM approach to analyse the links between terrorism and capitalism is important given that, as Jonathan Joseph (2011: 27) highlights: 'It is fair to say that CTS makes some reference to historical materialism but pays little attention to the nature of capitalist society.'

As HM is a diverse academic tradition and can cover a panoply of political and economic processes, it does not fit the scope of this chapter to discuss all the ways in which HM can be employed to analyse terrorism. Instead, we focus on four key ways in which an HM approach can be applied to terrorism research to uncover insights into terroristic violence and capitalist development. Firstly, we discuss how HM constitutes a political economy approach which entails close scrutiny of the interplay between political and economic aspects of terrorism at the subnational, national and international levels. Secondly, we highlight how Marxist assumptions regarding violence, capitalism and social relations can provide critical insights into the class aspect of terroristic violence. Thirdly, we argue that, through an appreciation of the often violent character of globalised capitalism, an HM framework provides a useful corrective to liberal scholarship which often assumes political violence to be inimical to economic development. In contrast, a HM framework allows us to analyse how violence, including terrorism, can be linked to the advancement of globalised capitalism. Finally, we discuss theories of imperialism in the context of terrorism and globalisation. We then proceed to discuss how we conduct our own research and provide examples of this research.

In terms of capitalist development, this chapter discusses what is commonly referred to as neoliberal globalisation, an economic model which, since the 1970s, has been fervently pushed by the US government and powerful international financial institutions such as the World Bank and the International Monetary Fund (IMF). During the 1980s (under former US President Ronald Reagan and UK Prime Minister Margaret Thatcher) and 1990s (after the fall of the Soviet Union), this neoliberal economic model rapidly expanded across the globe and today pervades the global political economy. Based on free market capitalism, this economic model was famously described by John Williamson as the 'Washington Consensus' and includes (*inter alia*) fiscal discipline, trade liberalisation, privatisation, liberalisation of foreign direct investment (FDI) and deregulation (e.g. Williamson 1990). As Blakeley (2009: 5) describes, neoliberal economics typically involves 'the opening up of previously closed economies to the forces of economic competition', with a focus on 'globalised rather than national economics' ensuring 'the globalisation of the political economy along specific lines'. With increases in income inequality and a reduction in labour's share of income, neoliberalism is described as a hegemonic political and economic project which, following a period of declining income disparity after the Great Depression and the Second World War, is re-establishing power and concentrations of wealth into the hands of the ruling elite (Chomsky 1999; Duménil and Lévy 2004; Harvey 2005; Birch and Mykhnenko 2010). Within this context, this chapter highlights how a HM approach can uncover important insights into neoliberal economics and terrorism.

An HM framework: a Marxist political economy approach

To elucidate the 'critical' aspects of historical materialism in the context of terrorism studies, it is first necessary to discuss the work of Karl Marx, the progenitor of the HM approach. While Marx did not refer to the term 'historical materialism' himself, through his critique of political economy he nonetheless articulated a materialist conception of history positing that the social relations of production have a broader constitutional effect on the 'general process of social, political and intellectual life' (Marx 1990: 175, footnote 35). In this way, capitalism should not be understood myopically: it is not simply an economic system, but constitutes a whole way of being and acting. Capitalism is thus a political, economic and social force that shapes and continually interacts with certain outcomes, including terrorism.

Building on the critical work of Marx, then, an HM framework of analysis constitutes a political economy approach to social inquiry. As Benjamin Cohen (2008: 80) observes, 'The "materialism" in historical materialism means placing economic relations and the social organization of production at the center of analysis.' The 'historical' component, as Robert Cox (1996: 88) describes, provides a 'theory of history in the sense of being concerned not just with the past but with a continuing process of historical change'. Importantly, then, the core component of an HM framework is its acknowledgement of the mutual constitution of the political and economic spheres. Indeed, one prominent historical materialist, William Robinson (2003: 43), has implored social and political analysis more generally to overcome the restrictive Weberian separation of 'markets' and 'states' as related but separate analytical concepts. Drawing from similar Marxian principles, numerous scholars have also advocated a political economy approach to the study of terrorism which is attentive to the interplay between these spheres (Herring and Stokes 2011; Porpora 2011; Herring 2008).

HM therefore provides terrorism scholarship a way of understanding and analysing the broader political and economic contexts in which terrorism occurs, including the historically specific dynamics of capitalist development. In the milieu of neoliberal globalisation, an HM approach moves beyond simply analysing states/non-state actors (political sphere) and markets (economic sphere) to encompass a range of political and economic entities and activities. For example, analysis can investigate links between a wide range of political actions (e.g. neoliberal policies, foreign aid, security and, crucially, political violence such as terrorism) and economic factors (e.g. trade agreements, economic growth, FDI, international trade, among many possibilities).

This provides a broader framework for explaining the structural logics of capitalist development (through such notions as neoliberal globalisation) and how these logics link with political violence (such as terrorism). Importantly, then, while most analyses of terrorism tend to focus on the political motivations behind terroristic violence, an HM approach instead allows for the study of both the political *and* economic motives underpinning such violence (see Maher and Thomson 2011). Therefore, by adopting a political economy framework acknowledging the inextricable linkages between the political and economic spheres, a fuller understanding of terrorism can be attained.

Bringing social relations and class into critical terrorism studies

Further drawing from Marx's materialist conception of history, the analysis of class relations is also central to an HM approach. Marx observed that the social relations of production underpin the very nature of class relations. He distinguished between the minority who own the means of production (namely the bourgeoisie or capitalist class) vis-à-vis the majority (namely the proletariat) who, to survive, are forced to sell their labour-power to this dominant, capitalist class. Moreover, the capitalist class extracts surplus value from the labour provided by the proletariat, which is integral to capitalist accumulation. In other words, the valorisation of capital is based on the production of commodities which contain more labour than the capitalist has paid for (Marx 1990: 769). This unequal ownership of the means of production and the exploitation by one class (bourgeoisie) of another (proletariat) produces class antagonisms and conflict. Indeed, such class antagonisms have been a driving force underpinning historical development; as Marx and Engels famously wrote: 'The history of all hitherto existing society is the history of class struggles'

(Marx and Engels 1992: 1). For our purposes here, this provides a class-based understanding of how certain political and economic structures are both contested and stabilised through political violence.

Terrorism is a specific tactic, within a spectrum of political violence, used by both bourgeois and proletariat sections of society in order to oppose or advance certain political and economic configurations. Within this, terrorism can be analysed as embedded within the context of unfolding dynamic class relations: a manifestation of social interaction predicated on the ownership of the means of production by the few who exploit the many. The study of terrorism from an HM perspective therefore requires examination of class hierarchies, class antagonisms and broader political and economic inequalities. Indeed, as Jonathan Joseph (2011: 34) has argued: 'Terrorism can only be understood by a thorough understanding of a complex set of social relations, the investigation of which require a lot more than just looking at beliefs and motivations.' Therefore, analysis should appreciate the complexities of class relations in the context of terrorism; as Herring (2008: 200) argues: 'The class role that terrorism plays may be functional or dysfunctional and driven by complex interaction of fractions of classes and elites (subnational, national, transnational) and progressive or reactionary opposition.'

In this light, one important implication of this approach is that terrorism is understood as a tactic that can be used by opposing class groups, rather than, say, simply a 'weapon of the weak' to challenge the state. HM thus helps to explain both non-state terrorism and state terrorism (discussed below) as interconnected in the contestation and stabilisation of capitalist social relations and the prevailing political and economic order (McKeown 2011; Porpora 2011: 53). Rather than understanding non-state (e.g. revolutionary) terrorism and state terror as separate categories unto themselves (regardless of how qualitatively different they may be), they are understood as occurring within the contours of unfolding capitalist development. Importantly, this implies that while terrorism can be used to contest oppressive modes of elite domination, it can also aid in the advancement of capitalism itself.

Linking terrorism to capitalist development

Another core component of Marx's analysis of capitalism is the understanding of capitalist development as a dialectical process within which violence, including terrorism, is a central component. As McKeown (2011) correctly points out, a Marxist theory of international social relations can broaden our knowledge of terrorism because it is essentially a theory which 'is rooted in the study of social conflict'. For example, Marx took issue with classical liberal thinkers such as Adam Smith for positing that the original accumulation of capital (and thus the very formation of the capitalist elite) was achieved through the diligence, intelligence and frugality of the elite, vis-à-vis the lazy and profligate majority (Marx 1990: 873). In contrast, Marx gave a distinct version of what he labelled the primitive accumulation of capital, which was underpinned by violence. Indeed, Marx (1990: 875) famously wrote that the historical transmogrification of the feudal system to a capitalist mode of production 'is written in the annals of mankind in letters of blood and fire'. Marx thus argued that the primitive accumulation of capital involved:

> The spoliation of the Church's property, the fraudulent alienation of the state domains, the theft of the common lands, the usurpation of feudal and clan property and its transformation into modern private property under circumstances of ruthless terrorism, all these things were just so many idyllic methods of primitive accumulation. They conquered the field for capitalist agriculture, incorporated the soil into capital, and created for the urban industries the necessary supplies of free and rightless proletarians. (Marx 1990: 895)

From a Marxist perspective, then, capitalism was violent in its incipiency and, in many places, continues to be violent today.[1]

We argue that this acknowledgement forms a very important critique (among others) of core assumptions regarding the economic effects of terrorism that currently pervade much of terrorism studies. That is to say, borrowing from the same classical liberal thinkers Marx critiqued, contemporary liberal scholarship tends to assume that political violence such as terrorism is inimical to economic growth and 'progress', especially in developing countries (for a good overview, see Cramer 2006; for studies, see Keefer and Loayza 2008; Sandler and Enders 2008; Gaibulloev and Sandler 2011). For example, studies suggest that terrorism inhibits a country's economic development by discouraging FDI, curtailing international trade, destroying infrastructure and redirecting public funds to finance security (for an overview, see Sandler and Enders 2008). Moreover, even when studies have acknowledged that not all terroristic violence is linked to economic decline, the possibility of some forms of terrorism to bolster economic processes is completely overlooked. This is exemplified in a recent study by Powers and Choi (2012), who attempt to show how different types of terrorism affect inflows of FDI. The authors argue that 'business related terrorism' (i.e. terrorism which targets the assets and employees of multinational corporations) has a negative impact on a country's ability to attract FDI inflows; so-called 'non-business related terrorism' (i.e. terrorism which does not target the interests of foreign companies) had no significant effect. What is entirely missing from these studies, and many others like it, is any consideration of what we might term 'pro-business terrorism', in other words how acts of terrorism can serve the interests of foreign capital and thus stimulate FDI inflows. What is also missing is how so-called 'non-business related terrorism', while not targeting the interests of investors, may in fact serve the interests of capital in an extended pattern of capital accumulation. For example, while the logic of capitalism often requires stability to promote predictability, instability caused through violence can also be of interest to foreign capital, especially if such violence can disrupt existing rights to assets (e.g. land or natural resources), exclude local interests and present new ownership and investment opportunities to foreign capital (Cramer 2006: 233). As Cramer (2006) has noted, violence has been and often still is 'part of the economy, not simply a brake on it', contrary to liberal assumptions.

We believe that an HM framework can provide a corrective to such oversights, and the acknowledgement of the often violent characteristics of capitalist expansion is an important step towards analysing terrorism through an HM lens. That is to say, an HM framework provides the conceptual and theoretical tools necessary to examine the use of terrorism in processes of capital accumulation and capitalist development. It aids researchers in tracing the violent tendencies of neoliberal globalisation by emphasising a political economy model of analysis which places class hierarchies (as well as other inequalities of power, for example gender relations) at the centre of investigation. Pertinent to terrorism debates, these class hierarchies are, according to a Marxist framework, typically manifested within the state. At this juncture, then, it is necessary to discuss the concept of state terrorism.

HM and state terrorism

We understand state terrorism as the 'intentional use or threat of violence by state agents or their proxies against individuals or groups who are victimised for the purpose of intimidating or frightening a broader audience' (Jackson *et al*. 2010: 3). Further, state terror involves deliberate acts of violence targeted at individuals that the state has a duty to protect (Blakeley 2010: 15). With its emphasis on class structures and the violent characteristics of capitalist development, an HM framework which is rooted in Marxist theory is particularly adept at analysing the role of the state in the context of terrorism.

Pertinently, the state itself is understood in the Marxist tradition to be a manifestation or expression of specific social relations. As Robinson argues, in

> Marx's view, the state gives a political form to economic institutions and production relations. Consequently, the economic globalization of capital cannot be a phenomenon isolated from the transformation of states and of class relations. The state is the congealment of particular and historically determined constellations of class forces and relations, and states are always embodied in sets of political institutions. Hence states are: (a) a moment of class and social power relations; and (b) a set of political institutions (an 'apparatus'). (Robinson 2003: 43)

Furthermore, from a Marxist perspective, the state is a tool of elite domination that typically serves the interests of the bourgeoisie often at the expense of the proletariat. As Marx and Engels (1992: 5) wrote: 'The executive of the modern state is but a committee for managing the common affairs of the whole bourgeoisie.' While the state has undoubtedly changed since the time of Karl Marx's life (1818–83), the global economic crisis has for many demonstrated Marx and Engels' point well: while some governments have increasingly implemented austerity measures to curb social spending, the same governments have provided munificent bailout packages for major banks.

In a similar light, terroristic violence perpetrated by states or groups sponsored by governments can serve the interests of the bourgeoisie vis-à-vis the proletariat.

For instance, constituting the 'first experiment with neoliberal state formation' (Harvey 2005: 7), the military junta of General Augusto Pinochet implemented and entrenched the neoliberal economic model in Chile through the widespread terrorisation of the civilian population. Pinochet's dictatorship (1973–90), wholly backed by the US, brutally repressed political, social and civilian groups deemed inimical to neoliberal free market capitalism, including leftist political groups, trade unions and peasant movements. Moreover, this type of terrorism is much more prevalent than non-state terrorism which challenges the interests of the bourgeoisie (Blakeley 2009).

In this regard, an HM framework is particularly useful in examining state terrorism. HM allows for sustained analysis of the political and economic structures that have enabled and conditioned state terror. It does so by situating state terrorism in relation to class frictions and elite concentration of power within and through the state. By adopting an HM framework, one can locate the structural sources of state terror within the broader schema of the historical development of capitalism, in which terror is used to make available and stabilise particular political and economic arrangements conducive to capitalist interests. As Robinson (2004: 137–8) highlights: 'Global capitalism requires an apparatus of direct coercion to open up zones that may fall under renegade control, to impose order, and to repress rebellion that threatens the stability or security of the system.' Counterinsurgency, for example, is a politico-military strategy that often results in terroristic means to stabilise beneficent political and economic structures (Stokes 2005; Hristov 2009; Maher and Thomson 2011). In summary, an HM framework can help to unpack how and why the state can represent an 'apparatus of direct coercion' through which elite capitalist interests are pursued using terroristic means.

Such an examination of the global dimensions of state terrorism also introduces notions of imperialism into this mix. Imperialism contextualises the hierarchical power relations between nations and classes internationally through which capitalist interests can be pursued. McKeown (2011: 77) states, for instance, that 'the theory of capitalist imperialism necessarily situates the use of state terrorism in an international capitalist system in which capital accumulation takes place within the context of international class conflict and/or cooperation between competing sets of ruling classes within both developed and underdeveloped countries.' In this way, scholars have been able to analyse state terrorism within the context of imperialist foreign policies in pursuit of sustaining favourable capitalist arrangements abroad. This is discussed in more detail below.

An HM framework applied

Hitherto, our own research follows these trends in examining the political and economic frameworks conditioning the use of state terror in Colombia. To recap, subscribing to the framework we have outlined above, our research (1) adopts a political economy approach that is attentive to the mutual constitution of the political and economic spheres; (2) investigates these political and economic processes in the context of antagonistic class relations; (3) acknowledges the often violent characteristics of globalised capitalism; and (4) incorporates theories of imperialism in order to analyse the global dimensions of state terror.

To apply this critical framework, we fall into what Cohen has described as the 'British School' of international political economy, namely an interdisciplinary approach which, in contrast to the 'American School', is 'less wedded to conventional social science methodology', is sceptical about 'rational choice' models and generally 'rejects a positivist epistemology' (Cohen 2009: 396). At the same time, such an approach pursues 'analytical eclecticism' and constitutes a 'pragmatic research style that is willing to borrow concepts, theories, and methods from a variety of scholarly traditions as needed to address socially important problems' (Cohen 2009: 400). In this light, we do acknowledge that critical theories could be open to certain methods (including variable-based regression analyses, for example) which can identify regularities in human behaviour and social phenomena. Nonetheless, we acknowledge that 'these methods are insufficient on their own because they cannot identify the deeper, underlying nature of reality and they reduce the causal powers and liabilities of things to their actual exercise' (Joseph 2011: 26).

We also advocate research designs which focus on detailed, individual case study analyses. This enables the use of process-tracing, whereby 'the researcher examines histories, archival documents, interview transcripts, and other sources to see whether the causal process a theory hypothesizes or implies in a case is in fact evident in the sequence and values of the intervening variables in that case' (George and Bennet 2005: 6). In the context of terrorism and economic development, processes may include (among others) economic growth, inflows of FDI, levels of international trade, trade agreements and, importantly, patterns of terroristic violence. In the following example, to investigate the links between terrorism and economic development through a method of process tracing we have mainly relied on descriptive statistics, economic data, accounts of observers 'on the ground' and other documentary evidence, which includes US and Colombian government reports and declassified US diplomatic cables, studies conducted by non-governmental agencies, as well as reports published by the UN and the Organisation of American States.

Case study: Colombia

Colombia has been embroiled in a civil war since at least the 1960s. Powerful armed groups within this civil war – including left-wing guerrillas and right-wing paramilitaries – are labelled as terrorist organisations by the US and the EU. These armed groups have indeed committed violent acts of terror, including torture, murder, massacres, kidnapping and widespread forced displacement. However, it is important to acknowledge the deep and well documented links between Colombia's security forces and right-wing paramilitary groups throughout the country (e.g. see Amnesty International 2004; Human Rights Watch 2010; Maher and Thomson 2011).[2] Moreover, Colombia's security forces have been complicit with and had direct involvement in civilian massacres and have been responsible for the extra-judicial killings of thousands of civilians. This includes the so-called 'false positives' scandal, whereby, since 1986, the Colombian armed forces have executed approximately 3,900 civilians and presented them as guerrilla insurgents killed in combat. These so-called 'false positive' executions intensified between 2002 and 2008 when 3,470 civilians were killed, representing 89 per cent of total 'false positive' deaths (see Colombia Reports 2013).

The impact of violence perpetrated by Colombia's armed actors is perhaps best highlighted by the number of internal displaced persons (IDPs) recorded by the government of Colombia (GOC). Indeed, forced displacement is an acute problem in Colombia, with the GOC recording more IDPs than any other country in the world (IDMC 2012). Currently, this number stands at 4–5 million people (depending on the source), over 10 per cent of Colombia's total population. Moreover, according to the GOC's own statistics, almost 80 per cent of forced displacement occurred between 2000 and 2009 (Acción Social 2011). Therefore forced displacement intensified during the 2000s.

In the midst of this endemic violence, Colombia's government has developed the country's economy according to a neoliberal economic model. Since 1991, in a process known as *la apertura económica* (the economic opening), and continuing to the present day, the Colombian government has fervently implemented neoliberal economic reforms, based *(inter alia)* on deregulation, privatisation, encouraging international trade and attracting foreign direct investors. Moreover, during periods of intensifying violence, the economy has exhibited robust economic growth, especially during the 2000s. For example, average GDP per capita was 2.5 per cent between 2000 and 2009, higher than the regional average of 1.8 per cent during this period (see World Bank n.d.). Similarly, since 2001, Colombia has attracted a very high level of FDI, with FDI stock rising from $15.4 billion in 2001 to $95.7 billion in 2011, an average annual growth rate of 21 per cent (UNCTAD n.d.). By using an HM framework, we thus inquire from the outset if terroristic violence has bolstered Colombia's economic growth and facilitated the entrenchment of the neoliberal economic model. This provides critical insights when compared to adopting a liberal framework, which, as noted, can overlook such crucial observations by assuming that economic growth declines with violence or occurs *in spite* of terrorism.

We argue that terrorism perpetrated by the state and its 'proxy army of paramilitary fighters' (Maher and Thomson 2011: 106) has created economic opportunities for both domestic and foreign capital in Colombia by clearing large swathes of land for commercial activities. Indeed, forced displacement should not be viewed as a vicissitude of armed combat between actors in Colombia's internal armed conflict. Rather, it is a concerted strategy of war to 'spread territorial control and diversify funding sources' and functions as 'a low cost and effective strategy for clearing out territories' (Ibáñez and Vélez 2008: 661). Moreover, forced displacement is a tactic most commonly employed by paramilitary groups (e.g. see Ibáñez and Vélez 2008: 661), followed by the military (Leech 2011: 131). In particular, forced displacement has cleared areas for oil exploration (Colombia's largest sector in terms of FDI and exports) and has opened up large areas of land needed for emerging agro-industrial export crops such as palm oil. This displacement has largely (but not exclusively) occurred in rural areas where the majority of Colombia's natural resources and agro-industrial projects are found. Thus there has been widespread displacement of *campesino* farmers and indigenous groups who often live in areas of economic interest. In short, we argue that: 'Large sections of Colombia's citizenry continue to abandon their lands as they are forcibly displaced from their homes, satisfying the voracious appetite of foreign (mainly US) multinational corporations (MNCs) for Colombian territory as the neo-liberal economic program is further entrenched in Colombian society' (Maher and Thomson 2011: 96).

In a similar light, we argue that state-paramilitary terror has systematically targeted groups deemed inimical to the expansion and entrenchment of Colombia's neoliberal economic model. While this includes the targeting of Colombia's left-wing guerrillas, who often attack the interests and employees of domestic and foreign companies, it is imperative to acknowledge the systematic targeting of civilian groups. This includes trade unions which seek to improve working conditions and wages, incurring additional costs for capital which ultimately lowers profitability. In fact, in 2010, more trade unionists were murdered in Colombia than the rest of the world combined (ITUC 2011). As with forced displacement, the right-wing paramilitaries are responsible for the majority of violence against Colombia's trade unionists, followed by Colombia's security forces (see, for example, ITUC 2012). The targeting of these groups has thus 'made Colombia very attractive to foreign investment as poor working conditions and low wages keep profit margins high' (Maher and Thomson 2011: 96). Further, it is important to note that, while clearing land for commercial activities, the high levels of forced displacement in Colombia are also aimed at 'impeding collective action, damaging social networks, and intimidating and controlling [the] civilian population' (Ibáñez and Vélez 2008: 662).

In light of the very high levels of forced displacement and widespread attacks on Colombia's organised labour movement, the implementation of Colombia's neoliberal economic model and strong economic development outlined above has not seriously tackled the acute levels of poverty and inequality in the country. In fact, while levels of inequality have undulated, wealth distribution in Colombia has worsened since Colombia's neoliberal economic model was implemented in 1991, when the richest 10 per cent of Colombia's population held a 39.5 per cent share of the country's total income; by 2010, the figure stood at 44.4 per cent (World Bank 2012). Economic growth in Colombia has therefore benefited domestic and foreign capital much to the expense of the wider Colombian population. In the context of security, this is especially the case for the millions of Colombia's citizens who have been forcibly displaced, the thousands of trade unionists who are systematically targeted by the state-paramilitaries, as well as the millions of Colombians who continue to live below the poverty line and who today realise a lower proportion of Colombia's income compared to when the neoliberal economic model was implemented in 1991.

A final component of this research focuses on the central role of US intervention. By adopting an HM lens, we are able to link Colombia's internally directed system of state terror to a transnational imperialist dimension. As the hegemon in the post-Second World War era, the US has played the lead managerial role in the global capitalist system (Panitch and Gindin 2004; Bromley 2006). Following the logic of capitalist imperialism, the US has served to underwrite the stability and fluid functioning of capitalism in the periphery, in order to maintain access to resources and markets. The US has done so through various methods; nevertheless, pertinent to this chapter, US administrations have often bolstered the military capability of allies within peripheral countries to thwart internal threats (Stokes and Raphael 2010; Blakeley 2009; Robinson 2003). In Colombia, the US government has granted substantial military aid packages (including military training) in order to armour Colombia's neoliberalisation from the country's left-wing guerrilla groups (the FARC and the ELN). Indeed, despite well documented links to paramilitary groups and continued human rights violations perpetrated by Colombia's public forces, since 2000 the US government has provided over $8 billion of aid to Colombia, the majority of which has been channelled into Colombia's security forces. While billed as an anti-narcotics programme, this aid has consistently had counterinsurgency motivations at its core (Hristov 2009; Stokes 2005). While the counterinsurgency effort has aimed primarily to destroy Colombia's insurgency, it has also systematically targeted progressive unarmed movements considered inimical to the implementation of neoliberal structural reforms. Moreover, while the state's security forces have been responsible for a large proportion of violations, a good deal of this state terror has been orchestrated by state-linked paramilitary groups, and often in concert with the Colombian armed forces. As Stokes and Raphael (2010: 71) argue, the US counterinsurgency doctrine has explicitly advocated tight relationships between state armed forces and the pervasive use of paramilitaries. Such terrorism has served to insulate Colombia's elite from the prospect of radical political change from 'below' and to maintain and advance capitalist political and economic structures underpinning the US-led global economy.

Conclusion

An HM lens provides a way to understand and examine terrorism and counter-terrorism as embedded within a wider set of dynamic and changing social relations. This moves beyond dominant dichotomous interpretations of state and non-state terrorism, political versus economic terrorism, and political or criminal terrorism as distinct categories. Instead, HM accounts for terrorism and other forms of violence as being embedded in and a manifestation of a set of complex and ever-changing social relations (Joseph 2011).

Importantly, such a framework acknowledges the marriage of the political and economic spheres, and how this can provide critical insights into terrorism. This includes the importance of class relations, the appreciation of capitalism as an often violent mode of economic development, and how the political and economic motivations underpinning some forms of terrorism can be integral to imperialism. The case of Colombia demonstrates this well: economic development has occurred during periods of intensifying violence. Rather than understanding this economic development as occurring *in spite of* terroristic violence, we have instead applied an HM approach which unpacks crucial links between violence and economic processes which more liberal frameworks often overlook. That is to say, we have argued that terrorism perpetrated by the Colombian armed forces and right-wing paramilitary groups, including widespread forced displacement and attacks on civilian groups deemed inimical to the neoliberal economic model, has stimulated levels of FDI, international trade and the resultant economic growth. Moreover, since 1991, this economic growth has been increasingly distributed unequally. It is primarily domestic and foreign investors that have benefited from this neoliberal model vis-à-vis the majority of Colombians, which is especially the case for the millions of Colombians affected by state and state-sponsored terrorism.

As we have argued, HM can be used to unveil valuable insights into the links between terrorism and capitalist development. In this light, and referring back to Joseph's observation outlined in the introduction to this chapter, CTS can benefit from an HM framework by paying careful attention to the nature of capitalism, especially in terms of how terrorism interacts with the social relations of production.

Notes

1. The application of primitive accumulation (and its closely related derivatives such as David Harvey's accumulation by dispossession) to contemporary debates can be contested (for example, see Glassman 2006). However, critical scholars typically converge in the acceptance that capitalist accumulation was violent in its incipiency and continues to be violent in many areas of the world. It is this broad framework which we employ throughout this chapter.
2. There are also well documented links between large sections of Colombia's political class and right-wing paramilitaries (e.g. IHRLC 2010). Such a discussion, however, does not fit the scope of this chapter, which instead focuses on the links between Colombia's security forces and paramilitary groups.

References

Acción Social (2011) *Sistemas de información. Estadísticas de la población desplazada. Registro único de población desplazada* [database online]. Online at: http://www.dps.gov.co/contenido/contenido.aspx?catID=621&conID=556&pagID=838 (accessed 11 September 2012).

Amnesty International (2004) *Colombia: Laboratory of War – Repression and Violence in Arauca*. Online at: http://www.amnesty.org/en/library/info/AMR23/004/2004 (accessed 10 September 2012).

Birch, K. and Mykhnenko, V. (2010) 'Introduction: A world the right way up', in Kean Birch and Vlad Mykhnenko (eds), *The Rise and Fall of Neo-Liberalism: The Collapse of an Economic Order?* London: Zed, pp. 1–20.

Blakeley, R. (2009) *State Terrorism and Neoliberalism: The North in the South*. London: Routledge.

Blakeley, R. (2010) 'State terrorism in the social sciences: theories, methods, and concepts', in Richard Jackson, Eamon Murphy and Scott Poynting (eds), *Contemporary State Terrorism: Theory and Practice*. London: Routledge, pp. 12–27.

Bromley, S. (2006) 'The logic of American power in the international capitalist order', in A. Colas and Saull, R. (eds), *The War on Terrorism and the American 'Empire' After the Cold War*. London: Routledge, pp. 44–64.

Cohen, B. J. (2008) *International Political Economy: An Intellectual History*. Princeton, NJ: Princeton University Press.

Cohen, B. J. (2009) 'The way forward', *New Political Economy*, 14 (3): 395–400.

Colombia Reports (2013) *Fact Sheets: False Positives*. Online at: http://colombiareports. com/false-positives/ (accessed 8 August 2013).

Cox, R. (1996) *Approaches to World Order*. Cambridge: Cambridge University Press.

Cramer, C. (2006) *Civil War Is Not a Stupid Thing: Accounting for Violence in Developing Countries*. London: Hurst.

Chomsky, N. (1999) *Profit Over People: Neoliberalism and Global Order*. New York: Seven Stories Press.

Duménil, G. and Lévy, D. (2004) 'The economics of US imperialism at the turn of the 21st century', *Review of International Political Economy*, 11 (4): 657–76.

Gaibulloev, K. and Sandler, T. (2011) 'The adverse effect of transnational and domestic terrorism on growth in Africa', *Journal of Peace Research*, 48 (3): 355–71.

George, A. L. and Bennet, A. (2005) *Case Studies and Theory Development in the Social Sciences*. Cambridge, MA: MIT Press.

Glassman, J. (2006) 'Primitive accumulation, accumulation by dispossession, accumulation by extra-economic means', *Progress in Human Geography*, 30 (5): 608–25.

Harvey, D. (2005) *A Brief History of Neoliberalism*. Oxford: Oxford University Press.

Herring, E. (2008) 'Critical terrorism studies: an activist scholar perspective', *Critical Studies on Terrorism*, 1 (2): 197–211.

Herring, E. and Stokes, D. (2011) 'Critical realism and historical materialism as resources for critical terrorism studies', *Critical Studies on Terrorism*, 4 (1): 5–21.

Hristov, J. (2009) *Blood & Capital: The Paramilitarization of Colombia*. Toronto, ON: Between the Lines.

Human Rights Watch (2010) *Paramilitaries' Heirs: The New Face of Violence in Colombia*. New York: Human Rights Watch.

Ibáñez, A. M. and Vélez, C. E. (2008) 'Civil conflict and forced migration: the micro determinants and welfare losses of displacement in Colombia', *World Development*, 36 (4): 659–76.

Internal Displacement Monitoring Centre (2012) *Global Overview 2011: People Internally Displaced by Conflict and Violence*. Geneva: IDMC.

International Human Rights Law Clinic (2010) *Truth Behind Bars: Colombian Paramilitary Leaders in U.S. Custody*. Berkeley, CA: University of California.

International Trade Union Confederation (ITUC) (2011) *Worldwide Survey: Repression of Union Rights and Economic Freedoms Across the Globe*. Online at: http://www.ituc-csi.org/ worldwide-survey-repression-of.html (accessed 8 July 2012).

International Trade Union Confederation (ITUC) (2012) *Colombia – 2012. In Practice*. Online at: http://survey.ituc-csi.org/Colombia.html#tabs-4 (accessed 11 September 2012).

Jackson, R., Murphy, E. and Poynting, S. (2010) 'Introduction: terrorism, the state and the study of political terror', in R. Jackson, E. Murphy and S. Poynting (eds), *Contemporary State Terrorism: Theory and Practice*. London: Routledge.

Joseph, J. (2011) 'Terrorism as a social relation within capitalism: theoretical and emancipatory implications', *Critical Studies on Terrorism*, 4 (1): 23–37.

Keefer, P. and Loayza, N. (eds) (2008) *Terrorism, Economic Development, and Political Openness*. Cambridge: Cambridge University Press.

Leech, G. (2011) *The FARC: The Longest Insurgency*. London: Zed Books.

McKeown, A. (2011) 'The structural production of state terrorism: capitalism, imperialism and international class dynamics', *Critical Studies on Terrorism*, 4 (1): 75–93.

Maher, D. and Thomson, A. (2011) 'The terror that underpins the "peace": the political economy of Colombia's paramilitary demobilisation process', *Critical Studies on Terrorism*, 4 (1): 95–113.

Marx, K. (1990) *Capital: A Critique of Political Economy*, trans. B. Fowkes, Vol. 1. London: Penguin.

Marx, K. and Engels, F. (1992) *The Communist Manifesto*. Oxford: Oxford University Press.

Panitch, L. and Gindin, S. (2004) *Global Capitalism and American Empire*. London: Merlin Press.

Porpora, D. (2011) 'Critical terrorism studies: a political economic approach grounded in critical realism', *Critical Studies on Terrorism*, 4 (1): 39–55.

Powers, M. and Choi, S.-W. (2012) 'Does transnational terrorism reduce foreign direct investment? Business-related versus non-business-related terrorism', *Journal of Peace Research*, 49 (3): 407–22.

Robinson, W. I. (2003) *Transnational Conflicts: Central America, Social Change, and Globalization*. London: Verso.

Robinson, W. I. (2004) *A Theory of Global Capitalism: Production, Class, and State in a Transnational World*. Baltimore, MD and London: Johns Hopkins University Press.

Sandler, T. and Enders, W. (2008) 'Economic consequences of terrorism in developed and developing countries: an overview', in P. Keefer and N. Loayza (eds), *Terrorism, Economic Development and Political Openness*. Cambridge: Cambridge University Press, pp. 17–47.

Stokes, D. (2005) *America's Other War: Terrorizing Colombia*. New York: Zed Books.

Stokes, D. and Raphael, S. (2010) *Global Energy Security and American Hegemony*. Baltimore, MD: Johns Hopkins University Press.

United Nations Conference on Trade and Development (n.d.) *Foreign Direct Investment* (online database). Online at: http://unctadstat.unctad.org/TableViewer/tableView.aspx.

Williamson, J. (1990) *What Washington Means by Policy Reform*. Online at: http://www.iie.com/publications/papers/paper.cfm?ResearchID=486 (accessed 8 October 2010).

World Bank (2012) *Income Share Held by Highest 10% – Colombia*. Online at: http://data.worldbank.org/indicator/SI.DST.10TH.10 (accessed 11 September 2012).

World Bank (n.d.) *Data*. Online at: http://data.worldbank.org/ (accessed 11 March 2013).

PART 3
Ethnography

4

TERRORISTS AS CO-PARTICIPANTS?

Outline of a research model

Harmonie Toros

Methodology can be understood as a series of conscious and unconscious choices made by scholars as they reflect upon and adapt to the conditions of research. In the field of qualitative research, a scholar will arguably never use the same methods twice as no research is ever replicable. One's broader methodological and epistemological stance, however, is likely to follow certain foundational principles. The aim of this chapter is to outline the rationale behind the choice of using what I term an *empathetic ethnographic approach* to the study of conflicts marked by terrorist violence, and engage with some of the key specificities, strengths and problems of this approach, in particular when investigating political violence.

I will begin by outlining the key reasons that have led me to adopt an ethnographic approach before examining its implications. The chapter puts forward – in initial broad strokes – a framework drawn from psychologist Carl Rogers' work in person-centred therapy for empathetic ethnographic investigations. In particular, I will examine how Rogers' three core conditions of empathy, congruence and unconditional positive regard can help ensure that – as far as possible – one speaks *with* research co-participants rather than *for* them. Both strengths and weaknesses of the framework become apparent when discussing direct experience researching political violence and the chapter concludes by sharing the challenges that emerged while attempting to use a yet-to-be formalised empathic ethnographic approach in field research with paramilitaries in Northern Ireland.

Why ethnography?

Raymond Morrow and David D. Brown (1994: 200) argue that methodological choices are also political and ideological. They are based on understandings of how structures and agents interact, how much importance to grant to each, and how one understands change in the social world and what drives it. Such choices are also based on what one understands as 'truth' and what kinds of 'truths' are available to scholars, in this case in the social sciences.

In formal terms, I adopt a minimal foundationalist approach that investigates key relationships – from broad structural ones to interpersonal ones – that frame the choices of individual agents. An actor's choice to use violence (or not) is therefore never disconnected from the complex web of social relations in which s/he is making such a choice. Such an approach – broadly based on Frankfurt School critical theory but also drawing on the work of French sociologist Pierre Bourdieu – believes scholars can investigate historically contingent 'truths' which can never be fully grasped but only approached by trying to arrive at the 'best' knowledge available at a certain moment in time and within the conditions of research. Linking back to the argument of Morrow and Brown, critical theory also defines itself by the stance that no knowledge and no research is apolitical.

Although not essential to all *critical* approaches to terrorism (see Stump and Dixit 2013), emancipation is at the heart of any approach based on the Frankfurt School (Wyn Jones 1999). However, unlike projects aimed at spreading 'universal' liberal (or indeed Marxist) practices across different political, social and cultural contexts, a critical theory-based understanding of emancipation is always context-specific. Indeed, the praxis toward Horkheimer's (1992: 246) broad aim of freeing human beings from slavery can only be understood by investigating each particular historical example. For Horkheimer (1992: 216), one needs to engage in 'an aggressive critique not only against the conscious defenders of the status quo but also against distracting, conformist, or utopian tendencies within his own household.'

For this, one needs a methodology that allows for the specificities of each context to emerge. It requires that researchers come to understand the aspirations of their research co-participants (so-called 'subjects') as well as the constraints impeding the realisation of their aspirations. What does emancipation mean to them? What does it entail? What are the hurdles they identify? What are the hurdles that are not explicitly identified by the actors but that may nonetheless be contributing to the structural violence surrounding them?

As argued by Lee Jarvis and Michael Lister, answering such questions requires that researchers aim to speak *with* rather than speak *for* their co-participants (Jarvis and Lister 2013: 172). The essential question is *how* does one try to achieve this aim of allowing research co-participants to speak their words with the researcher.

Before we examine how such an approach can be envisaged, however, it is important to note that 'speaking *with*' is unlikely to ever mean that the researcher and her/his co-participants will have an equal say in any research. 'It is the investigator who starts the game and who sets up its rules: it is most often she who, unilaterally and without any preliminary negotiations, assigns to the interview its objectives and uses,' Pierre Bourdieu (1996: 19) states, noting the asymmetry in the relationship. Often, even the best-intentioned researcher will have a greater role in constructing the narrative at hand particularly during the writing up phase as the lived experience of the field research is cut and pasted into sections and subsections that make up PhDs, books and articles. The words of co-participants are transformed from being the primary constituting elements in their narrative to being 'quotes' or supporting evidence used in the narrative of the researcher.

Furthermore, the longer the researcher is away from co-participants, the more difficult it is to re-evoke the experiential knowledge acquired in the field. With the passage of time, the researcher forgets how the words inscribed in notes or even recorded on tape were spoken – the context of the meeting, the micro-political events of that day that may or may not have impacted on the interview and/or observation. Statements become truncated as the researcher forgets why a particular sentence was important to the speaker or to illustrate the context. The asymmetry that results from the interview or observation is further deepened 'every time the investigator occupies a higher place in the social hierarchy of different types of capital, especially cultural capital' (Bourdieu 1996: 19).

There are also times when research co-participants will occupy a higher place in the social hierarchy than the researcher. This can create a power differential during the field research at the expense of the researcher, who may be forced to interview such co-participants in circumstances of the latter's choosing. This can be particularly problematic when investigating political violence as co-participants could have the extreme power of life and death over the researcher. Thus complete equality in research – as in any other social practice – is likely unachievable.

Carl Rogers and speaking *with* co-participants

With this in mind, Rogers[1] offers three key guiding principles or 'core conditions' that can help researchers in their attempt to speak with co-participants: empathy, congruence and unconditional positive regard. Rogers' work in psychotherapy was based on the principle that 'the client knows best': s/he 'knows what hurts and where the pain lies and it is the client who, in the final analysis, will discover the way forward' (Mearns and Thorne 2013: 2). In this 'person-centred approach' the counsellor acts as 'a non-directive companion rather than as a guide or an expert on another's life' (Mearns and Thorne 2013: 2). It requires counsellors to be 'fully present' in the moment – engaging emotionally as well as cognitively – with the other, rather than extracting oneself to make a diagnosis.

I argue that speaking *with* rather than *for* another person requires the same emotional and cognitive commitment from the researcher. The researcher needs to be 'fully present' in an attempt to 'understand' as much of the co-participant as possible. To achieve this, empathy, congruence and unconditional positive regard are particularly useful.

Empathy, understood in the person-centred approach as 'to learn what it feels like to be in the client's skin and to perceive the world as the client perceives it' (Mearns and Thorne 2013: 13) – is both emotional and cognitive. Indeed, Naomi Head argues that it may be understood as a relational process 'whereby cognition and affect play out in interpersonal exchanges through which participants can generate shared new meanings' (Head 2011: 19). Meanings are indeed being renegotiated in all interaction between social actors, even when actors are not 'explicitly seeking to renegotiate their relations' (King 2000: 428). As such, researchers are required to open themselves up to this renegotiation – they need to be willing to negotiate meanings with their co-participants to be able to create shared meanings.

Congruence – or being true – is arguably a prerequisite for such a relational process to be established. In Rogers' words (1990: 224), being congruent means that 'within the relationship [the therapist] is freely and deeply himself, with his actual experience accurately represented by his awareness of himself. It is the opposite of presenting a façade, either knowingly or unknowingly.' Indeed, Rogers (1990: 224) adds: 'It should be clear that this includes being himself even in ways which are not regarded as ideal …' For researchers, this means being true to one's co-participants, which can involve acknowledging ignorance, fear, mistrust or on the opposite side of the spectrum sympathy, love and everything in between. Of course, as Rogers points out for therapy, the aim is not for the therapist or researcher 'to express or talk out his own feelings', although this may be required if they are standing in the way of building an empathetic relationship.

The third condition of unconditional positive regard can lead to some confusion. Indeed, Rogers (1990: 225) himself accepts that the phrase 'may be an unfortunate one, since it sounds like an absolute, an all-or-nothing dispositional concept.' It also may lead some to believe that the therapist or the researcher must only 'think well of' clients or co-participants respectively. In fact, having unconditional positive regard means to accept the other in their entirety, including their positive and negative attributes, their consistencies and inconsistencies. For the therapist, it means 'caring for the client as a *separate* person, with permission to have his own feelings, his own experiences' (Rogers 1990: 225). For the researcher, this can be equated with accepting co-participants as *separate* and whole persons, with multiple identities, feelings and experiences. It also means 'caring for' the co-participants in the sense of trying as far as possible to follow Mary Anderson's 'Do no harm' principle. Bourdieu (1996: 19, emphasis in original) indeed advises researchers 'to do all in our power … *to reduce as much as possible the symbolic violence which is exerted*' through the power asymmetry separating interviewer and interviewee.

Thus, although research is not being equated with therapy, the three core conditions for person-centred therapy put forward by Rogers can serve as core conditions for critical theory-based researchers seeking to *speak with* rather than *for* their co-participants. Empathy allows researchers to put themselves, as much as possible, in the shoes of their co-participants – a relational process they are only able to engage in if they are congruent with the latter. In this relational process, researchers attempt as much as possible to recognise co-participants in their uniqueness and their entirety – they offer unconditional positive regard for them while trying to ensure that the often-present power differential between the parties is as mitigated as possible.

Empathy for *terrorists*? Congruence with *terrorists*? Unconditional positive regard for *terrorists*?

How do these core conditions fare when researching political violence? Should one empathise with actors who have carried out violent attacks on soft targets? How can one have 'unconditional positive regard' for actors who make means-ends calculations with the lives of civilians?

As noted by Nicholas J. Wheeler (2013) in his work on empathy and trust in international relations, empathy does not necessarily lead to positive feelings toward another. Indeed, actors can use their capacity to empathise with their opponent to better defeat them. Empathy therefore does not imply 'sympathy' for armed actors. It does, however, require researchers to be able to put themselves in the other's shoes. This in turn requires of researchers to see and accept the humanity of their co-participants. Empathy demands that researchers start any interaction with another by saying: 'They are like me, human.'

Such an approach is in direct contrast with many traditional terrorism scholars who explicitly separate 'terrorists' from law-abiding and moral citizens, such as themselves. Scholars often stress the barbaric or savage nature of the violence carried out by terrorists, in particular religious terrorists, who, as Magnus Ranstorp (1996: 54) argues, are seen as lacking 'in any moral constraints' (see also Toros and Mavelli 2014 forthcoming). Indeed, 'terrorists' are presented as so other, that it is not only empathy but indeed any form of communication that is banned. Leading terrorism scholar Paul Wilkinson (2001: 80), for example, wrote against any dialogue with 'terrorists' on the grounds that the 'idea that such criminals should be accepted as legitimate interlocutors for their professed aims would surely cause general revulsion and in my view is totally unacceptable.' Such an approach, however, bars researchers from any access to the lived experience that brings actors – human beings – to engage in political violence.

Recognising the humanity of one's research co-participants means having unconditional positive regard for them. One accepts them as a whole individual, an individual with positive and negative feelings, with the power to heal as well as the power to hurt. One thus accepts that violent actors have the potential for non-violent action as they are whole humans. Unconditional positive regard also means ensuring that one's entrance into their lives does not create harm – for example by leading to their arrest or identification by opposing armed groups, be they state or non-state. The latter condition can be particularly difficult when investigating outlawed armed groups or their sympathisers as the presence of a researcher can be used by authorities of opposing groups to identify members. Nevertheless, empathy and unconditional positive regard are not impossible in research on terrorism and political violence and hinge on recognising the humanity of all actors one is engaged with – even the violent ones.

It is also possible to be congruent in such research. One can be open and entirely present in observations and interviews. One can acknowledge fear and discomfort, for example. However, as Jacob Stump and Priya Dixit (2013: 81) point out, researchers also need to present themselves to co-participants in a way that 'makes sense to the audience at hand'. This may involve carefully selecting the language researchers use in interactions with co-participants. This is particularly important when researching outlawed groups who are likely to be very suspicious of researchers as potential state informants. Even without this suspicion, how researchers present their research will have a direct impact on how they are perceived by the community and they need to take care that language that is true or congruent to them is not saying something very different to co-participants.

Empathy, congruence and unconditional positive regard: a research experience

Although I had not yet come across the work of Rogers when I undertook a three-month fieldwork stay in Northern Ireland, the concept of empathy was very much a part of my approach to research co-participants. I also struggled with questions surrounding congruence and unconditional positive regard. The research – aimed at gathering data for one of two case studies for my doctoral dissertation – investigated whether and how dialogue can contribute to the transformation of actors engaged in terrorist violence. From February to May 2007, it involved a series of 22 face-to-face interviews, an informal conversation and a telephone conversation, as well as several days of participant observation of meetings between loyalist and republican former and current paramilitaries. It was greatly facilitated by the support of InterAction Belfast – my 'gatekeeper' – and in particular Noel Large, a community worker and former Ulster Volunteer Force (UVF) gunman. Noel, whom I had met during a research trip to Belfast in 2004 with my Masters class from the University of Bradford and have come to consider a personal friend, explicitly and implicitly vouched for me, assuring others that I was a legitimate researcher who had the interests of peace in Northern Ireland at heart.

My research directly investigated the role of talking in triggering empathy and humanisation of actors labelled as 'terrorists' (see Toros 2012) and involved interviewing actors from across the conflict spectrum on whether and how empathy and humanisation played a role in their relations. I was acutely aware of the reflexive loop that I had placed myself in: I was talking to 'terrorists' to see whether 'talking to terrorists' could transform them and others. I believed I was open to be transformed by the dialogue. Indeed, I begin the conclusion of my book by saying that my research had transformed me from an arrogant and naive one investigating whether 'we' could talk *to* 'terrorists' to convince them to end their violent means to a more collaborative one.

> Actually talking with people who have taken part, ordered or sanctioned terrorist violence radically changed the question being asked. I realised that one could not simply talk *to* 'terrorists' but rather one talks *with* them – they are far from passive actors waiting to be redeemed and may have as much to teach us as they have to learn from us. [...] It is not only *their* violence that needs to be transformed, but also ours: the counterterrorist violence and the structural violence to which we are often accomplices, if only by our silence and inertia. (Toros 2012: 189)

Arriving at this conclusion required that research 'subjects' become co-participants, with a recognition of their agency and essentially of their humanity.

Importantly, the humanisation of (wo)men involved in past and present violence was not overall an emotionally difficult or transforming process as long as the violence they had been or were engaged in remained aimed at nameless people unknown to me. This changed and led to what Antonius Robben and Carolyn Nordstrom (1995) aptly call a 'fieldwork crisis' when I realised I had been in a dialogue with a man sentenced for taking part in a very public and documented attack. I could for the first time put a name and face to the victims of the man I had engaged with professionally as a researcher but also in a social setting as I had gone to the pub with several former and current paramilitaries after a meeting.

Suddenly the phrase 'He is like me, human' became extremely difficult to bear as I had seen photographs and video footage showing the terror of the faces of his victims when they realised they would likely be killed and later their half-naked mutilated bodies lying dead in a parking lot of West Belfast. I was grappling, trying to find ways in which 'he is not like me' or more precisely 'I am not like him.' One could be tempted to conclude from this that empathy cannot be (or should not) extended to violent actors or actors guilty of particularly vicious crimes. That there is indeed a qualitative difference between 'them' and 'us'.

However, Robben and Nordstrom state: 'A fieldwork crisis, as personal as it is political and theoretical, may deepen the understanding of ethnographers, of the people with whom they associate, and of the violence they study' (1995: 14). Indeed, potentially the better lesson to learn may be that empathy is not easy. Empathy, particularly with actors who perpetrate extreme violence, is actually very difficult and represents a personal challenge. In this case, it confronted me with difficult questions, such as: 'If I can sit down for a pint with a "terrorist" what does that say about my moral compass?' But it also leads to more fundamental questions: 'What would make me capable of such violence? What would be my breaking point?' By asking myself these questions, I felt a little of the extreme personal discomfort and pain experienced by those of whom I demand the willingness to enter into a dialogue and empathise with 'terrorists'. Until them, this discomfort and pain were feelings I could cognitively conceive of but had not felt personally. Ethnographic research was thus essential for me to achieve a deeper – though still partial and flawed – knowledge of the emotional and moral strain that can emanate from dialogue with violent actors.

Congruence was also at times a challenge during my fieldwork in Northern Ireland. For certain matters, it was simple to be open and fully present. For example, I often told my interviewees that I had no position on whether Northern Ireland should remain part of the United Kingdom or unite with the Republic of Ireland. I indeed have no real position on the question – a neutrality that appeared to reassure rather than irritate my interlocutors. On other matters, however, congruence was more difficult. In particular, the republican movement's complete rejection of the term 'terrorist' and 'terrorism' meant that I would not use the term in any of my interactions with republicans. It became very quickly clear that even though I qualified my use of the term – I do not believe in labelling armed groups as 'terrorists' as it reduces complex human beings into single-identity cardboard cutouts – and argued that I was investigating dialogue with actors 'labelled as terrorist', republican interlocutors often objected to the term without hearing how I was using it. I therefore said I was investigating dialogue in contexts of political violence, while knowing that in my final product – the PhD thesis and book – I would be replacing 'political violence' with 'terrorism'. I chose to tell a story 'that makes sense to the audience at hand' rather than complete congruence, taking the risk that some co-participants may feel betrayed if and when they discovered that my thesis and book would be about dialogue with groups involved in 'terrorist' violence.

Final thoughts

> 'S/he does what s/he can. What s/he can't, s/he doesn't do.' (Alberto Manzi)

Gayatri Chakravorty Spivak (1988: 271) is right in saying that our efforts to call into question the positionality of researchers 'can never suffice' to counterbalance the structural violence caused by (often white) researchers investigating the violence of those in the Global South, be it the Global South of Belfast, Los Angeles or Cotabato City. Even when my co-participants occupy a higher place in the social hierarchy of the context of the field research, I know that I can return to my ivory tower to apply for promotion based on publications that I write – cutting, pasting and building 'original' and 'innovative' narratives about other people's lives. There is no escape from our position as narrators with the final say on what is said and how.

I hope, however, not to be guilty of 'meaningless piety' (Spivak 1988: 271). In my defence – and I do need to defend myself for having the gall to enter other people's lives, to question them and then take their words – all I can say is that if methodology is a series of conscious and unconscious choices made by scholars, my approach is based on the conscious choice of trying to speak *with* co-participants rather than speak *for* research subjects, of trying to mitigate the structural violence often present in the positionality of researchers vis-à-vis co-participants, and to engage in research that keeps as a constant overall aim the freeing of human beings from slavery.

To this end, I have argued here that Rogers' three core conditions of his person-centred therapy provide helpful guidelines for an empathetic ethnographic practice. In my research, I *need to* empathise with co-participants, try as much as possible to put myself in their place, and be open to renegotiating my truths and understandings in order to create shared new meanings with them. I *need to* be congruent with my co-participants. I must be truthful – offering a negotiated truth that is both true and comprehensible to my audience – and fully present in the moment. I *need to* have unconditional positive regard for my co-participants, by which I mean accept them as complex, entire human beings with positive and negative feelings, capable of hurting and healing. I *need to* also care for my co-participants to ensure that my intrusion into their lives causes a little harm as possible.

Such conditions are likely to be difficult in any research and one must be cautious of perpetuating the 'terrorism' exceptionalism that has marred much work in the field. Nonetheless, engaging with violent actors – state and non-state actors who have often willingly targeted non-combatants – makes empathy, congruence and unconditional positive regard a constant challenge for researchers. As was exemplified in the brief illustration of fieldwork in Northern Ireland, it can challenge how researchers understand their co-participants, themselves and ultimately what it means to be human. It is this difficulty, however, that may produce knowledge that challenges established 'truths' about terrorism and political violence, about actors engaged in such violence, and how it may be transformed. It is precisely its difficulty that may make an empathetic ethnographic approach worthwhile. Finally, such an approach may help us to keep in mind the secret of Antoine de Saint-Exupéry's (1943: 63) fox in *The Little Prince*: 'It's quite simple: One sees clearly only with the heart. Anything essential is invisible to the eyes.'

Note

1. I am grateful to Phill Gittins for introducing me to the work of Carl Rogers. It is important to note that I am not arguing that research or the relationships between researchers and co-participants are a form of therapy or are therapeutic for any of the parties. I am using Rogers' person-centred framework and his three core conditions of empathy, congruence and unconditional positive regard as a useful general framework to outline my approach to research.

References

Bourdieu, P. (1996) 'Understanding', *Theory, Culture and Society*, 13 (2): 17–37.

de Saint-Exupéry, A. (1943) *The Little Prince*. London: Egmont.

Head, N. (2011) *The 'Other Side of the Coin': Theorising the Role of Deception in Trust, Empathy, and Dialogue*. Paper presented at the British International Studies Association Conference, Manchester, May.

Horkheimer, M. (1992) *Critical Theory: Selected Essays*. New York: Seabury Press.

Jarvis, L. and Lister, M. (2013) 'Vernacular securities and their study: a qualitative analysis and research agenda', *International Relations*, 27 (2): 158–79.

King, A. (2000) 'Thinking with Bourdieu against Bourdieu: a "practical" critique of the habitus', *Sociological Theory*, 18 (3): 417–33.

Mearns, D. and Thorne, B. (2013) *Person-Centred Counselling in Action*. London: Sage.

Morrow, R. A. and Brown, D. D. (1994) *Critical Theory and Methodology*. Thousand Oaks, CA: Sage.

Ranstorp, M. (1996) 'Terrorism in the name of religion', *Journal of International Affairs*, 50 (1): 41–62.

Robben, A. C. G. M. and Nordstrom, C. (1995) 'The anthropology and ethnography of violence and sociopolitical conflict', in C. Nordstrom and A. C. G. M. Robben (eds), *Fieldwork under Fire: Contemporary Studies of Violence and Survival*. Berkeley, CA: University of California Press, pp. 1–23.

Rogers, C. (1990) 'The necessary and sufficient conditions of therapeutic personality change', in H. Kirschenbaum and V. Land Henderson (eds), *The Carl Rogers Reader*. London: Constable, pp. 219–35.

Spivak, G. (1988) 'Can the subaltern speak?', in C. Nelson and L. Grossberg (eds), *Marxism and the Interpretation of Culture*. Basingstoke: Macmillan Education, pp. 271–313.

Stump, J. and Dixit, P. (2013) *Critical Terrorism Studies: An Introduction to Research Methods*. London: Routledge.

Toros, H. (2012) *Terrorism, Talking and Transformation: A Critical Approach*. Abingdon: Routledge.

Toros, H. and Mavelli, L. (2014) 'Collective evil and individual pathology: the depoliticization of violence against Afghan civilians', *International Politics*, 51 (4): 508–24.

Wheeler, N. J. (2013) 'Investigating diplomatic transformations', *International Affairs*, 89 (2): 477–96.

Wilkinson, P. (2001) *Terrorism Versus Democracy: The Liberal State Response*. London: Frank Cass.

Wyn Jones, R. (1999) *Security, Strategy, and Critical Theory*. Boulder, CO: Lynne Rienner.

Wyn Jones, R. (2005) 'On emancipation: necessity, capacity and concrete utopias', in K. Booth (ed.), *Critical Security Studies and World Politics*. Boulder, CO: Lynne Rienner, pp. 215–36.

5

ECOLOGIZING 'TERRORISM'

Attending to emergent pathways of ethnographic fieldwork, writing, and analysis

Yamuna Sangarasivam

Introduction

Ethnographic methodology invites the researcher into the possibilities for participating in multi-sited, collaborative, and politically engaged forms of scholarship and knowledge production. The production of subjectivities is at the heart of ethnographic practice. A study of 'terrorism'[1] calls for an especially careful and conscientious practice of research and representation of transnational and transcultural subjectivities when 'the field' is constituted as a person, an entire group or nation of people, a form of political action and political violence, a trope, a political ideology, and a site of war. As a qualitative methodological practice, ethnographic fieldwork is implicated in the production of knowledge about who is constituted as a 'terrorist' and what actions constitute the 'global war on terror.' I came to adopt an ethnographic methodology as an anthropologist endeavoring to disturb the neat grid of logic that relies on the binary of good versus evil while placing terrorism in opposition to patriotism, nationalism, freedom, and democracy. The continued expressions and experiences of violence named as terrorism by state and non-state entities present the inexorable need to re-examine the ideas and assumptions in that grid that predominantly define national security and justifies the deployment of military force to engage in war. As researchers, we are not outside of this grid. Our subjectivities are implicated in the pursuit and production of knowledge about terrorism. Ethnographic methodologies allow researchers to see and understand 'terrorism' from different perspectives, including: people who are witnesses to the violence of 'terrorism,' state and not-state agents who are prosecuting the global war on terror, and the people who are named and criminalized as terrorists.

At the core of academic studies focused on the problem of 'terrorism' lies the necessity of recognizing the continued experiences of colonialism and the consequent counter-struggles for liberation. Ethnographic research practices allow for the narrative encounter and exposition of these experiences and struggles of both the colonizer and the colonized who are caught in the crossfires of political violence in which 'terrorism' is assigned a unique value. What is essential to our understanding of how we justify our methodological stance – that is, how we choose specific methods, how we collect and analyze our ethnographic data, and how we situate our research within and across disciplinary boundaries – is the reality that we are *not* objective participants and observers carrying an ontological and epistemological privilege of neutrality. Rather, apprehending our role in 'the imperial contest itself,' researchers exist within the ecology of terrorism. Edward Said recognized that this

> is a cultural fact of extraordinary political as well as interpretive importance, because it is the true defining horizon, and to some extent, the enabling condition of such otherwise abstract and groundless concepts like 'otherness' and 'difference'. The real problem remains to haunt us: the relationship between anthropology as an ongoing enterprise and, on the other hand, empire as an ongoing concern. (Said 1989: 217)

Particularly because ethnographic research practices require the making and sustaining of relationships with living beings, places, and material realities in imperial settings, researchers are politically accountable for the consequences of representing and participating in the space, time, and fluidity of ecological systems within which terrorism is experienced. In attending to the normative challenges presented to the researcher by the construction of a racialized, 'terrorist' Other, this chapter examines pathways of ethnographic inquiry and analyses that emerge by ecologizing 'the terrorist' and 'terrorism' as a site of fieldwork.

Ethnography, ecography, and epistemologies of place

Ecologizing 'terrorism' begins with approaching the study of 'terrorism' as a place that ethnographers inhabit along with other living beings. Rather than conceptualizing terrorism simply as a morally reprehensible form of violence creating a threat to personal and national security, an ecological approach invites the researcher to be in a relationship with 'terrorism' as a place that is inscribed with local and global histories and futures that are interconnected. How does ethnography intersect with ecography to inform how we conduct research? What is at stake for whom in the collecting and constructing of knowledge about terrorists and terrorism? Ethnographers can intersect with ecographers by attending to the ways that we engage with the environment – our site of fieldwork. The practice of ethnography is predicated on the ability of the researcher to create relationships with community members with the intention of building enough trust to invite people to engage in conversations, tell their stories, and share their insights and analyses that become ethnographic data. Conventionally, the ethnographer would situate and organize the information embedded in this data into larger historical, political, economic, and cultural contexts to develop an analysis about terrorism. By inviting the ethnographer to build a relationship with 'terrorism' as a *place* where both 'terrorists' and ethnographers emerge from, inhabit, and disperse out of, a practice of ecologizing 'terrorism' allows for non-conventional ways of understanding people who choose violence as means of communicating their histories, identities, and futures that intersect with ours.

The concept of ecologizing 'terrorism' emerges from the theoretical and methodological practices of Jamon Alex Halvaksz and Heather E. Young-Leslie in their study of political economy and ecology from ecographers in Papua, New Guinea and in the Kingdom of Tonga. In studying with Saia Fifita, a Tongan elder, Young-Leslie developed the concept of ecography 'to describe the ontology she was learning from her interlocutors for speaking selves, surroundings, history, future, and present into being' (Halvaksz and Young-Leslie 2008: 201). With an ecographic approach, researchers studying 'terrorism' can endeavor to recognize, learn from, and narrate the ontology they have studied from interlocutors for people and places that are categorized as 'terrorists' and 'terrorism.' From this standpoint, 'terrorism' can be studied as a place where speaking selves – including the research/ethnographer – come into being by critically engaging with interlocutors for people who inscribe their surroundings, their present, their histories, and their futures through not only the practice of violence but also through the practice of love for land/soil, family, kinship, heritage, and more, to signify the integrity of agency and sovereignty that may or may not transcend the place(s) of nationalism.

Through this method of learning an ontology – a way of being, becoming, and thriving in an ecosystem – as a practice of integrating ecographic thinking with ethnographic research, 'terrorism' is made visible as a *place* where ethnographers and their interlocutors coexist within the imperial contest. As Halvaksz and Young-Leslie assert, 'ecographic thinking is therefore political and generative of new lines and movements between conventions of places [i.e. nationalism and 'terrorism'], humans, and animals' (Halvaksz and Young-Leslie 2008:186). Ecologizing 'terrorism' is related to conventional ethnographic approaches by the fundamental concerns about issues of power and constructions of authority in the process of representation that is linked to the political practice of knowledge production and dissemination. The practice of learning an ontology by integrating ecographic thinking with ethnographic research also enables researchers to 'be attentive to our historical practice of projecting our cultural practices onto the other … [by mapping] how and when and through what cultural and institutional means other people started claiming epistemology for their own' (Rabinow 2009 [1986]: 24).

The cultural value of terrorism

Terrorism is of cultural value to empire. As a place where imperial sentiments of nationalism and patriotism are nurtured and galvanized, terrorism is of cultural value for creating and maintaining a cohesive and unified national identity that elides the 'dilemmas, contradictions, and vulnerabilities of empire' (Lutz 2006: 607).

In forwarding a critical need for ethnographic methods that 'prioritize connections of patriarchy and white supremacy with the projects of empire,' Catherine Lutz argues for ethnographic research methods that can 'make the human and material face and frailties of imperialism more visible, and in so doing, to make challenges to it more likely' (2006: 594).[2] Ecographic thinking allows for a methodology that invites us to research and generate new lines and movements between the subject positions and social locations of 'terrorists,' ethnographers, and agents of imperial armies – including soldiers, mercenaries, private military contractors, and cultural analysts who 'provide socio-cultural knowledge' for the US Army's Human Terrain System missions, the Department of Defense, the State Department, and other Intelligence Community agencies.[3] An ecographic methodology invites ethnographers to excavate how the cultural value of terrorism as a place informs one's own constructions of national and transnational identity(ies) in relation to the interlocutors that we seek out to engage with and learn from not just in the local contexts of particular field sites, but also from the globalizing contexts of imperialism. Specifically, this means to generate fluid lines and movements between who we are vis-à-vis our national/transnational identities and who we perceive as terrorists. Through this process of understanding the importance of 'geographical disposition' and 'temporality' in constructing ethnographic authority, researchers can be guided by Said's concern for how ethnographic representations (of terrorists and terrorism) are deployed and circulated as public media images that in turn shape the domains of policy-making and policy enactment: 'How does work on remote or primitive or "other" cultures, societies, people [i.e. terrorists] in Central America, Africa, the Middle East, various parts of Asia, feed into, connect with, impede, or enhance the active political processes of dependency, domination, or hegemony?' (1989: 218). For example, in my study of Tamil nationalism and the armed struggle of the Liberation Tigers of Tamil Eelam (LTTE), an ecographic method of perceiving, formulating questions, and engaging in conversations with LTTE cadres and Tamil community members invites both myself and my interlocutors to observe how we are constructing our own emergent national and transnational identities as we critically examine the mutual shaping of the Tamil nationalist movement as a 'terrorist' organization by the US, its European allies, and the LTTE. This critical examination generates new lines and movements of thinking about how the US-sponsored global 'war on terror' necessitates the enduring 'inequalities, cultural values, and contradictions' of imperial projects, which in turn, inform and potentially feed nationalist wars (Lutz 2006: 607).

Racism, in conjunction with 'Islamophobia,' is an example of the enduring inequalities and contradictions that inform the cultural value of terrorism as a place to reunify and consolidate the sentiments of nationalism and patriotism. Calling a person a terrorist or categorizing an entire group/nation of people as terrorists in the everyday flow of conversation harkens back to the days when 'nigger' was once used in the flow of normative speech in the US to signify the racist cultural value of white supremacy and apartheid policies of racial segregation: policies and values that defined not only the social and cultural norms but also the notions of freedom and democracy for white people in the United States. The obvious contradictions surrounding the violent subjugation, discrimination, and oppression of African-Americans and people of color, juxtaposed with assertions of freedom and democracy for white people in support of white supremacy, was rendered invisible. To call a person 'nigger' was a way to sanction both structural and direct forms of violence – from the denial of citizenship and participation in electoral processes to the practice of ritualized lynching that marks the history of the United States.[4] Similarly, to call a person a terrorist authorizes the use of extreme state-sponsored violence that is performed as a part of the US-sponsored global war on terror that contradicts the values of freedom and democracy: the military invasions of sovereign countries such as Iraq and Afghanistan, along with the orchestrated lynching of Saddam Hussein and the assassinations of Osama bin Laden and Muammar al-Gaddafi, the militarized enclosure of the globe via the establishment of CIA black-sites in member states of the European Union, in North Africa, the Middle East and Asia, the maintenance of concentration camps in Guantanamo Bay, the policies of extraordinary rendition, indefinite detention, and torture of largely people of Islamic heritage, and the targeted killing of people with drone strikes for the exigencies of US national security. These actions and policies exemplify empire as an ongoing concern, while exposing the racial inequalities and contradictions that inform the cultural value of terrorism as a place where ethnographers and their interlocutors inhabit.

In seeking recognition from the international community, namely the United States and its European allies, for the rights to national self-determination, the LTTE learned and practiced similar enduring inequalities, cultural values, contradictions, and brutalities of Islamophobia in their infamous expulsion of Tamil-Muslim community members from the Jaffna peninsula. In October of 1990, after establishing the de facto administration and territory of Tamil Eelam by claiming the northern province of Sri Lanka from both the Sri Lankan and Indian military forces, the LTTE forcibly expelled approximately 75,000 Tamil-Muslim community members from their ancestral homes and lands in the northern province by identifying them as a threat to 'national security.'[5] To justify their policy of expulsion, the LTTE drew on the evidence of Tamil-Muslim cadres who had defected from their movement to join the Sri Lankan military and paramilitary forces that were responsible for the disappearances, torture, and massacres of Tamil civilians. As a form of functional and self-justifying violence,[6] the LTTE carried out counter-massacres in Muslim communities. The Saddam Hussein Nagar, also known as the 'Saddam Hussein model village of Eravur' (Jeyaraj 2012) was among the targeted sites for these counter-massacres. The former president of Iraq had donated funds and humanitarian relief aid to rebuild the village and its mosque in 1978 after a cyclone devastated and displaced the community. Hence, the place was named in his honor, 'Saddam Hussein Nagar.' In a BBC report after the capture and impending execution of Saddam Hussein in 2003, J. Abdul Jawad, a Saddam Hussein village community member, said 'I can only understand [his capture] as one more [example] of US high-handedness and dictatorship' (BBC 2003). He spoke as an ecographic interlocutor, articulating the connections and contradictions of terrorism, US imperialism, environmental disaster, and international aid from Saddam Hussein who is demonized in the US and Europe and who is memorialized in a model village in Sri Lanka that Mr Jawad calls home.

The cultural value of terrorism seeps through the facade of distinctions and disparate histories, alliances, and commitments to a singular national identity while revealing the 'cost of empire on human bodies and social worlds' (Lutz 2006: 598): the LTTE massacre of Tamil-Muslim community members in the model village that Saddam Hussein built after a devastating natural disaster; the expulsion and targeted violence against Tamil-Muslim community members by LTTE cadres along with the apathy and fear of bystanders within the Hindu and Christian Tamil communities; Tamil-Muslim paramilitary cadres who collaborated with the Sri Lankan military forces in abducting, torturing, and killing Tamil civilians; US invasions of Iraq since 1990, the execution of Saddam Hussein and the sympathy for him by Tamil-Muslim community members – this collage of interconnected histories, experiences, and social worlds are linked by the cultural value of terrorism as a place where the costs of empire is inscribed on the bodies of human subjects that links Iraq and Sri Lanka by the global reach of US imperial wars. The Islamophobia that informs the imperial constructions of terrorists and terrorism was imitated by the LTTE with their policy of expulsion and violence against Tamil-Muslim community members in the name of national security. Caught in the contradiction of seeking empire's recognition of their struggle for national self-determination, the LTTE was and is proscribed as a terrorist organization by the US and its European allies, precisely because of its tactic of targeted assassinations and massacres of civilians – the distinction lies in the asymmetry of imperial military technology and power. The US employs aerial bombardments and drone attacks to carry out its assassinations and massacres, while non-state political movements like the LTTE employ guerilla warfare and 'suicide bombers.'[7] In this way, the US and its European allies, and the LTTE mutually shape the Tamil nationalist movement as a terrorist organization. Ethnographers engaged in ecologizing 'terrorism' witness these colluding and colliding social worlds while examining how their own bodies are inscribed while apprehending their role in the imperial contest itself.

Ecologizing 'terrorism'

The date 27 November is designated by the LTTE as *Maaveerar Naal* (Great Heroes Day). In 2008, Velupillai Prabhakaran, the leader of the LTTE, delivered what would be his last yearly address to the Tamil people within Sri Lanka and in the Tami diaspora who commemorated this day in honor of the thousands of men, women, and children who participated in and gave up their lives for the Tamil nationalist struggle. *Maaveerar Naal* was observed in northern Sri Lanka and in the Tamil diasporic communities of North America, Europe, and Australia. *Maaveerar Naal* commemorations have been banned in Sri Lanka since May 2009, when Sri Lankan government forces militarily crushed the armed struggle of the LTTE with assistance from India, Pakistan, and China. The commemorations continue, though, in the Tamil diaspora. Young-Leslie's concept of ecography invites us to learn from Prabhakaran as an ecographer who calls on Tamil national and transnational community members to remember not only the sacrifices of the people that died in the collective struggle for the creation of Tamil Eelam, but also to make the critical connections between local and global histories and futures that continue to inscribe the lives of Tamil people living in Sri Lanka and in diasporic communities across the globe. Prabhakaran begins his speech by calling on the Tamil people to 'commemorate this auspicious day with a whole-hearted love for our courageous heroes who sacrificed their lives, while inspiring our life with integrity, for the dawning of Tamil Eelam' (Prabhakaran 2008).[8] He completes the frame to his speech by concluding with the recognition of community members in the Tamil diaspora and the critical role they play in maintaining the integrity of the struggle for justice and liberation: 'In this historic context, in whichever corner of the globe that Tamils are living in, in whichever flag that Tamils are raised under, raise your voices with determination for the liberation of our homeland, and strengthen the hand of our movement's freedom struggle' (Prabhakaran 2008).

The cultural poesis and politics of Prabhakaran's speech illustrates what James Clifford describes as 'the constant reconstitution of selves and others through specific exclusions, conventions, and discursive practices' (Clifford 1986: 24). Prabhakaran's discursive practice distinguishes him as a leader of the Tamil nationalist movement and as an ecographic historian whose pedagogy incorporates local epistemologies and global political processes to situate the LTTE's armed struggle. He details the history of the LTTE's efforts to participate in repeated peace negotiations while connecting to the Tamil community's historic attempts to participate in representative parliamentary politics with successive Sri Lankan governments throughout the past sixty years of struggle for Tamil civil rights. He links the discriminatory rule of the Sri Lankan state with histories of European colonial interventions that inform the contemporary political and military landscapes of war and dispossession. His discursive practice implicates the US and its European allies that

> denigrated our freedom movement as a terrorist organisation. They put us on their black list and ostracized us as unwanted and untouchable. Our people living in many lands were intimidated into submission by oppressive limitations imposed on them to prevent their political activities supporting our freedom struggle.[9]

Of significance in Prabhakaran's discursive practice is the way he tells the story of how a deeply rooted national consciousness comes into being by one's bodily emergence from, relationship with, and return to *munn* (the soil). An ecographic method allows the soil to be perceived as a living being that informs the cultural poesis and politics of ethnographers and their interlocutors. Prabhakaran narrates the ontology of soil by generating epistemological movements between the subject positions and social locations of LTTE cadres who have died and the soil that they and we the listeners are called to be in a relationship with:

It is in this soil that our courageous heroes were born, were raised, and it is where they lived. It is in this soil that their footprints leave an impression. Their breath is blended here. It is in this soil that our nation lived for generations through time … The soil within which they rest, is the soil that we are duty-bound to care for. For us, it is the soil that we belong to and that belongs to us. (Prabhakaran 2008)

Through the cultural poesis and politics of Prabhakaran's speech, we can witness the soil as a living being where speaking selves come to know and to inscribe their environments, their past, present, and future with a knowledge that soil preserves and promotes – a knowledge for love of kinship, family, and the integrity of agency that transcends territorial boundaries. Ecographers, like Prabhakaran, 'actively distill human-environment relations, forming – and cutting – networks to make sense of the world' (Halvaksz and Young-Leslie 2008: 188). He situates 'terrorism' in the ontology of *munn* (soil) to make sense of the exclusionary practice that feeds a protracted war with devastating consequences of human death and environmental destruction.

This ontology of *munn* in conjunction with the need for an independent state emerged in my conversation with Maathini and Vasanthi, Tamil women who identified themselves and their families as internally displaced persons from the eastern city of Batticaloa. We were seated next to each other at the inaugural Tamil National Resurgence Convention, *Ponngu Tamil*, which was organized by the LTTE in Vavuniya on 27 July 2005. I asked their permission to record our conversation. They agreed with a trace of hesitation. We both were taking risks as we were all being observed by agents of the Sri Lankan military and paramilitary forces as well as members of the LTTE. We took the risk of being detained, of these recordings being confiscated, and consequently being interrogated, and even being disappeared by soldiers of the Sri Lankan army who were patrolling the parameters of the area where the LTTE convened hundreds of people to rally in support of Tamil national independence. The town of Vavuniya was largely administered by the Sri Lankan Army because it was a significant territorial demarcation point between the territory of Sri Lanka and the de facto territory of Tamil Eelam, in the Northern Province, that was claimed by the LTTE between 1990 and 1995. More than a thousand Tamil national activists, academics, religious leaders, and representatives of Tamil political organizations gathered at the Vairavapuliyankulam Children's Park, where people convened to listen to parliamentary representatives from the Tamil National Alliance, leaders of the Up-Country People's Front, and the Western Province People's Front, the representatives of the LTTE, as well as representatives of local non-governmental organizations who were invited to speak and participate in the convention.[10] One of the LTTE's principal aims of the Convention was to seek reconciliation and solidarity with the Tamil-Muslim community. In 2002, Prabhakaran issued a formal apology to the Tamil-Muslim communities in the North and East, admitting the injustices of the movement's policy of expulsion. Consequently, Tamil-Muslim community members slowly began their repatriation to their homelands in the north. When I asked Maathini about her thoughts on the Convention, she analyzed the Tamil nationalist struggle by telling a story of the plight of women under military occupation.

> We need an independent state, my child. The reason is this. Now, you can capture and kill a resistance fighter who carries arms and weapons and do whatever. But women like us, they [the soldiers of Sri Lankan army] raped and tortured. Anyway, with all these atrocities, we kept asking for peace, peace, peace, and they kicked us with their feet and now these masked men – they mask their faces and they kill our people. So we say, one country cannot be divided in two. Only one king can rule. But if that very same king is deceitful and practices atrocities against his own people, then we need a separate state. We are from Batticaloa. Our properties, our freedom, our lives were all erased by the brutality of the Sri Lankan Army and so we ran to the safety of LTTE held areas. They have taken care of us. The atrocities that we witnessed and learned about from our neighbors and village community members are unspeakable. They [Sri Lankan soldiers] broke into our homes and grabbed our boys and men from us, right in front of our eyes. One woman was dragged by her hair and her young daughter screamed after her mother as the solders dragged her to the road and took her away. Later we learned that she was taken to a shop where one of the commanders of the Special Forces was. Her screams were heard throughout the neighborhood as she was being raped. Her young daughter stood outside the door of the shop screaming. When they were done, they came out to the child and said, 'you want your mother? Well, here she is' and the kid screamed at the sight of her mother's mutilated body. Both the mother and the child were burned to death. The soldiers wanted to teach us a lesson for supporting the movement. Before, each household would know that surely one of their kids is likely to join the movement. Now entire households and families are joining the movement by seeking refuge in LTTE-controlled areas like Wanni where we have lived as displaced people for all these years. We had to leave our *munn* (soil), to arrive here, displaced to survive.

Vasanthi joined to add her experiences and analysis to the story.

> Truth be told, the possibility of violence at this convention is imminent. Life could be lost, even. We left our husbands and kids to come here. It is our love for Tamil Eelam that brings us here and we need to inform the world. To demonstrate that we need a separate state of Tamil Eelam is why were are here, even ready to disregard our life. We have confidence in Prabhakaran that he will show us the way. When you return to foreign states, you must educate and inform the people outside, of our struggle here.

Survival and displacement, rape and torture, refuge and resistance, *munn* and Tamil Eelam, along with faith in Prabhakaran as a leader in the nationalist struggle, are all juxtaposed in the ecographic analyses that Maathini and Vasanthi shared. In the process of telling their stories and analyses, they invite us to stand in solidarity with them to bear witness to the cost of empire on human bodies and social worlds – theirs and ours. As an anthropologist attending the inaugural Tamil National Resurgence Convention, I am not outside the imperial contest that defines the LTTE as a terrorist organization and that consequently informs those moments of being in conversation with Maathini, Vasanthi, and others who risked their lives and livelihoods to be present to witness and support this historic moment. I was given a responsibility by Maathini, Vasanthi, and others whom I had the privilege to learn from in my ethnographic research: your responsibility in collecting and sharing our stories, our histories, our present, and our aspirations for the future are not for your personal and career advancement alone. For once you enter into relationship with us here, on this soil, you are accountable for the knowledge that you gain and the knowledge that you produce for others to learn about who we are and our struggle here. This is my translation via 'a contrapuntal interweaving of tellings' (Tyler, 2009 [1986]: 126) of Maathini and Vasanthi's request to 'educate and inform the people outside, of our struggle here.' It is my translation of Tamil language into English and it is also my translation of their analyses and retelling of their experiences and their stories.

> '[C]ultural translation' is inevitably enmeshed in conditions of power – professional, national, international. And among these conditions is the authority of ethnographers to uncover the implicit meanings of subordinate societies. Given that this is so, the interesting question for inquiry is … how power enters into the process of 'cultural translation,' seen both as a discursive and as a non-discursive practice. (Asad 2009 [1986]: 163)

Solidarity is an implicit meaning that I bring to this analysis of ethnographic subjectivities. In the construction of these subjectivities, power enters into the process of 'cultural translation.' Issues of positionality and power are principally centered on how, why, and by whom knowledge is constructed and thereby become of epistemological and ontological significance and concern.

In my 'cultural translation' of solidarity, there is an interplay of authenticity, authority, and invention between myself as the ethnographer and Vasanthi as an ecographer. We both can claim and re-present an authentic experience of participating in the Tamil Resurgence Convention but our subject positions and social locations radically differ and delineate the limitations of this solidarity that I choose to claim via the discursive practices of splicing my voice into the flow of analyzing and translating Vasanthi's words while constructing her as an ecographer. She did not authorize this particular remix of our discussion and dialogue that I present here. She and Maathini, and many others that I interviewed as a part of my ethnographic study, remained in Sri Lanka as internally displaced people while I retained the privileges of a round-trip ticket and a US passport that brought me back to the United States. Here, 'outside' the war zone where there isn't the imminent threat of detention and disappearance by Sri Lankan military or paramilitary forces, I write an ethnographic account and analysis of our discussion and experiences of war, displacement, survival, integrity, and a need to understand a Tamil nationalist struggle. My 'ethnographic self-fashioning' (Clifford 1988: 92–113) is mutually constituted – myself in relation to the interlocutors that I choose to engage with and learn from in the context of fieldwork. This self-fashioning is a critical aspect of how a researcher accesses 'the field' of research whose geographical, ontological, and epistemological boundaries remain ambiguous throughout the process of research and writing. Feminist anthropologists and postcolonial scholars[11] working at the nexus of the modern and postmodern turn in anthropology have critically transformed the process of ethnographic research by calling attention to how researchers assert their authority to represent cultural Others while being attentive to 'seeing power as productive and permeative of social relations and the production of truth in our current regime of power' (Rabinow 2009 [1986]: 241).[12] How a researcher reveals her/his subject position and social location in the context of conducting interviews becomes a critical component of constructing ethnographic knowledge and narrative authority. I am Tamil. I am an 'American,' though there is ambivalence in claiming this identity because I am consistently perceived as a visitor in communities within the United States even after living here for more than thirty years. I am a transnational woman who navigates multiple personal and political identities. When I am in Sri Lanka, extended family members embrace me as a child of our community. Simultaneously, I am perceived and called a 'white woman' by Tamil boys in our neighborhood and on the streets of Jaffna where I am apparently known as 'an outsider' and 'an American.' All this and more contribute to my ethnographic subjectivity and self-fashioning. My identity is mutually constituted as a Tamil woman belonging and yet foreign to Tamil society in Sri Lanka. And so did Maathini and Vasanthi see me as 'one of them'? I didn't ask. It is implicitly understood that I am and I am not.[13] When they address me as *pillai* ('child') it is a linguistic signifier of community belonging. When they ask me to relate their stories and tell 'the people outside, of our struggles here,' we both understand that the lines of difference, privilege, and power are clear for we know that I will not stay but will return to the United States and to my life and sense of home here.[14] These and many other experiences that I bring to 'the field' of writing and representation position me as an anthropologist studying 'terrorism' from a set of specific yet ambiguous 'structural location[s] from which one has a particular vision' of who is a terrorist and what constitutes terrorism (Rosaldo, quoted in Roth [1989: 556]). As such, 'ethnographic self-fashioning presupposes lies of omission and of rhetoric, it also makes possible the telling of powerful truths' (Clifford 1988: 112). Careful attention to the construction of ethnographic authority and self-fashioning is certainly an implication for researchers employing a politically engaged ethnographic methodology.

Advocacy is an important aspect of politically engaged scholarship that informs the ethnographic practice of anthropologists working in national and international contexts (Herzfeld 2010; Low and Engle Merry 2010; Johnston 2001; Kirsch 2002; Sanford and Angel-Ajani 2006; Speed 2006). Activism, social critique, collaboration, teaching, and public education, sharing, and support are also forms of engaged anthropology that has transformed the practice of ethnographic research and representation by anthropologists who are critically conscious of social inequalities that intersect with cultural and political processes.[15] Nancy Scheper-Hughes calls for 'a politically committed and morally engaged anthropology … [that] must be ethically grounded' (1995: 410). Her departure from the 'traditional role of the anthropologist as neutral, dispassionate, cool and rational, objective observer of human condition' to a 'politically and morally engaged *companheira*' (or to 'accompany') with community members in their struggle for civil rights, emerged from her fieldwork with disenfranchised women and children in Brazil and South Africa (1995: 410–11). Maathini, Vasanthi, and other Tamil community members invited me to accompany them in their struggles to be free from the destructions of war and to live in their ancestral homelands with dignity and safety, so that they too can realize the dream of a prosperous future for their families.

Ecographic thinking invites us to critically understand our role as politically engaged and ethically grounded ethnographers collecting the histories, testimonies, lived experiences, and analyses of community members who are living within situations of war. Our work as ethnographers at the nexus of ecography and anthropology is political and holds the potential to generate new lines and movements of dialogue, resistance, and understanding between and within the conventional places and spaces of imperial wars. Maathini, Vasanthi, and Prabhakaran were speaking as ecographers, asserting their agency by promoting an epistemology of place and soil – Tamil Eelam and *munn* – to articulate their understanding of how their stories link with ours here in the US, the center of imperial power. How shall we apprehend our role as ethnographers in the imperial contest where the cultural value of terrorism serves to construct and organize knowledge about policies of exclusion and expulsion from a life of integrity and dignity? How will we stand in solidarity with people who bear the cost of empire on their bodies and social worlds that intersect with ours? As Edward Said noted in what's at stake for anthropologists and others engaging in ethnographic studies, 'representation becomes significant, not just as an academic or theoretical quandary but as a political choice' (Said 1989: 224). Ecologizing 'terrorism' invites us to integrate ecographic thinking into the practice of an ethically grounded, politically engaged anthropology. Ecographic thinking allows us to recognize our interlocutors as ecographers who are 'individuals situated at a nexus of information and events, bisected by time, and possessing an intimacy with their environment' that we come to inhabit through the privilege of ethnographic research. Through the method of learning an ecographic ontology, 'terrorism' is made visible as a cultural value and as a place where empire coexists with agency and sovereignty, with nationalism and patriotism, with torture and expulsion, and with freedom and democracy.

Notes

1. 'Terrorism' is placed within quotation marks to signify that it is not a concept to be taken for granted as reality defined by state agents alone but rather as an ideology and a political tool to categorize and authorize state-sponsored violence in the context of imperial global wars. As an aspect of ethnographic writing practice, I make a distinction between

'terrorism,' 'terrorist' – as a way of representing a critical reading of these terms – and terrorism and terrorist (without quotation marks) as a way of representing a conventional, uncritical, and popular reading and consumption of these terms both within and beyond academic discussions.

2. In apprehending our roles as researchers within the imperial contexts of the US-sponsored global war on terror, we can reposition ourselves within an ecology of terrorism by beginning with, for example, Lutz's definition of empire: '… a constellation of state and state-structured private projects successfully aiming to exert wide-ranging control, through territorial or more remote means, over the practices and resources of areas beyond the state's borders. This influence can be exercised through direct military and political intervention, the threat of intervention, the mediation of proxy states, or multilateral institutions in which the imperial power is the dominant member' (2006: 594).

3. See Kamari M. Clarke's 'Toward a Critically Engaged Ethnographic Practice' (2010) for a discussion of the increased engagement of anthropologist and other social science researchers as cultural analysts in the Human Terrain System (HTS) mission and the subsequent debates within the American Anthropological Association (AAA) that resolved to disapprove the HTS program as a violation of the AAA's code of ethics. Clarke argues for anthropologists to 'use the tools of our discipline in principled forms of engagement with a range of publics, including the state, our corporations, and those nonstate actors whose actions may produce violence.' Her analysis of an engaged anthropology draws from her experience of accepting 'the offer to share some of my ethnographic knowledge and political criticisms with US Army decision makers' (2010: S303). For further discussion, debates, and critique of the uses of ethnographic research and anthropology's engagement and collaboration with the United States military and intelligence agencies, see Forte (2011), Price (2005, 2007, 2008), and Lutz (2008).

4. My intention here is to question the signifying power of authorizing the extreme violence of extraordinary rendition, indefinite detention, torture, and death by labeling and condemning a person as a terrorist. I am not asking the reader to equate 'nigger' (a linguistic creation of white Americans to name people with dark skin) with terrorist by assuming an unconscious erasure of racial violence that marks the history of slavery, segregation, and the denial of human rights in the United States. Though it is beyond the scope of this chapter to analyze the intersections of racism and the US-sponsored global 'war on terror,' I invite the reader to question why terrorist, as a label, was not invoked and why racial profiling as a policy and tactic was not ordered to carry out mass raids, searches, indefinite detentions, and extraordinary renditions to Guantánamo Bay of politically suspicious white men, particularly those who maintained so-called extremist politics. Consider, for example: the labeling of Ted Kaczynski as the 'Unabomber,' the labeling of Jared Lughner as 'a 22-year-old man in the shooting rampage' (Murray and Horwitz 2011) that critically wounded Congresswoman Gabrielle Giffords and killed six people including US District Judge John M. Roll, the labeling of James Holmes as 'a gunman' (Rowlands and Spellman 2012) who killed 12 people in a mass shooting at a movie theater in Aurora, Colorado, and the labeling of Timothy McVeigh and Terry Nicholas as 'Timothy McVeigh' and 'Terry Nicholas,' and that, according to a *Washington Post* report, 'Americans were shocked to learn that the prime suspects in the Oklahoma City bombing were not foreign terrorists but men from the nation's heartland' (Russakoff and Kovaleski 1995). Though an empirical study is needed of the extent to which skin color and racialized religious identification, such as Islamophobia, are tied to the label terrorist, racial profiling of non-white people has been established as a means by which government agents have sought to identify and punish suspected terrorists nationally and internationally. For example, consider the racialized identity of detainees at Guantánamo Bay throughout the ongoing global war on terror. The Center for Constitutional Rights (CCR) has documented several cases where people were indefinitely detained and tortured 'merely because of their race, religion, and national origin.' Additionally, the CCR, as part of a federal, class action lawsuit, *Turkmen v. Ashcroft*, has documented information with 'allegations that former Attorney General Ashcroft ordered the INS and FBI to

investigate individuals for ties to terrorism by, among other means, looking for Muslim-sounding names in the phonebook' (CCR 2010).

5. For an analysis of the expulsion, displacement, and history of Tamil-Muslim communities in Sri Lanka, see Cathrine Brun (2003) and Dennis B. McGilvray (2008). See also Nathalie Peutz's (2006) detailed ethnographic account and analysis of the legal processes and consequences of expulsion and deportation experienced by the increasing criminalization of displaced persons seeking asylum in the context of the global war on terror.

6. In her analysis of the practices of rape and torture of Somali people by Canadian Peacekeeping troops 'who saw themselves as colonizers, civilizing the natives and imposing order on the 'chaos of tribal warfare,' Sherene Razack (2000: 130) draws on Hugh Ridley's definition of the intersecting practices of 'functional violence – the teach-the-natives-a-lesson violence' – and self-justifying violence, 'meted out by [the colonizer] to prove something about himself' (Ridley 1983: 141).

7. A problematic, colonial label and category: for a detailed analysis and deconstruction of 'suicide bombing' see Asad (2007).

8. This and other excerpts of Prabhakaran's speech that was presented in Tamil are my translation into English. Unless otherwise noted, all interviews presented in this chapter were conducted in Tamil and are included here with my translations.

9. This excerpt is from the LTTE's official English translation of Prabhakaran's speech: http://velupillaiprabhakaran.wordpress.com/2012/11/08/leader-v-prabakarans-heros-day-speech-2008-2/.

10. For details of this and other *Ponngu Tamil* Tamil National Resurgence Conventions that took place in Switzerland, Australia, Canada, and Sri Lanka, see Tamilnation.org: http://tamilnation.co/diaspora/ponguthamil.htm.

11. See Asad (1973), Behar and Gordon (1995), Clifford (1988), Narayan (1993), Said (1978), Stacy (1988), Sundar (2004), Tyler (1986), Visweswaran (1994, 1997).

12. A critically conscious practice of reflexivity emerged from the analyses of power and domination exercised by anthropologists working in colonial contexts. In these colonizing situations, 'the field' includes, perhaps even begins at, the body of researchers/ethnographers who constitute themselves and are constituted by others in particular time-space continuums.

13. Solidarity in the contexts of politically engaged and ethically grounded scholarship does not imply or demand that researchers endeavor to become or be perceived as 'one of them.'

14. In my discussions with fellow Tamil community members, I have told my own stories of displacement and racial discrimination that I have and continue to experience in the United States. These are stories that I choose not to retell here in this chapter. Nor do I choose to tell the stories of my experiences at military checkpoints and other experiences of living and studying within a war zone.

15. Setha M. Low and Sally Engle Merry discuss the history and dilemmas of engaged anthropology in the United States in their introduction to a special issue of *Current Anthropology* that was published after the debates within the American Anthropological Association around the involvement of anthropologists in the US military's Human Terrain System projects 'for pacification in the wars in Afghanistan and Iraq' (2010: S206).

References

Asad, T. (ed.) (1973) *Anthropology and the Colonial Encounter*. London: Ithaca Press.

Asad, T. (2007) *On Suicide Bombing*. New York: Columbia University Press.

Asad, T. (2009 [1986]) 'The concept of cultural translation in British social anthropology,' in *Writing Culture: The Poetics and Politics of Ethnography*, eds J. Clifford and G. E. Marcus. Berkeley, CA: University of California Press, pp. 141–64.

Behar, R. and Gordon, D. (eds) (1995) *Women Writing Culture*. Berkeley, CA: University of California Press.

British Broadcasting Corporation (BBC) (2003) *Gloom in Saddam's Sri Lanka Village*, 13 December. Available at: http://news.bbc.co.uk/2/hi/south_asia/3323455.stm.

Brun, C. (2003) 'Local citizens or internally displaced persons? Dilemmas of long term displacement in Sri Lanka,' *Journal of Refugee Studies*, 16 (4): 376–97.

Catherine, L. (2006) 'Empire is in the details,' *American Ethnologist*, 33 (4): 593–611.

Center for Constitutional Rights (2010) *Former Detainees Join Federal Court Challenge to Post-9/11 Racial Profiling and Abuse of Muslim, Arab and South Asian Men*, 13 September. Available at: http://ccrjustice.org/newsroom/press-releases/former-detainees-join-federal-court-challenge-post-9-11-racial-profiling-and-abuse-of-muslim-arabs.

Clark, K. M. (2010) 'Toward a critically engaged ethnographic practice,' *Current Anthropology*, 51 (2): S301–S312.

Clifford, J. (1986) 'Introduction: partial truths,' in J. Clifford and G. E. Marcus (eds), *Writing Culture: The Poetics and Politics of Ethnography*. Berkeley, CA: University of California Press, pp. 1–26.

Clifford, J. (1988) *Predicament of Culture: Twentieth-Century Ethnography, Literature, and Art*. Cambridge, MA: Harvard University Press.

Forte, M. C. (2011) 'The human terrain system and anthropology: a review of ongoing public debates,' *American Anthropologist*, 133 (1): 149–53.

Halvaksz, J. A. and Young-Leslie, H. E. (2008) 'Thinking ecographically: places, ecographers, and environmentalism,' *Nature and Culture*, 3 (2): 183–205.

Herzfeld, M. (2010) 'Engagement, gentrification, and the neoliberal hijacking of history,' *Current Anthropology*, 51 (supplement 2): S259–S267.

Jeyaraj, D. B. S. (2012) '22nd Anniversary of Northern Muslim expulsion by LTTE,' *Daily Mirror*, 3 November, electronic document. Online at: http://www.dailymirror.lk/opinion/dbsjeyaraj-column/23182-22ndnanniversary-of-northern-muslim-expulsion-by-ltte.html.

Johnston, B. R. (2001) 'Anthropology and environmental justice: analysts, advocates, mediators and troublemakers,' in C. Crumley (ed.), *New Directions in Anthropology and the Environment*. Walnut Creek, CA: AltaMira, pp. 132–49.

Kirsch, S. (2002) 'Anthropology and advocacy: a case study of the campaign against the Ok Tedi Mine,' *Critique of Anthropology*, 22: 175–200.

Low, S. M. and Engle Merry, S. (2010) 'Engaged anthropology: diversity and dilemmas: an introduction to Supplement 2,' *Current Anthropology*, 51 (supplement 2): S203–S226.

Lutz, C. (2006) 'Selling ourselves? The perils of Pentagon funding for anthropology,' *Anthropology Today*, 24 (5):

McGilvray, D. (2008) *Crucible of Conflict: Tamil Muslim Society on the East Coast of Sri Lanka*. Durham, NC: Duke University Press.

Murray, S. and Horwitz, S. (2011) 'Rep. Gabrielle Giffords shot in Tucson rampage; federal judge killed,' *Washington Post*, 9 January. Available at: http://www.washingtonpost.com/wp-dyn/content/article/2011/01/08/AR2011010802422.html.

Narayan, K. (1993) 'How native is a "native" anthropologist?' *American Anthropologist*, 95 (3): 671–86.

Peutz, N. (2006) 'Embarking on an anthropology of removal,' *Current Anthropology*, 47 (2): 217–41.

Prabhakaran, V. (2008) '(Maaveerar Naal)' *Eelam View*, 27 November. Available at http://www.eelamview.com/wp-content/uploads/2012/11/Prabakaran-Heros-day-speech-2008-tamil.pdf.

Price, D. (2005) 'America the ambivalent: quietly selling anthropology to the CIA,' *Anthropology Today*, 21 (6): 1–2.

Price, D. (2007) 'Buying a piece of anthropology, Part 1: Human ecology and unwitting anthropological research for the CIA,' *Anthropology Today*, 23 (3): 8–13.

Price, D. (2008) *Anthropological Intelligence: The Deployment and Neglect of American Anthropology in the Second World War*. Durham, NC: Duke University Press.

Rabinow, P. (2009 [1986]) 'Representations are social facts: modernity and post-modernity in anthropology,' in J. Clifford and G. E. Marcus (eds), *Writing Culture: The Poetics and Politics of Ethnography*. Berkeley, CA: University of California Press, pp. 234–61.

Razack, S. (2000) 'From the "clean snows of Petewawa": the violence of Canadian peace-keepers in Somalia,' *Cultural Anthropology*, 15 (1): 127–63.

Ridley, H. (1983) *Images of Imperial Rule*. New York: St. Martin's Press.

Roth, P.A. (1989) 'Ethnography without tears', *Current Anthropology* 30(5): 555–61.

Rowlands, T. and Spellman, J. (2012) 'James Holmes called university 9 minutes before shooting, attorney says,' CNN, 31 August. Available at: http://www.cnn.com/2012/08/30/justice/colorado-shooting/.

Russakoff, D. and Kovaleski, S. F. (1995) 'An ordinary boy's extraordinary rage,' *Washington Post*, 2 July. Available at: http://www.washingtonpost.com/wp-srv/national/longterm/oklahoma/bg/mcveigh.htm.

Said, E.W. (1978) *Orientalism*. New York: Pantheon.

Said, E.W. (1989) 'Representing the colonized: anthropology's interlocutors,' *Critical Inquiry*, 15 (2): 205–25.

Sanford, V. and Angel-Ajani, A. (2006) *Engaged Observer: Anthropology, Advocacy, and Activism*. New Brunswick, NJ: Rutgers University Press.

Scheper-Hughes, N. (1995) 'The primacy of the ethical: propositions for a militant anthropology,' *Current Anthropology*, 36 (3): 409–40.

Speed, S. (2006) 'At the crossroads of human rights and anthropology: toward a critically engaged activist research,' *American Anthropologist*, 108: 66–76.

Stacy, J. (1988) 'Can there be a feminist ethnography,' *Women's Studies International Forum*, 11 (1): 21–7.

Sundar, N. (2004) 'Toward an anthropology of culpability,' *American Ethnologist*, 31 (2): 145–63.

Turkmen v. Ashcroft, 915 F. Supp. 2d 314 (E.D.N.Y. 2013)

Tyler, S. (2009 [1986]) 'Post-modern ethnography: from document of the occult to occult document,' in J. Clifford and G. E. Marcus (eds), *Writing Culture: The Poetics and Politics of Ethnography*. Berkeley, CA: University of California Press, pp. 122–40.

Visweswaran, K. (1994) *Fictions of Feminist Ethnography*. Minneapolis, MN: University of Minnesota Press.

Visweswaran, K. (1997) 'Histories of feminist ethnography,' *Annual Review of Anthropology*, 26: 591–621.

PART 4

Discourse Analysis

6

CRITICAL DISCOURSE ANALYSIS[1]

Richard Jackson

Introduction

Discourse analysis has been an established research method in international relations (IR) for some time now (see Milliken 1999). Emerging from within constructivist poststructuralist, feminist, and postcolonial approaches to IR, discourse analysis has been employed in the analysis of, among many others: identity construction and war (Campbell 1998; Doty 1993; Hansen 2006; Jabri 1996; Jackson 2004; Kaufman 2001; Mertus 1999; Wilmer 2002); national security and the decision to use force (Campbell 1992; Katzenstein 1996; Weldes 1999; Williams 1998); national security cultures (Gusterson 1998); and norms and arms control (Price 1997).

However, before September 11, 2001, studies which employed forms of discourse analysis were relatively rare within the terrorism studies field (for notable exceptions, see Zulaika 1984; Zulaika and Douglass 1996; Gold-Biss 1994; Leeman 1991; Livingston 1994). Since then, and based on these earlier works, discourse analytic studies have proliferated and now constitute an important body of research within the broader field. Today, research on terrorism-related subjects utilizing discourse analytic approaches, broadly speaking, can be divided into five main strands. First, there is an increasingly large literature which examines the discursive construction of terrorism and counter-terrorism within political rhetoric, both since and prior to the war on terror (see, among others, Brulin 2012; Collins and Glover 2002; De Castella *et al.* 2009; Holland 2012; Jackson 2005, 2007c, 2011a; Jarvis 2009; McCrisken 2011, 2012; Murphy 2003; Tuman 2003; Winkler 2006). Second, there is a growing body of research on the social and cultural construction of terrorism in the media (see, among others, Altheide 2006; Croft 2006; Jenkins 2003; Norris *et al.* 2003; Scanlan 2001; Silberstein 2002; Spencer 2010, this volume). A third strand of the literature critically analyses academia, the terrorism studies field itself and the sociology of terrorism knowledge (see, among others,

Burnett and Whyte 2005; Gunning and Jackson 2011; Hellmich 2011; Hellmich and Behnke 2012; Jackson 2007a, 2009a, 2012a; Miller and Mills 2009; Stampnitzky 2013). Fourth, there is a small but growing literature which examines the language and discourse of terrorist leaders, groups and associated movements (see, among others, Devji 2005; Euban 2002; Finn 2012; Fricano 2012; Wiktorowicz and Kaltner 2003). Finally, there are a wide variety of discourse-focused, critical studies on counter-terrorism and related issues such as risk, torture and 'radicalization' (see, among others, Amoore and de Goede 2008; Coaffee et al. 2009; Githens-Mazer and Lambert 2010; Jackson 2007b; Vaughan-Williams 2007).

This literature is diverse in terms of its methodological orientation, ranging from light constructivist studies of political rhetoric or media content, to mainstream constructivist narrative analysis, metaphor analysis, formal forms of critical discourse analysis (CDA), and poststructuralist and Foucault-inspired genealogical and deconstructive analyses. While all these approaches share a focus on language, text, and social practice, they often entail different ontological and epistemological assumptions, and employ contrasting methodologies. Nevertheless, this rich and diverse literature has greatly advanced our understanding of both how to better research contemporary terrorism and counter-terrorism using the tools of discourse analysis, and the origins, nature, ideology, and wider social effects of the terrorism discourse itself.

In this chapter, I briefly explain why I have employed the method of critical discourse analysis (CDA) in my ongoing analysis of the broader political, academic, and social field of terrorism, how I practically go about the research, and some of the challenges involved in employing this kind of methodological approach. I also provide a brief description of some of the key findings of my research into the discourse of the war on terror and contemporary counter-terrorism, in particular, highlighting some of the main effects and real-world ideological consequences of the discourse.

The utility of discourse analysis in the study of terrorism

My initial decision to employ CDA in the study of terrorism grew out of research I conducted on the social construction of intrastate war and organized political violence (Jackson 2004). Adopting a constructivist approach to conflict analysis (see Jackson 2009b), I examined the role of political and social narratives and discursive formations in constructing the hostile identities and socially accepted norms necessary for initiating and sustaining political violence within a particular context. After observing the spread and practices of the largely unopposed global war on terror after 2001, I became interested to discover whether the same kinds of narratives and discursive processes used in civil wars were employed by US political elites to generate social consensus and legitimacy for the war on terror. I discovered that they were (Jackson 2005). In particular, I was interested in the way identity construction – of both the 'terrorist other' and the 'counter-terrorist self' – generated both legitimacy and the strategic logic of the global campaign (see Jackson 2007a). I was also interested in how the war on terror was transformed into a durable social structure or 'truth regime,' and whether it was therefore likely to change any time soon (see Jackson 2011a, 2014a).

At the same time, inspired by Zulaika and Douglass's (1996) deconstruction of the dominant 'terrorism mythography' that had existed since the 1980s, I was intrigued by a series of noticeable contradictions in the broader terrorism discourse. For example, how was it that individuals such as Nelson Mandela, Yasser Arafat, and Sean McBride could transmute from being widely condemned 'terrorists' to Nobel Peace Prize winners? How could the United States offer support to terrorist groups such as the Afghan mujahideen one day, and then sanction and condemn them as evil terrorists the next? How could so-called state sponsors of terrorism and officially designated terrorist groups move on and off the US State Department's official list according to changing political interests rather than behavioral changes? How could the very same acts of violence, such as aircraft hijackings or bombing of public places, be denied the label of 'terrorism' when committed by state actors? Moreover, how had the meaning of the word 'terrorism' shifted from being a description of state repression during the French Revolution to being solely a description of non-state religious extremist groups? Similarly, in more concrete terms, why were fatalities at the hands of terrorists considered to be so nationally important that they required a costly war on terrorism, when other kinds of fatalities, such as those caused by gun crime or domestic violence, were not? Why did so many people fear being killed by terrorists when their statistical chances of dying in that way were demonstrably miniscule in comparison to other risks? And why was society prepared to expend hundreds of thousands of lives and literally trillions of dollars, as well as give up civil liberties, fighting a limited and highly subjective threat such as terrorism?

These questions suggested that there was a great deal more to 'terrorism' than simply acts of political violence committed by small groups of dissidents – acts which could be objectively identified, measured, and analyzed using empirical methods. Rather, they suggested that terrorism was a much broader and more complex cultural-political discourse made up of a series of narratives, metaphors, predicates, labels, assumptions, and discursive formations. Moreover, it was a discourse that changed and shifted over time and place. That is, it was historically and spatially contingent: what particular actions were considered to be 'terrorism' and which actors were considered to be 'terrorists' was not self-evident and objectively measureable, but socially constructed within particular cultural, political, and historical contexts. Therefore, it seemed clear that understanding the thing currently known as 'terrorism' necessitated a theoretical and methodological approach based, in large part, on the critical analysis of discourse understood as related texts and social practices. Crucially, understanding how 'terrorism' has been socially constructed could also provide important clues and explanations for how counter-terrorism and the war on terror has been devised, legitimized, and practiced.

Employing CDA in terrorism research

Every methodological approach has a deeper set of theoretical assumptions embedded within in it. These assumptions relate to the nature of reality, the relationship between the object under analysis and the researcher, the nature and status of knowledge, the purpose of research, the nature of causality, and so on. Discourse analysis is no different. Its aim is to illustrate and describe the relationship between discursive or textual phenomena, and social processes and practice. In particular, it is concerned with representation – how people, things, and processes are represented through discourse – and the political consequences of adopting one mode of representation over another.

Discourse analysis is employed within a range of different research paradigms, including poststructuralist, postmodernist, feminist, postcolonial, and social constructivist. However, all forms of discourse analysis have a shared set of theoretical assumptions or commitments about the nature and consequences of language, text, discourse, and social practices (Milliken 1999; see also Jorgensen and Phillips 2002). Broadly speaking, these shared commitments include: an understanding of language as constitutive or productive of meaning rather than simply descriptive of an external reality; an understanding of discourse as involving structures of signification which construct social realities, particularly in terms of defining subjects and establishing their relational positions within a broader social system of signification; an understanding of discourse as being productive of subjects authorized to speak and act, legitimate forms of knowledge and political practices, and, importantly, common sense within particular social groups and historical settings; an understanding of discourse as necessarily exclusionary and silencing of other modes of representation; and an understanding of discourse as historically and culturally contingent, intertextual, open-ended, requiring continuous articulation and re-articulation and therefore, open to destabilization and counter-hegemonic struggle.

As a consequence of these shared commitments and broader theoretical assumptions about discourse and how it constructs social meaning, identities, relationships, forms of legitimate knowledge and the like, discourse analytic research on terrorism also implicitly or explicitly adopts a social constructivist ontology in relation to its primary subject, 'terrorism.' That is, scholars in this tradition assume that 'terrorism' and 'terrorists' derive their ontological status primarily from their existence as commonly used rhetorical terms and cultural constructs – that 'terrorism' is fundamentally a social fact rather than a brute fact (Jackson *et al.* 2011). In other words, while *political violence* is obviously experienced as a brute fact by its direct victims, its wider cultural-political meaning and its analytical-descriptive or legal status – as an act of 'war,' 'crime,' 'insurgency,' or 'terrorism,' for example – is decided by socially negotiated agreement and inter-subjective practices involving political authorities, investigators, judges, the media, academic experts, and others (Jenkins 2003). This is why some acts of violence are not classified as acts of terrorism even when they seemingly share the characteristics of other violent acts which are considered 'terrorism' and why some actors are never referred to as 'terrorists' even when they commit identical acts to other 'terrorist' groups.

From this perspective, just as 'races' do not have an independent ontological existence but classifications of humankind do, so too 'terrorism' does not exist as an objective, externally recognizable phenomenon, but classifications of different forms of political violence do (Sluka 2002: 23). As two well-known terrorism experts put it, 'The nature of terrorism is not inherent in the violent act itself. One and the same act ... can be terrorist or not, depending on intention and circumstance' (Schmid and Jongman 1988: 101). As already noted, it also depends on historical context and juncture: who is a terrorist – Menachem Begin, Nelson Mandela, Osama bin Laden – and which acts of political violence are considered acts of terrorism – the assassination of Archduke Ferdinand, Hiroshima, the Lockerbie bombing – are not independently verifiable facts, but interpretations liable to change over time, place and observer.

In other words, discourse analytic approaches view 'terrorism' as an empty signifier and argue that the thing itself cannot be known with any real certainty, only the way in which it has been discursively constructed through language usage and social practices (Zulaika and Douglass 1996). Within academia, but also in the wider social and political sphere, this means that 'terrorism' is a quintessential example of a 'contested concept', because it lacks 'one clearly definable general use ... which can be set up as the correct or standard use' (Gallie 1955–6: 168). This is reflected in the well-worn observation that there are now over 200 hundred definitions of terrorism currently in use by scholars, governments, and international organizations (Jackson 2011b). In the end, because 'terrorism' exists in society as a socially constructed (and highly pejorative) label for particular acts of political violence, scholars who employ discourse analysis as their primary research method suggest that it is the language games and representational practices and processes of the term which should be the primary focus of academic research, not necessarily the thing itself which does not exist independently of the discourses which construct and enclose it (Hulsse and Spencer 2008; Zulaika and Douglass 1996, 2008).

In addition to these broader theoretical commitments and assumptions, critical discourse analysis (CDA) entails a number of more specific assumptions relating to epistemology and the research process. For example, although there are different approaches to CDA (see Fairclough 2010; van Dijk 2001, 2008; Jorgensen and Phillips 2002), the version of CDA which I generally employ subscribes to a notion of social causality that takes reasons as causes, in the sense that norms and rules structure or constitute – that is, 'cause' – the things that people and institutions do (Adler, 1997: 329). In other words, understanding the social and material structures which shape identities and which are antecedent to action does important explanatory work which can lead to causal stories about how discourses affect social actions and practices (see Yee 1996; Banta 2013). In this sense, CDA aims at a particular sort of explanatory approach which rejects the search for laws in favor of contingent generalizations which focus on the question, 'how-possible?', rather than simply 'why?' (Doty 1993; Alkopher 2005). Additionally, and in opposition to other discourse analytic approaches, CDA adopts an explicit commitment to the notion of emancipation (see McDonald 2009). Despite objections to the term and its past implication in hegemonic projects, and drawing on critical theory, CDA scholars for the most part see emancipation as a process of trying to construct 'concrete utopias' by realizing the unfulfilled potential of existing structures, freeing individuals from structural constraints, and the democratization of the public sphere (Wyn Jones 2004: 229–32). In other words, like other explicitly 'critical' approaches, including critical terrorism studies (CTS) itself, CDA involves an underlying conception of a different social and political order (Wyn Jones 2004: 217–20; see also Jackson *et al.* 2009). The purpose of discourse analysis is more than analytical; it is also openly normative.

As a practical outworking of all the assumptions described above, the form of CDA I employ proceeds in the following stages. The first stage entails the collection and close examination of texts representative of the particular part of the 'terrorism' discourse I am interested in studying, particularly texts by actors presumed to be authoritative or authorized speakers of the dominant discourse. For example, in researching the political and academic discourse of terrorism in Western society, I examine the following texts: (1) official speeches, interviews, memos, and documents of senior policy-makers and political leaders; (2) books, articles, and reports by major think tanks, public intellectuals, and journalists; and (3) academic books and scholarly articles related to the subject. Each text is examined for the themes, labels, assumptions, narratives, predicates, metaphors, inferences, and arguments it deploys and the kinds of existing cultural-political narratives, texts and, cultural repertoires it draws upon. In other words, this stage of the research involves descriptively mapping the contours of the discourse in the chosen texts. Employing a kind of 'grounded theory' approach, the analysis is assumed to be completed or validated when it is found that adding new texts generates no new categories or insights outside of those developed through the examination of the earlier texts.

The second stage of the research involves subjecting the descriptive findings of the textual analysis to what I term a first- and second-order critique (see Jackson 2007a). A first-order or immanent critique looks for the internal contradictions, mistakes, misconceptions, and instabilities within and between texts in order to critique the discourse on its own terms, and expose the events and perspectives that it fails to acknowledge or address, or indeed actively subjugates (Jackson 2012b). The point of this kind of internal critique is not necessarily to establish the 'correct' or 'real truth' of the subject, but rather to destabilize dominant interpretations and demonstrate the inherently contested, shifting, and political nature of the discourse.

A second-order critique entails employing social theory and wider research findings to reflect on the broader political and ethical consequences – the ideological effects, as it were – of the representations and constructions of the discourse. For example, it may involve an exploration of the ways in which the terrorism discourse functions as a 'symbolic technology' (Laffey and Weldes 1997) wielded by particular elites and institutions in order to: structure the primary subject positions, accepted knowledge, commonsense and legitimate policy responses to 'Islamic terrorism' (see Jackson 2007a); construct the legitimacy and social consequence of employing particular counter-terrorism practices (see Jackson 2007b); exclude and delegitimize alternative knowledge and practices towards counter-terrorism (see Jackson 2012b); and construct and maintain a hegemonic 'regime of truth' and broader social order (see Jackson 2005). Within both phases of the research, a range of specific discourse analytic methods can be useful, including genealogical analysis, predicate analysis, narrative analysis, and deconstructive analysis. Importantly, the exposure and destabilization of dominant forms of knowledge opens up critical space for the articulation of alternative and potentially emancipatory forms of knowledge and practice.

An example of CDA: deconstructing the war on terror

The majority of my discourse analytic research has been focused on analyzing and deconstructing the political, social, and academic discourse of the war on terror. For example, I began by analyzing the dominant political discourse which constructed and legitimized the 'war on terrorism' as the accepted response to the attacks on September 11, 2001 (Jackson 2005), the roots of the Bush administration's discourse in Reagan's first 'war on terrorism' (Jackson 2006), as well as the way in which a dominant '9/11' narrative was constructed largely by political elites as the primary interpretation of the events, and the demonstrable effects that this had on counter-terrorism and society more generally (Jackson 2009c). I also examined specific aspects of the war on terrorism discourse, including: the particular narratives and discursive constructions of political and academic understandings of 'Islamic terrorism' (Jackson 2007a); the narratives and justifications for employing torture as a central practice in counter-terrorism (Jackson 2007b); the way the terrorism threat was narrated and constructed as an existential threat to Western societies (Jackson 2007c, 2013); the narratives surrounding so-called 'terrorist sanctuaries' after 9/11 (Jackson 2007d); and the social embedding of the war on terror discourse and consequent possibilities for discursive change (Jackson 2011a, 2014a). Lastly, I have also examined academic discourses of terrorism and counter-terrorism, the way in which they overlap with dominant political discourses, and the ideological effects of discursively constructing 'terrorism' in certain ways (Jackson 2007a, 2009a, 2012b). Much of this research has been confirmed by, and confirms, other discourse analytic studies (see, among many others, Croft 2006; Hodges 2011; Holland 2012; Jarvis 2009; McCrisken 2011, 2012; Murphy 2003; Tuman 2003; Winkler 2006).

There is not the space here to outline all the main findings of this wider body of research. However, among others, some of the central narratives of the war on terror discourse I have mapped and analyzed in these works include: the '9/11' attacks were an 'act of war' and represent a clear turning point in history; non-state terrorism poses a significant and existential threat to modern societies that without significant investment in counter-terrorism could be catastrophic to Western states; contemporary terrorism poses a 'new' and more serious kind of threat because today's terrorists are driven by religious extremism, are unconstrained in their targeting of civilians, aim at mass killing, and are willing to use weapons of mass destruction; people become terrorists through a process of radicalization; the contemporary struggle against terrorism is an example of the struggle of good against evil, civilization against barbarism, and liberty against totalitarianism; the struggle against terrorism is a just cause which will result in eventual victory; and the 'new' and catastrophic threat posed by terrorism justifies 'new' and aggressive measures such as using 'enhanced interrogation,' restricting the rights of terrorist suspects, and mass surveillance.

In many cases, these narratives are also wrapped up in, or directly appeal to, pre-existing social and political narratives, metaphors, and cultural repertoires, such as popular understandings of good and evil, the Pearl Harbor and World War II 'good war' narratives, the notion of 'the enemy within,' Cold War myths of sleeper cells, and mostly importantly the 'war' metaphor. Moreover, many of these narratives have their genealogical roots in earlier wars on terrorism and periods of counter-terrorism. In addition, within this broader war on terror discourse, a number of specific new narratives have been constructed around a mythology of al Qaeda – its nature, scope, and capabilities – and so-called 'jihadists' and suicide bombers more generally.

More importantly than simply describing and mapping these narratives, metaphors, and discursive constructions through the analysis of written and spoken texts about terrorism, my research has also sought to explore and explain the material and practical *effects* of this discourse. I have done this in a number of ways. First, I have examined the means and processes by which the terrorism discourse has become materially embedded in institutions, law, culture, and security architecture and practices. The enactment of new terrorism laws, the construction of mass surveillance programs, the establishment of the Department of Homeland Security, and the installation of security measures and machines at airports, public buildings and elsewhere, are all examples of this process. In other words, the discourse has directly resulted in the construction of new institutions, laws, and material structures (such as the concrete bollards erected in front of public buildings designed to protect against car-driven bombs).

Second, in these studies I have explored how the core narratives about terrorism have affected counter-terrorism policies by enabling and constraining specific policy responses. For example, employing the 'war' metaphor enables the use of military force as a primary response to acts of terrorism, while inscribing terrorists as 'evil' constrains the option of engaging in political dialogue with them. As such, one of the key findings of my research relates to the way in which certain kinds of knowledge about terrorism, specifically about how to respond to it nonviolently (see Jackson 2012b), and certain alternative narratives about the war on terror (see Jackson 2011a), have been suppressed and successfully delegitimized by dominant political actors. In addition, I have explored how certain narratives have been employed instrumentally by political elites to legitimize and justify specific measures, such as torture and mass surveillance. These narratives are often designed to appeal to the cultural context of the audience and function to delegitimize alternative narratives.

Finally, drawing upon social theory and broader critical research, I have examined how the narratives and discourse of the war on terror can be directly linked to widespread human rights abuses (such as the Guantánamo detentions, the Abu Ghraib scandal, rendition, preventive detention, drone strikes, and the like), the construction and maintenance of national identity and the shaping of public opinion on security issues, the consolidation of state power and the control of dissent and protest, and the promotion of external political projects (such as expanding the US military presence in the Middle East and elsewhere, strengthening friendly regimes, exerting greater financial controls, surveillance of other states and international organizations, and the like). In sum, linking discourses and practices in this way entails using social theory and the assumptions of CDA to tell a kind of causal story (see Banta 2013; Yee 1996) about the way in which language and text enables and constrains action, and how the combination of widely accepted narratives and practices creates a dominant terrorism 'regime of truth.'

Finally, in keeping with the explicitly normative aims of CDA, my research has attempted to deconstruct and challenge the core narratives of the war on terror, especially those that have directly resulted in human rights abuses. As such, these studies have challenged and destabilized most of the core narratives about terrorism and counter-terrorism, demonstrating that they are full of contradictions, are often empirically unsupported within the discourse itself, and are ethically damaging in their wider effects. Crucially, such a deconstruction opens up intellectual and political space for debating and considering alternative ways of thinking about, and responding to, terrorism and political violence.

Conclusion: the challenges of discourse analytic approaches

There is no doubt about the advantages of employing discourse analytic approaches in terrorism research. Not only does this rich literature provide real insights into the way in which the war on terror and counter-terrorism has evolved to become a dominating truth regime over the past decade, but it also helps us to better understand the human rights abuses that have become so prevalent against terrorist suspects, the many contradictions and inconsistencies in the discourse and practice of counter-terrorism, and the ways in which counter-terrorism has been materialized into wider liberal forms of governance.

However, notwithstanding these obvious advantages, discourse analytic approaches also pose a number of challenges and display some current weaknesses. Perhaps the greatest challenge relates to the issue of causality and the causal inferences that can be drawn from discourse analysis. While it is relatively straightforward to map and describe narratives, metaphors, frames, and discourses, it is much more challenging to convincingly show how they generate causal effects in the real world. Demonstrating the causal effects of discourse requires substantial theoretical and empirical efforts (see Banta 2013; Yee 1996). To date, terrorism-related discourse analysis has tended to sidestep this challenge by focusing on the articulation of discourse rather than its reception and causal effects. Moreover, most of this work has tended to focus on elite producers of discourse, such as political, academic, and media elites, and has largely ignored the way ordinary people and subaltern groups consume, mediate, and articulate their own discourses of terrorism. In particular, there is little discourse analytic research to date on alternative discourses of terrorism and discursive resistance to the dominant terrorism discourse. Adding these domains and processes to the analysis would fill out the broader picture and provide a more dynamic account of the terrorism discourse, avoiding the inaccurate impression of a top-down, linear process of elite articulation and passive mass acceptance.

The discourse of terrorists and their supporters also remains relatively understudied compared to analyses of the discourse of Western political leaders and counter-terrorism practitioners, particularly in terms of the way in which terrorists construct their discourse in response to the dominant discourse. In part, the challenge of such research lies in gaining access to sufficient quantities and types of terrorist texts beyond their public statements, and then in being able to analyze them with sufficient background knowledge of language, culture, and context. However, the existence of some notable studies of terrorist discourse demonstrates that this challenge is far from insurmountable (see, for example, Devji 2005; Finn 2012; Wiktorowicz and Kaltner 2003).

Another important analytical challenge lies in the frequently narrow focus within discourse analytic approaches on language and text alone, to the neglect of the material world and the material aspects of discourse (see Boivin 2008; Purvis and Hunt 1993). Among others, such approaches have been criticized for failing to explore how materiality shapes, and is itself shaped by, discourse, and indeed for failing to contextualize how the historical-material conditions of contemporary capitalism and strategic power have thus far shaped the war on terror discourse (Herring and Stokes 2011; Porpora 2011). For example, there is room for exploring the ways in which technological developments – including the rise of capabilities for mass surveillance and drone technology, among others – have interacted with, and shaped, contemporary counter-terrorism discourse.

Finally, CDA in particular poses a key normative challenge, namely how to engender progressive discursive *change* at the political and social levels, particularly once a discourse has become materially embedded, self-perpetuating and socially and politically dominant? This is, of course, also an analytical challenge which I have tried to explore elsewhere in relation to US counter-terrorism policy (see Jackson 2011a, 2014a), that is how do we account for, and predict, changes in dominant discourses? While it is important to deconstruct and challenge dominant discourses through academic research and publishing, it is questionable whether such work can by itself generate wider changes in political, media, and popular discourses. CDA scholars working in the field need to consider other modes of discursive struggle and resistance to the terrorism truth regime, including media engagement and artistic endeavors such as films, theater, novels, comics, video games, and the like. This is one of the reasons why I have recently published a novel entitled *Confessions of a Terrorist* (Jackson 2014b) which deliberately challenges the dominant cultural and political representation of terrorists. As a popular novel, it has an arguably greater chance of influencing the media and popular cultural than an academic text.

Note

1. This chapter synthesizes and expands material drawn from Jackson (2005, 2007a) and Jackson *et al.* (2011).

References

Adler, E. (1997) 'Seizing the middle ground: constructivism in world politics,' *European Journal of International Relations*, 3 (3): 319–63.

Alkopher, T. (2005) 'The social (and religious) meanings that constitute war: the Crusades as realpolitik vs. socialpolitik,' *International Studies Quarterly*, 49: 715–37.

Altheide, D. (2006) *Terrorism and the Politics of Fear*. Lanham, MD: Alta Mira Press.

Amoore, L. and de Goede, M. (2008) *Risk and the War on Terror*. London: Routledge.

Banta, B. (2013) 'Analysing discourse as a causal mechanism,' *European Journal of International Relations*, 19 (2): 379–402.

Boivin, N. (2008) *Material Cultures, Material Minds: The Impact of Things on Human Thought, Society and Evolution*. Cambridge: Cambridge University Press.

Brulin, R. (2012) 'Defining "terrorism": the 1972 General Assembly Debates on "international terrorism" and their coverage by the *New York Times*,' in B. Hawks (ed.), *Societies Under Siege: Media, Government, Politics and Citizens' Freedoms in an Age of Terrorism*. Cambridge: Cambridge Scholar Press.

Burnett, J. and Whyte, D. (2005) 'Embedded expertise and the new terrorism,' *Journal for Crime, Conflict and the Media*, 1 (4): 1–18.

Campbell, D. (1992) *Writing Security: United States Foreign Policy and the Politics of Identity*. Minneapolis, MN: University of Minnesota Press.

Campbell, D. (1998) *National Deconstruction: Violence, Identity, and Justice in Bosnia*. Minneapolis, MN: University of Minnesota Press.

Coaffee, J., O'Hare, P. and Hawkesworth, M. (2009) 'The visibility of (in)security: the aesthetics of planning urban defences against terrorism,' *Security Dialogue*, 40 (4–5): 489–511.

Collins, J. and Glover, R. (eds) (2002) *Collateral Language: A User's Guide to America's New War*. New York: New York University Press.

Croft, S. (2006) *Culture, Crisis and America's War on Terror*. Cambridge: Cambridge University Press.

De Castella, K., McGarty, C. and Musgrove, L. (2009) 'Fear appeals in political rhetoric about terrorism: an analysis of speeches by Australian Prime Minister Howard,' *Political Psychology*, 30 (1): 1–26.

Devji, F. (2005) *Landscapes of the Jihad: Militancy, Morality, Modernity*. Ithaca, NY: Cornell University Press.

Doty, R. (1993) 'Foreign policy as social construction: a post-positivist analysis of U.S. counterinsurgency policy in the Philippines,' *International Studies Quarterly*, 37: 297–320.

Euban, R. (2002) 'Killing (for) politics: *Jihad*, martyrdom, and political action,' *Political Theory*, 30 (1): 4–35.

Fairclough, N. (2010) *Critical Discourse Analysis: A Critical Study of Language*, 2nd edn. London: Pearson Education.

Finn, M. (2012) *Al-Qaeda and Sacrifice: Martyrdom, War and Politics*. London: Pluto.

Fricano, G. (2012) 'Horizontal and vertical honour in the statements of Osama bin Laden,' *Critical Studies on Terrorism*, 5 (2): 197–217.

Gallie, W. B. (1955–6) 'Essentially contested concepts,' *Proceedings of the Aristotelian Society*, 56: 167–98.

Githens-Mazer, J. and Lambert, R. (2010) 'Why conventional wisdom on radicalization fails: the persistence of a failed discourse,' *International Affairs*, 86 (4): 889–901.

Gold-Biss, M. (1994) *The Discourse on Terrorism: Political Violence and Subcommittee on Security and Terrorism, 1981–1986*. New York: Peter Lang.

Gunning, J. and Jackson, R. (2011) 'What's so "religious" about "religious terrorism"?' *Critical Studies on Terrorism*, 4 (3): 369–88.

Gusterson, H. (1998) *Nuclear Rites: A Weapons Laboratory at the End of the Cold War*. Berkeley, CA: University of California Press.

Hansen, L. (2006) *Security as Practice: Discourse Analysis and the Bosnian War*. London: Routledge.

Hellmich, C. (2011) *Al-Qaeda: From Global Network to Local Franchise*. London: Zed.

Hellmich, C. and Behnke, A. (eds) (2012) *Knowing al-Qaeda: The Epistemology of Terrorism*. Farnham: Ashgate.

Herring, E. and Stokes, D. (2011) 'Critical realism and historical materialism as resources for critical terrorism studies,' *Critical Studies on Terrorism*, 4 (1): 5–21.

Hodges, A. (2011) *The 'War on Terror' Narrative: Discourse and Intertextuality in the Construction and Contestation of Sociopolitical Reality*. Oxford: Oxford University Press.

Holland, J. (2012) *Selling the War on Terror: Foreign Policy Discourses after 9/11*. Abingdon: Routledge.

Hulsse, R. and Spencer, A. (2008) 'The metaphor of terror: terrorism studies and the constructivist turn,' *Security Dialogue*, 39 (6): 571–92.

Jabri, V. (1996) *Discourses on Violence: Conflict Analysis Reconsidered*. Manchester: Manchester University Press.

Jackson, R. (2004) 'The social construction of internal war,' in R. Jackson (ed.), *(Re) Constructing Cultures of Violence and Peace*. Amsterdam and New York: Rodopi.

Jackson, R. (2005) *Writing the War on Terrorism: Language, Politics and Counterterrorism*. Manchester: Manchester University Press.

Jackson, R. (2006) 'Genealogy, ideology, and counter-terrorism: writing wars on terrorism from Ronald Reagan to George W. Bush Jr,' *Studies in Language and Capitalism*, 1: 163–93.

Jackson, R. (2007a) 'Constructing enemies: "Islamic terrorism" in political and academic discourse,' *Government and Opposition*, 42 (3): 394–426.

Jackson, R. (2007b) 'Language, policy and the construction of a torture culture in the war on terrorism,' *Review of International Studies*, 33: 353–71.

Jackson, R. (2007c) 'Playing the politics of fear: writing the terrorist threat in the war on terrorism,' in G. Kassimeris (ed.), *Playing Politics With Terrorism: A User's Guide*. New York: Columbia University Press, pp. 176–202.

Jackson, R. (2007d) 'Critical reflection on counter-sanctuary discourse,' in M. Innes (ed.), *Denial of Sanctuary: Understanding Terrorist Safe Havens*. Westport, CT: Praeger Security International, pp. 21–33.

Jackson, R. (2009a) 'Knowledge, power and politics in the study of political terrorism,' in R. Jackson, J. Gunning, and M. Breen Smyth (eds), *Critical Terrorism Studies: A New Research Agenda*. Abingdon: Routledge, pp. 66–83.

Jackson, R. (2009b) 'Constructivism and conflict resolution,' in J. Bercovitch, V. Kremenyuk, and I. W. Zartman (eds), *The Sage Handbook on Conflict Resolution*. Thousand Oaks, CA: Sage, pp. 172–89.

Jackson, R. (2009c) 'The 9/11 attacks and the social construction of a national narrative,' in M. Morgan (ed.), *The Impact of 9-11 on the Media, Arts and Entertainment: The Day that Changed Everything?* New York: Palgrave Macmillan, pp. 25–35.

Jackson, R. (2011a) 'Culture, identity and hegemony: continuity and (the lack of) change in US counter-terrorism policy from Bush to Obama,' *International Politics*, 48 (2/3): 390–411.

Jackson, R. (2011b) 'In defence of "terrorism": finding a way through a forest of misconceptions,' *Behavioral Sciences of Terrorism and Political Aggression*, 3 (2): 116–30.

Jackson, R. (2012a) 'Terrorism studies and academia,' in J. Bailes and C. Aksan (eds), *Weapon of the Strong: Conversations on US State Terrorism*. London: Pluto Press, pp. 118–31.

Jackson, R. (2012b) 'Unknown knowns: the subjugated knowledge of terrorism studies,' *Critical Studies on Terrorism*, 5 (1): 11–29.

Jackson, R. (2013) 'The politics of terrorism fear,' in S. Sinclair (ed.), *The Political Psychology of Terrorism Fears*. Cambridge: Cambridge University Press, pp. 267–82.

Jackson, R. (2014a) 'Bush, Obama, Bush, Obama, Bush, Obama …: the war on terror as a durable social structure,' in M. Bentley and J. Holland (eds), *Obama's Foreign Policy: Ending the War on Terror*. Abingdon: Routledge, pp. 76–90.

Jackson, R. (2014b) *Confessions of a Terrorist: A Novel*. London: Zed Books.

Jackson, R. and McDonald, M. (2009) 'Constructivism, US foreign policy and the "war on terrorism,"' in I. Parmar, L. Miller and M. Ledwidge (eds), *New Directions in US Foreign Policy*. London: Routledge, pp. 18–31.

Jackson, R., Breen Smyth, M., and Gunning, J. (eds) (2009) *Critical Terrorism Studies: A New Research Agenda*. London: Routledge.

Jackson, R., Jarvis, L., Gunning, J., and Breen-Smyth, M. (2011) *Terrorism: A Critical Introduction*. Basingstoke: Palgrave Macmillan.

Jarvis, L. (2009) *Times of Terror: Discourse, Temporality and the War on Terror*. Basingstoke: Palgrave Macmillan.

Jenkins, P. (2003) *Images of Terror: What We Can and Can't Know About Terrorism*. New York: Aldine de Gruyter.

Jorgensen, M. and Phillips, L. (2002) *Discourse Analysis as Theory and Method*. London: Sage.

Katzenstein, P. (ed.) (1996) *The Culture of National Security: Norms and Identity in World Politics*. New York: Columbia University Press.

Kaufman, S. (2001) *Modern Hatreds: The Symbolic Politics of Ethnic War*. London: Cornell University Press.

Laffey, M. and Weldes, J. (1997) 'Beyond belief: ideas and symbolic technologies in the study of international relations,' *European Journal of International Relations*, 3 (2): 193–237.

Leeman, R. (1991) *The Rhetoric of Terrorism and Counterterrorism*. New York: Greenwood Press.

Livingston, S. (1994) *The Terrorism Spectacle*. Boulder, CO: Westview Press.

McCrisken, T. (2011) 'Ten years on: Obama's war on terrorism in rhetoric and practice,' *International Affairs*, 87 (4): 781–801.

McCrisken, T. (2012) 'Justifying sacrifice: Barak Obama and the selling and ending of the war in Afghanistan,' *International Affairs*, 88 (5): 993–1007.

McDonald, M. (2009) 'Emancipation and critical terrorism studies,' in R. Jackson, M. Breen Smyth, and J. Gunning (eds), *Critical Terrorism Studies: A New Research Agenda*. London: Routledge, pp. 109–23.

Mertus, J. (1999) *Kosovo: How Myths and Truths Started a War*. Berkeley, CA: University of California Press.

Miller, M. and Mills, T. (2009) 'The terror experts and the mainstream media: the expert nexus and its dominance in the news media,' *Critical Studies on Terrorism*, 2 (3): 414–37.

Milliken, J. (1999) 'The study of discourse in international relations: a critique of research and methods,' *European Journal of International Relations*, 5 (2): 225–54.

Murphy, J. (2003) '"Our mission and our moment": George W. Bush and September 11,' *Rhetoric and Public Affairs*, 6 (4): 607–32.

Norris, P., Kern, M., and Just, M. (eds) (2003) *Framing Terrorism: The News Media, the Government, and the Public*. New York: Routledge.

Porpora, D. (2011) 'Critical terrorism studies: a political economic approach grounded in critical realism,' *Critical Studies on Terrorism*, 4 (1): 39–55.

Price, R. (1997) *The Chemical Weapons Taboo*. Ithaca, NY: Cornell University Press.

Purvis, T. and Hunt, A. (1993) 'Discourse, ideology, discourse ideology, discourse ideology …,"' *British Journal of Sociology*, 44 (3): 473–99.

Scanlan, M. (2001) *Plotting Terror: Novelists and Terrorists in Contemporary Fiction*. Charlottesville, VA: University of Virginia Press.

Schmid, A. and Jongman, A. (1988) *Political Terrorism: A New Guide to Actors, Authors, Concepts, Databases, Theories and Literature*. Oxford: North Holland.

Silberstein, S. (2002) *War of Words: Language, Politics and 9/11*. London: Routledge.

Sluka, J. (2002) 'Comment: what anthropologists should know about the concept of "terrorism,"' *Anthropology Today*, 18 (2): 22–3.

Spencer, A. (2010) *The Tabloid Terrorist: The Predicative Construction of New Terrorism in the Media*. Basingstoke: Palgrave Macmillan.

Stampnitzky, L. (2013) *Disciplining Terror: How Experts and Others Invented Terrorism*. Cambridge: Cambridge University Press.

Tuman, J. (2003) *Communicating Terror: The Rhetorical Dimensions of Terrorism*. London: Sage.

van Dijk, T. A. (2001) 'Critical discourse analysis,' in D. Schiffrin, D. Tannen, and H. Hamilton (eds), *The Handbook of Discourse Analysis*. London: Blackwell.

van Dijk, T. A. (2008) *Discourse and Power*. London: Palgrave Macmillian.

Vaughan-Williams, N. (2007) 'The shooting of Jean Charles de Menezes: new border politics?' *Alternatives: Global, Local, Political*, 32 (2): 177–95.

Weldes, J. (1999) *Constructing National Interests: The United States and the Cuban Missile Crisis*. London: University of Minnesota Press.

Wiktorowicz, Q. and Kaltner, J. (2003) 'Killing in the name of Islam: Al-Qaeda's justification for September 11,' *Middle East Policy*, X (2): 76–92.

Williams, M. (1998) 'Identity and the politics of security,' *European Journal of International Relations*, 4 (2): 204–25.

Wilmer, F. (2002) *The Social Construction of Man, the State, and War: Identity, Conflict, and Violence in the Former Yugoslavia*. London and New York: Routledge.

Winkler, C. (2006) *In the Name of Terrorism: Presidents on Political Violence in the Post-World War II Era*. Albany, NY: State University of New York Press.

Wyn Jones, R. (2004) 'On emancipation: necessity, capacity, and concrete utopias,' in K. Booth (ed.), *Critical Security Studies and World Politics*. Boulder, CO: Lynne Rienner.

Yee, A. (1996) 'The causal effect of ideas,' *International Organization*, 50 (1): 69–108.

Zulaika, J. (1984) *Basque Violence: Metaphor and Sacrament*. Reno, NV: University of Nevada Press.

Zulaika, J. and Douglass, W. (1996) *Terror and Taboo: The Follies, Fables, and Faces of Terrorism*. London: Routledge.

Zulaika, J. and Douglass, W. (2008) 'The terrorist subject: terrorism studies and the absent subjectivity,' *Critical Studies on Terrorism*, 1 (1): 27–36.

7

METAPHOR ANALYSIS AS A METHOD IN TERRORISM STUDIES

Alexander Spencer

Introduction

Metaphor analysis has by now become a fairly well established discourse analytical method in political science in general and in international relations in particular (Beer and de Landtsheer 2004a; Kornprobst *et al.* 2008; Carver and Pikalo 2008).[1] A growing amount of research is applying metaphor analysis to aspects of international politics such as European integration (Chilton and Ilyin 1993; Hülsse 2003; Drulak 2006), immigration (Santa Ana 1999; Charteris-Black 2006), security policy (Thronborrow 1993; Mutimer 1994), war (Paris 2002; Hartmann-Mahmud 2002) and more recently terrorism (Hülsse and Spencer 2008; Spencer 2010, 2012; Schwarz-Friesel and Kromminga forthcoming).

In line with constructivist and poststructuralist theories the central and unifying element of almost all metaphor analytical approaches is that the aspect which is to be researched, in our case terrorism, is not understood as a physical fact but as a social construction (Jackson 2005; Gunning 2007). The central notion on which this chapter is based is that terrorism is constituted through discourse and in particular through the metaphors we use about or in connection with terrorism. This does not mean that such a perspective denies the 'real' existence of terrorism. There are real people who conduct real actions, but what these people and their deeds mean is a matter of interpretation. It is this interpretation through metaphors which constitutes a certain group of people as 'terrorists', constructing them in a particular fashion and thereby influencing our reactions to them.

This chapter applies metaphor analysis to the issue of terrorism in order to show how certain constructions of 'the terrorist' in the media make certain counter-terrorism policies possible while others remain outside of the realm of those means considered appropriate. In pursuit of this aim the first part of the chapter will outline the method of metaphor analysis. The second part then illustrates this method by applying it to the German media discourse on terrorism found in the tabloid newspaper the *Bild* and draws out four conceptual metaphors which constitute terrorism as a 'war', as a 'crime', as 'uncivilised evil' and as a 'disease'. Thereby the chapter shows that metaphors do not only describe reality but they actively take part in the construction of the world as we see it, think of it and ultimately react to it. By projecting understandings from one conceptual area such as war, crime, uncivilised evilness or disease to a different area such as terrorism, metaphors make certain counter-measures such as military, judicial or immigration policies appear appropriate while other means such as negotiations are placed outside of the options considered sensible.

Metaphor analysis as a method

What exactly is a metaphor? The Oxford English Dictionary (2005: 1103) describes a metaphor as 'a figure of speech in which a word or phrase is applied to an object or action to which it is not literally applicable'. In an etymological sense the term 'metaphor' comes from the Greek word *meta* meaning beyond or above and the word *pherein* meaning carrying or bearing. Sam Glucksberg (2001: 3) has pointed out that '[f]rom this deceptively simple root, metaphor has come to mean different things to different people, so much so that specialists in the area are often temporarily confounded when asked for a definition of *metaphor*' (emphasis in original). Andrew Ortony (1979: 3) has argued that '[a]ny serious study of metaphor is almost obliged to start with the works of Aristotle' as '[h]is discussion of the issue, principally in the Poetics and in the Rhetoric, have remained influential to this day'. According to Aristotle metaphors are a transference, naming one thing in terms of another (Mahon 1999). Metaphor 'consists in giving the thing a name that belongs to something else' (Aristotle 1982: 1457b). A couple of hundred years later and around a thousand kilometres to the north-west, Cicero similarly stated that metaphors happen 'when a word applying to one thing is transferred to another, because the similarity seems to justify the transference' (cited in Purcell 1990: 39).

The general idea of what a metaphor is has more recently been discussed by a vast range of different scholars from very different disciplines using a varying degree of complexity to express their understandings. In fact, '[m]etaphor has by now been defined in so many ways that there is no human expression, whether in language or any other medium, that would not be metaphoric in *someone's* definition' (Booth, 1978: 50, emphasis in original). For example, Kenneth Burke (1945: 503) quite simply believes metaphors to be 'a device for seeing something in terms of something else' and Susan Sontag (1989: 93) describes metaphors as 'saying a thing is or is like something-it-is-not'. Paul Ricœur (1978: 80) argues that 'metaphor holds together within one simple meaning two different missing parts of different contexts of this meaning' and most recently Jonathan Charteris-Black (2004: 21) has defined a metaphor as 'a linguistic representation that results from the shift in the use of a word or phrase from the context or domain in which it is expected to occur to another context or domain where it is not expected to occur, thereby causing semantic tension'. So metaphors do not simply substitute one term for another, but create a strong perceptual link between two things (Bates 2004).

Most of these 'definitions' mentioned above which focus on the transference of something to something else would, however, include a large number of other linguistic tools such as analogies, similes and metonymy. 'Analogies' make comparisons between one thing and another and involve an inference that if two or more things are the same in one aspect they are probably the same in others. While metaphors draw comparisons from different realms of experience (across-domain comparisons), analogies generally draw comparisons from the same realm of experience (within-domain comparisons) (Vosniadou and Ortony 1989:7). Nevertheless, they are similar to metaphors as they involve understanding something in terms of something else. As Keith Shimko (1994: 660) points out, in 'a purely cognitive sense, there is very little difference between analogies and metaphors. Indeed, because the dynamics of analogical and metaphorical thought are alike, many cognitive psychologists usually fail to distinguish between the two (not because they cannot, but because doing so is often unnecessary)'. An example of a historical analogy is a comparison between the events of 9/11 and Pearl Harbor. In contrast, a 'simile' explicitly uses the words 'as' or 'like' to compare two things. Although, like metaphors and analogies, it makes a comparison, it is different because it allows these two things to remain distinct from each other despite their similarities. The first of the following sentences is an example of a simile while the second is a metaphor:

> 'Al-Qaeda is as well armed as an army'.
> 'Al-Qaeda is an army of terrorists'.

While metaphors involve two things that are similar but also different from each other in our conceptual system, metonymies involve two things which are closely related to each other in our conceptual system. With metonymies one uses one thing, for example 'Washington', to stand for another thing such as 'the American government'. For example:

> 'Washington decided to impose sanctions on Sudan'.
> 'Bin Laden attacked New York and Washington on September 11th'.

Metaphors and metonymies both involve a substitution of one term for another but metaphors are based on similarity while metonymies are based on contiguity. In the case of metonymies, the things which are compared have a 'stand-for relationship' within a single conceptual domain while the elements in the case of metaphors have an 'is-understood-as relationship' between two conceptually distant domains (Kövecses 2002: 227).

Despite these differences, most scholars, especially in political science and IR, generally adopt a very broad definition of metaphor to include these other linguistic devices such as analogies, similes and metonymy. Metaphor has become an 'all-purpose connector term' (Gozzi 1999: 55). This is understandable as the general idea of understanding something with the help of something else is central to all these linguistic tools.

Essentially, the definition one adopts depends very much on what one considers metaphors capable of and maybe it will become clearer what a metaphor is when examining what metaphors actually do (Glucksberg 2001: 3). Traditionally metaphors were considered 'convenient labels that accurately describe the nature of world politics' (Chilton and Lakoff 1999: 56). Alternatively they were deemed to be a purely rhetorical tool which replaces one word with another and serves little purpose but to make speech sound nice (Chilton 1996a: 359; Charteris-Black 2004: 25). '[M]etaphor has been considered a mere ornamental use of language, a pretty turn of phrase rippling along on the surface of discourse' (Gozzi 1999: 9). In other words, a metaphor was seen as a 'superficial stylistic accessory' and a way of decorating discourse without affecting its meaning (Beer and de Landtsheer 2004b: 5). Traditional terrorism research would probably think of metaphors in this way and consider them unimportant, seeing them as only words and rhetoric and therefore irrelevant for political analysis on a subject of such life-threatening importance.

In contrast to this rhetorical understanding of metaphor, cognitive linguistics goes further and argues that metaphors are more than just words. In particular, Lakoff and Johnson (1980) are among the most influential scholars in this respect as they have managed to export the study of metaphor from linguistics into other disciplines such as psychology, sociology and political science. For them, the 'essence of metaphor is understanding and experiencing one kind of thing in terms of another' (Lakoff and Johnson 1980: 5). In their groundbreaking book *Metaphors We Live By* they argue that metaphors structure the way people think and that the human conceptual system as such is fundamentally metaphorical. '[T]he way we think, what we experience and what we do everyday is very much a matter of metaphor' (Lakoff and Johnson 1980: 297). They believe that metaphors make humans understand one conceptual domain of experience in terms of another by projecting knowledge about the first familiar domain onto the second more abstract domain. 'Metaphors [...] are devices for simplifying and giving meaning to complex and bewildering sets of observations that evoke concern' (Edelman 1971: 65). The central idea here is that metaphors map a source domain, for example WAR, onto a target domain, for example TERRORISM, and thereby make the target domain appear in a new light. Sometimes the source and target domain are referred to as 'tenor' and 'vehicle' or as 'primary subject' and 'secondary subject' (Cameron 1999: 13; Black 1979). This idea is commonly captured in the following way:

TARGET DOMAIN (A) IS SOURCE DOMAIN (B)
TERRORISM IS WAR
TERRORISM IS CRIME

Here we have to distinguish between two kinds of metaphors: the *metaphoric expression* and the *conceptual metaphor*. The conceptual metaphor, in our case TERRORISM

IS WAR or TERRORISM IS CRIME, involves the abstract connection between one 'conceptual domain' (Lakoff 1993: 208–9) and another by mapping a source domain (WAR) and a target domain (TERRORISM). Mapping here refers to 'a set of systematic correspondences between the source and the target in the sense that constituent conceptual elements of B correspond to constituent elements of A' (Kövecses 2002: 6). 'Thus, the conceptual metaphor makes us apply what we know about one area of our experience (source domain) to another area of our experience (target domain)' (Drulak 2005: 3). Conceptual metaphors do not have to be explicitly visible in discourse. However, metaphorical expressions are directly visible and represent the specific statements found in the text which the conceptual metaphor draws on. For example:

> 'The West is facing a *terrorist army* led by Osama bin Laden'
> 'Osama bin Laden and his *lieutenants* are planning an attack'

Here the metaphors 'terrorist army' and 'lieutenants' are two different metaphorical expressions which both draw on the same conceptual metaphor of TERRORISM IS WAR. In other words: 'The conceptual metaphor represents the conceptual basis, idea or image that underlies a set of metaphors' (Charteris-Black 2004: 9).

The metaphorical formula A IS B applied to the conceptual metaphor mentioned above is, however, slightly misleading and not totally accurate as it suggests that the whole target domain is understood in terms of the whole source domain. However, this cannot be the case as concept A cannot be the same as concept B. The mapping between the two domains is only ever partial as not all characteristics of concept A are transferred to concept B. In fact, it is commonly accepted in the realm of metaphor analysis that through the use of metaphor 'people make *selective distinctions* that, by highlighting some aspect of the phenomenon, downplay and hide other features that could give a different stance' (Milliken 1996: 221, emphasis in original). Similar to media framing, they draw attention to certain aspects of a phenomenon and invite the listener or reader to think of one thing in the light of another. Thereby they influence policy and in our case counter-terrorism policy. Metaphors 'limit what we notice, highlight what we do see, and provide part of the inferential structure that we reason with' (Lakoff 1992: 481). As Chilton and Lakoff (1995: 56) point out, metaphors 'are concepts that can be and often are acted upon. As such, they define in significant part, what one takes as 'reality', and thus form the basis and the justification for the formulation of policy and its potential execution.' Metaphors structure the way people define a phenomenon and thereby influence how they react to it: they limit and bias our perceived policy choices as they determine basic assumptions and attitudes on which decision-making depends (Milliken 1996; Chilton 1996a; Mio 1997).

These assumptions have led to two distinct types of metaphor analysis. The first which is in line with many aspects found in critical discourse analysis (CDA) takes the premises mentioned above and argues that metaphor analysis can reveal the hidden agenda, ideology, thought or intentions of the person using the metaphors

(Fairclough 1992: 194; Musolff 2000: 4). Among these Jonathan Charteris-Black (2004) has developed a critical approach to metaphor analysis which argues that metaphors are potentially powerful weapons as they can influence the way we perceive a certain social reality. Metaphors have the potential to influence human beliefs, attitudes and consequently their actions. Critical metaphor analysis therefore wants to 'demonstrate how particular discursive practices reflect socio-political power structures' (Charteris-Black 2004: 29). The second kind of metaphor analysis does not try and reveal these secrets and the thinking behind the metaphor but concentrates on the reconstruction of how these metaphors shape and effect reality (Tonkiss 1998; Hülsse 2006). Rather than asking the question of who is responsible for certain metaphors and why these metaphors are used, this approach focuses on the 'reality' which follows from these metaphors. This is in line with the kind of discourse analysis which has been put forward by, among others, David Campbell (1998), Roxanne Lynn Doty (1993), Jennifer Milliken (1999) and Lene Hansen (2006). Drawing on Michel Foucault, these scholars share a concept of discourse which is 'above' individual discourse-participants. Discourse constitutes actors and structures what they can meaningfully say or do. Accordingly, actors have very limited agency. Rather than being able to use words intentionally and manipulate discourse to further their own purposes, they are themselves inextricably bound up with discourses that leave them little room for individuality. What they say and what they do is to a large extent determined by discourse. The main focus is on how discourse shapes the world, i.e. the actors, their self-understandings and their actions. The second part of this chapter follows this strand of researchers and wants to examine the 'reality' and policies which follow from the use of certain metaphors rather than the reasons for that use.

Obviously we have to be careful when talking about the idea that metaphors shape or cause policy and in particular counter-terrorism policy as they are only one among many linguistic devices, even taking a broad understanding of the term, which play a role in the discursive construction of reality. As Andrew Anderson (2004: 91) points out '[w]hen metaphors are said to *cause* political phenomena, political science often objects' (emphasis in original). 'The nature of metaphor does not lend itself easily to rigorous demonstrations of causality. Metaphorical power may exist, but it is hard to nail down' (Beer and de Landtsheer 2004b: 7). It is therefore very important to realise that metaphors do not cause a certain counter-terrorism policy in a positivist sense where the metaphor is the independent and the policies are the dependent variable. Metaphors do not entail a clear set of policies, but open up space for policy possibilities. Metaphors offer a discursive construct which frames the situation in a certain way. 'Metaphors are more likely to influence policy indirectly through their impact on the decision maker's general approach to an issue; they will be part of the conceptual foundation, not a detailed policy map' (Shimko 1994: 665). As metaphors help construct reality in a certain way they are able to define the limits of common sense, the limits of what is considered possible and logical, while excluding other options from consideration (Hülsse 2003: 225).

So how does one actually carry out metaphor analysis? There are a number of scholars who offer a range of different detailed plans of how to carry out a metaphor analysis (Gibbs 1999; Schmitt 2005). Although their emphasis varies, the key components remain similar. First, one selects a text or rather a series of texts such as works or speeches of a particular author or politician, news reports or television programs (Ricœur 1981). Second, the researcher starts identifying narrative elements which provide the context for metaphors such as actors, actions or settings. Third, one starts collecting the metaphorical expressions used in this corpus to talk about the narrative elements. In a fourth step one notes common and recurring metaphors and organises them into clusters which are then generalised into conceptual metaphors underlying the discourse. The frequency of the different conceptual metaphors is crucial as an indicator for their importance in the discourse. The more common the metaphor is, the more influence it is bound to have on the construction of reality and ultimately on policy (Charteris-Black 2004: 34). In the final step these metaphors are inductively interpreted. This interpretation is intuitive and undoubtedly subjective (Lule 2004: 182).[2] But there have been a number of suggestions of how such an interpretation of metaphors could be carried out in a 'scientific' and controlled way. For example, Ronald Hitzler (1993: 230) has used what he refers to as 'artificial stupidity' while Rainer Hülsse (2003: 228) takes up Umberto Eco's (1994) suggestion to interpret a metaphor like someone who had encountered it for the very first time. This without doubt is a difficult endeavour as 'metaphors are typically culturally-loaded expressions, whose meaning has to be inferred through reference to shared cultural knowledge' (Littlemore 2003: 273). Therefore there is a danger that people from one cultural background do not understand a metaphor from another especially if they attribute different associations to the source domain (Charteris-Black 2003; Deignan 2003). So the interpretation of metaphors is predominantly down to the intuition of native speakers and individual analysts embedded in the corresponding cultural sphere (Pragglejaz Group 2007: 25).

The illustrative metaphor analysis in the following part wants to avoid the charges of being arbitrary in two ways. Firstly, it focuses solely on the most common metaphors, and secondly it reassures the intuitive interpretation with the help of dictionaries. The assumption is that dictionaries store common knowledge about a phenomenon (Pragglejaz Group 2007). So if we want to know about the social construction of terrorism in discourse, we can examine the metaphors used and establish the kind of source and target domains of the underlying conceptual metaphors by checking the meaning of these metaphors in dictionaries. For example, the 'commando' metaphor is important in the terrorism discourse after 9/11, so to find out how this particular metaphorical expression constitutes the terrorist actor one consults the definitions of 'commando' provided in dictionaries. One here can find the following definitions:

'A soldier specially trained for carrying out raids' (Oxford Dictionary of English)

'A military unit trained and organized as shock troops especially for hit-and-run raids into enemy territory' (Merriam-Webster)
'An amphibious military unit trained for raiding' (Collins English Dictionary)

These definitions of the metaphor 'commando' construct him or her as something military, elite, well trained and deadly. Ultimately, words such as soldier, military unit and troops automatically come to mind and with these connotations one thinks of those actors as being involved in war. Obviously the definitions dictionaries offer vary to a certain extent but they represent a legitimate spectrum of interpretations which avoids the accusation of interpreting metaphors arbitrarily. As Rainer Hülsse (2006: 404) points out, with such techniques which spell out 'what appears to be obvious, i.e. the deautomatization of the usually automatic projection from source to target, one can reconstruct the reality constructions of metaphors'.

Metaphors of terrorism in the German newspaper *Bild*

This part of the chapter plans to illustrate the method of metaphor analysis by examining German media discourse on terrorism in the popular daily tabloid newspaper *Bild* and consider how these constructions allow for particular counter-terrorism options. The central idea behind analysing the media rather than the political elite is that the media, and in particular the widely read tabloid media, give an insight into the construction of terrorism possibly held by large portions of the general public as it is widely accepted that newspapers such as *Bild* are major agenda setters and hugely influential on public opinion. As very few people follow parliamentary debates or listen to public speeches by politicians most get their ideas about how the world is through the media. And although it is clear that the media discourse is influenced by the political elite, the same is true vice versa. Overall the analysis of metaphors in a widely read media discourse can offer a good indication of the general understanding of a phenomenon. It is important to point out that the social and political context of the data such as the ideological orientation of the newspaper does not play a major role in the analysis. As mentioned above it is concerned mainly with the resulting 'realities' of metaphor use rather than the reasons for why particular metaphors are used. The *Bild* newspaper serves as an example as many of the following metaphors can also be found in other media outlets and political statements (see Table 7.1).

The following paragraphs will focus on the metaphorisation of terrorism in the *Bild* newspaper by analysing one month of articles following five large attacks perpetrated by al-Qaeda: 9/11 in 2001, the bombings in Bali in 2002, the attacks in Istanbul in 2003, the train bombings in Madrid in 2004 and the London Tube attacks in 2005. *Bild* was chosen due to the fact that it has the largest readership in Germany with around 12 million readers and it can therefore from a cognitive perspective be considered to have a lot of influence on people's perception of terrorism. These events were chosen not only due to their fairly large nature and their focus on a Western target, but also because they offer a fairly regular timeline which

TABLE 7.1 Headlines of German newspapers after 9/11

Newspaper	Headline on the 12 September 2001
Süddeutsche Zeitung	Terror-War against America
Die Tageszeitung	War against the USA
Rheinische Post	War against civilization
Neues Deutschland	Terrorwar against the USA. Thousands of dead in New York
Financial Times Deutschland	'That is a second Pearl Harbor'
Schweriner Volkszeitung	The world is shocked – War against civilization
Junge Welt	Declaration of war against the USA
Express	War against America
Neue Ruhr Zeitung	The world under shock. War against the USA
Sächsische Zeitung	Inferno in the USA: Devastating terror-waves with thousands of dead
Thüringische Landeszeitung	Declaration of war against the world

indicates the regularity of the predicative constructions of terrorism. The timeframe of one month after each incident for selecting articles was chosen as further research beyond this time period did not add further kinds of conceptual metaphors. The four most salient conceptual metaphors over this timer period included: TERRORISM IS WAR, TERRORISM IS CRIME, TERRORISM IS UNCIVILISED EVIL and TERRORISM IS DISEASE.

Terrorism as war

A very common conceptual metaphor found in the media discourse following all five events between 2001 and 2005 in the German tabloid understood terrorism as a war.[3] Although the most famous is the 'war on terror' metaphor, there are a large number of other metaphorical expressions which reinforce this understanding. For example, in Germany the attacks of 9/11 were considered 'kamikaze attacks' and the event was metaphorised as a second 'Pearl Harbor'.[4] This understanding of terrorism as a war was further strengthened by describing the terrorists as 'al-Qaeda warriors' or 'terror commandos' in a 'terrorist army' made up not only of 'soldiers' but 'battle-hardened' 'veterans'.[5] The attacks are considered a 'declaration of war' to the Western 'alliance' in a conflict which includes 'battlefields' or 'war zones'.[6] Like a general, Osama bin Laden is 'commanding' his 'private army' made up of 'terror-' or 'combat troops' from the safety of his 'camouflaged' 'command centre'.[7]

Constituting terrorism as a war calls for a military response. As early as 1987 Jeffrey Simon of the RAND corporation realised the importance of the war metaphor in the fight against terrorism: 'Equating terrorism with war effectively ends any debate over whether military responses are justified. If a nation is at war it must respond militarily to attack' (Simon 1987: 9). Germany's initial reaction to al-Qaeda and Osama bin Laden fits this metaphorical understanding of terrorism as a war very well, as it openly supported US military action in Afghanistan and the country quickly offered nearly 4,000 troops in support (Hyde-Price 2003). This 'war' under-standing was also mirrored by the public. In September 2001, 58 per cent favoured German military participation in a war against terrorism (Katzenstein 2002a: 429). So the war metaphor influences the public's perception of the enemy and makes a military response appear logical. The illustrative metaphor constitutes reality. As Sarbin points out: 'An important feature of the war metaphor is that problems engendered by terrorist acts can be solved through the deployment of military forces' (Sarbin 2003: 150–1). So more than anything the public associates war with violence, insecurity and the application of military force to achieve victory and solve the threat of terrorism. If the problem is considered to have military dimen-sions, a military solution seems appropriate.

Terrorism as crime

A second conceptual metaphor found constructs terrorism as crime. While many in the literature on terrorism point to the almost dichotomous relationship between the war and the criminal justice model of engaging terrorism (Crelinsten and Schmid 1992), the discourse on terrorism in the media contains both metaphorical expressions of war and crime at the same time. So in Germany, Osama bin Laden is not only a soldier but also a 'thug' and the al-Qaeda 'army' is also a 'gang' full of 'criminal' 'murderers' or 'killers'.[8] The 'criminal attacks' were 'murderous' 'crimes' which left behind not only a 'war zone' but also a 'murder' 'crime scene'.[9] Not only were the 'commandos' responsible for these 'terror murders' but responsibility is attributed to the 'offender' bin Laden and his 'accomplices'.[10]

The conceptual metaphor TERRORISM IS CRIME makes a judicial response seem appropriate. As Peter Sederberg points out, while 'the view that terrorism is war leads its proponents to favor repressive responses; the view that terrorism is crime leads its proponents to favor legal solutions' (Sederberg 1995: 299–300). This, however, does not mean that the two understandings are dichotomously opposed to each other in all aspects. In fact, both conceptual metaphors seem to overlap to a certain extent as a legislative response can make sense in both TERRORISM IS WAR and TERRORISM IS CRIME. Similar to the concep-tual metaphor TERRORISM IS WAR and the military responses, the under-standing of terrorism as something criminal made a legal response by Germany appear logical after 9/11.

In Germany the government quickly passed a large number of new anti-terror laws and alterations to existing legislation against the terrorist 'criminal'. Most directly this is noticeable in the first two so-called 'security packages' (*Sicherheitspakete*), which made adjustments to more than 100 regulations in 17 different laws and a number of administrative decrees (Katzenstein 2002b). It increased the powers of the intelligence and security services giving the Federal Criminal Police Office a stronger position, removing its reliance on the police forces of the *Länder* for data collection. As the security expert Victor Mauer pointed out, although this prompted concerns about civil liberties and excessive intrusion, the 'new legislation reflects that the lion's share of counter-terrorism against transnational terrorist threats is to be conducted on the law enforcement and intelligence fronts [... after all] terrorists are regarded as criminals' (Mauer 2007: 63). This general understanding of terrorism as something criminal is also very clearly visible in German public opinion. For example, in November 2001 over 70 per cent of the German population seemed to support the second security package.[11]

Terrorism as something uncivilised and evil

A third important conceptual metaphor in Germany constitutes terrorism by al-Qaeda as something uncivilised and evil. In Germany, the terrorist becomes 'barbaric' 'bomb-barbarians' and terrorism becomes 'barbarianism' perpetrated by 'inhuman' 'terror beasts'.[12] In addition, the terrorist and bin Laden are not only constructed as a 'monstrous' 'hydra' or a 'terror monster' but the embodiment of 'evil'.[13] Osama bin Laden and his terrorists become the 'devil', who causes 'diabolical' 'infernos', 'apocalyptic' 'terror-hells' or the 'apocalypse' itself.[14]

The conceptual metaphor UNCIVILISED EVIL does a number of things and predicates terrorism in a number of ways. Most importantly, the metaphors signal a stark political difference. Predicating the terrorists as uncivilised or evil leads to a concrete and clear polarisation, as it outcasts the actor and his/her actions and dichotomises and antagonises them (the out-group) and us (the in-group) (Lazar and Lazar 2004). For example, the metaphor 'barbarian' constitutes terrorism not only as something 'other' but as something explicitly foreign; something that comes from outside one's own country or cultural hemisphere. Similar to the term 'Islamist' the expression 'barbaric' gives the terrorist construction something foreign without assigning a concrete nationality. So, in addition to the dehumanisation of the evil metaphors the terrorist actor is de-Westernised. Interestingly, Marina Llorente has noted that 'most violent acts by Westerners tend not to be labelled 'barbaric'. A good example is the case of the Oklahoma City bomber Timothy McVeigh, whose action was not categorised in terms of 'barbarism', presumably because he belonged to the 'civilised' part of the world' (Llorente 2002: 45). The understanding, inherent in the conceptual metaphor TERRORISM IS UNCIVILISED EVIL characterises terrorism as something foreign and makes policies which target and keep the otherness outside of the self − such as tighter border and immigration controls − appear appropriate.

In Germany, the notion of linking terrorism to the foreign 'other', and with this to the idea of migration, was visible from the beginnings of the political debate after 9/11 as politicians from the conservative parties, the liberals and the social democrats all immediately linked terrorism to immigration and called for tighter controls. The most obvious means of stopping these 'evil' 'barbarians' from entering the 'civilised' world is the securing of one's borders. In the time since 9/11 Germany has done precisely that; it has tightened its borders and increased resources for the Federal Border Guards (prior to 2005 known as the *Bundesgrenzschutz*, BGS) responsible for protecting Germany's borders from 'evil' 'savages'. Following 9/11 the budget for the border guards was substantially increased in 2002 by around 120 million euros and it purchased new high-tech helicopters and patrol boats and recruited and trained more personnel to patrol Germany's borders and embassies abroad against foreign terrorists. As Diez and Squire point out, these policies are 'indicative of a direct linkage between terrorism and migration in the German case' (Diez and Squire 2008). This link and the understanding of terrorism can also be seen in opinion polls. For example, 79 per cent of the German population agreed with Interior Minister Schily's idea following the train bombings in Madrid of making the deportation of suspicious foreigners quicker and easier.[15]

Terrorism as disease

The final conceptual metaphor underlying the discourse constitutes terrorism as disease. In the German tabloid one encountered metaphors which constituted terrorism as 'sick', 'crazy' or even the 'plague'.[16] By metaphorising the terrorist and Osama bin Laden as an 'insane' 'mad man' who plots 'terror-insanity' in his 'sick head' the source domain DISEASE is projected onto the target domain TERRORISM.[17]

Similar to the metaphors of 'uncivilised' 'evil', metaphors of 'disease' indicate a deep political rift. For example, one should consider the interpretation that disease, similar to the metaphors of evil and the uncivilised mentioned above, is something one cannot reason with. This is especially true when we consider the notion of 'madness' as a disease. While negotiations and ceasefire agreements do make sense if we constitute the terrorist as a soldier in a war, they are absurd in a conflict with an army of 'lunatics' who lack the ability for rational thought. One can simply not trust the 'insane', be they soldiers or criminals. A psychological study by Emily Pronin et al. showed that people were far less likely to advocate the use of diplomacy against terrorists if these were depicted as irrational (Pronin et al. 2006). Not only can one not negotiate with the insane or with diseases such as cancer, but many other illnesses such as the plague are in fact contagious. So any kind of contact with the 'disease' of terrorism runs the risk of the 'disease-riddled' terrorist infecting you. Therefore terrorists should not be talked to but rather isolated and quarantined as '[c]ontact with them is polluting' (Zulaika and Douglass 1996: 62). Overall, the construction of terrorism as a 'disease' suggests that certain policies such as engagement or negotiations are not considered as possible options.

In contrast to the other concrete policies mentioned above, it is obviously more difficult to indicate the non-existence of a policy. However, one may gain some insight into the implications of the conceptual metaphor TERRORISM AS DISEASE when we consider Osama bin Laden's negotiation offer made in April 2004[18] which the German government vehemently opposed. Chancellor Schröder and a large number of other politicians vigorously rejected such a truce as '[t]here cannot be negotiations with terrorists […] like Osama bin Laden'.[19]

Conclusion

Overall the aim of this chapter was to introduce metaphor analysis to the methodological tool kit in terrorism studies. By taking up insights from cognitive linguistics, metaphor analysis can tell us how terrorism is constructed in discourse by transferring insights from one familiar conceptual domain onto a more abstract domain and thereby give a new understandable meaning to the unfamiliar. Thereby metaphoric constructions of terrorism make some counter-terrorism policies appear appropriate (for example military strikes) while others fall outside of the options considered suitable (for example negotiations). By understanding terrorism in the form of metaphors and thereby critically reflecting on the existing facts about terrorism, one is able to question what was previously considered unthinkable responses. It is in particular the ability of metaphor analysis to unmask the constituted impossibilities which call for further research as this can highlight reactions previously ignored such as the possibility of engagement and negotiations with al-Qaeda and open up new areas of research that were previously considered taboo.

Notes

1. This chapter draws on Spencer (2010).
2. One has to note that the decision on what is metaphorical and what is not is also down to interpretation. On this point see in particular Low (1999: 49): 'There is always going to be a measure of subjectivity or randomness in identifying expressions.'
3. The following metaphors are examples of the various metaphors found in the *Bild* newspapers. Due to a lack of space only one example reference will be noted for each metaphorical expression.
4. *Bild*, 'Gibt es jetzt Krieg, Herr Scholl-Latour?', 12 September 2001; *Bild*, 'Kriegserklärung an die Menschheit', 12 September 2001.
5. *Bild*, 'Die Spur führt zu Al Qaida', 15 March 2004; *Bild*, 'Neue Terror-Kommandos unterwegs?', 15 September 2001; *Bild*, 'Das FBI jagt bin Laden mit 180 Spionage-Satelliten', 14 September 2001; *Bild*, 'Nach 26 Tagen schlagen die US-Streitkräfte zu', 8 October 2001; *Bild*, 'Der Bergbunker von Osama bin Laden', 15 September 2001; *Bild*, 'Das FBI jagt bin Laden mit 180 Spionage-Satelliten', 14 September 2001.
6. *Bild*, 'Das ist bin Ladens Kriegserklärung', 25 September 2001; *Bild*, 'Ein abscheuliches Verbrechen', 25 October 2002; *Bild*, 'Mitternacht stand das Paradies in Flammen', 14 October 2002; *Bild*, 'Großer Gott steh uns bei!', 12 September 2001.
7. *Bild*, 'Wir werden Madrid mit Leichen spicken', 17 March 2004; *Bild*, 'Wo steckt bin Laden?', 19 September 2001; *Bild*, 'Das sind die Pass-Fälscher von Terror-Chef bin Laden', 28 September 2001; *Bild*, 'Wir sind bereit zu sterben', 25 October 2002; *Bild*, 'Überall blutüberströmte, weinende Menschen', 21 November 2003; *Bild*, 'Der Angriff', 8 October 2001.
8. *Bild*, 'Wer steckt hinter dem Anschlag', 8 July 2005; *Bild*, 'Terroristen ermorden ägyptischen Botschafter', 8 July 2005; *Bild*, 'Mr. President, treffen Sie die Schuldigen, nicht die Unschuldigen', 17 September 2001; *Bild*, 'So feige! So sinnlos! Ihr Mörder!', 12 March 2004; *Bild*, 'Er war's!', 14 July 2005.
9. *Bild*, 'Schily fordert Raster-Fahndung in ganz Europa', 27 March 2004; *Bild*, 'Um 8.51 Uhr zerfetzte es die erste U-Bahn', 8 July 2005; *Bild*, 'Ein abscheuliches Verbrechen', 25 October 2002; *Bild*, 'Das ist Deutschlands gefährlichster Häftling', 23 October 2002; *Bild*, 'Ich sah, wie Trümmer eine Frau enthauptet haben', 14 October 2002.

10. *Bild*, 'Verdammte 11. Angst vor Attentaten am Ostersonntag', 7 April 2004; *Bild*, 'Kriegserklärung an die Menschheit', 12 September 2001; *Bild*, 'Was passiert mit den Leichen der zerfetzten Attentäter?', 19 July 2005.
11. 'Deutschland TREND November 2001', conducted by Infratest dimap for the ARD. Online at: http://www.infratest-dimap.de/uploads/media/dt0111.pdf (accessed 5 June 2012).
12. *Bild*, 'Die Spur führt zu Al Qaida', 15 March 2004; *Bild*, 'Jagt auf die Bomben-Barbaren', 9 July 2005; *Bild*, 'Jetzt sind wir alle Amerikaner weil ...', 13 September 2001; *Bild*, 'Terror-Bestie lebte acht Jahre in Deutschland', 14 September 2001.
13. *Bild*, 'Putin versetzt Luftabwehr in Gefechtsbereitschaft', 12 September 2001; *Bild*, 'Mitten ins stolze Herz Spaniens', 12 March 2004; *Bild*, 'Ist bin Laden schön aus Afghanistan geflohen?', 22 September 2001; *Bild*, 'Besiegen sie das Böse?', 19 September 2001.
14. *Bild*, 'In New York erlebten wir die Handlanger des Teufels', 21 September 2001; *Bild*, 'War es Osama bin Laden', 14 October 2002; *Bild*, 'Um 8.51 Uhr zerfetzte es die erste U-Bahn', 8 July 2005; *Bild*, 'Gibt es jetzt Krieg, Herr Scholl-Latour?', 12 September 2001; *Bild*, 'Ich überlebte die Terror-Hölle', 15 October 2002; *Bild*, 'Die Woche der Apokalypse', 17 September 2001.
15. 'Deutschland Trends April 2004', Infratest dimap conducted for the ARD. Online at: http://www.infratest-dimap.de/uploads/media/dt0404.pdf (accessed 5 June 2012).
16. *Bild*, 'Deutschland weint mit Amerika', 12 September 2001; *Bild*, 'Putin versetzt Luftabwehr in Gefechtsbereitschaft', 12 September 2001; *Bild*, 'Was uns die Spanier lehren', 16 March 2004.
17. *Bild*, 'So quälen sie die Geiseln von Moskau', 26 October 2002; *Bild*, 'Wer sind die barbarischen Bombenleger?', 12 March 2004; *Bild*, 'Terror-Irrsinn!', 25 March 2004; *Bild*, 'Wird heute bin Ladens Gehirn verhaftet?', 20 March 2004.
18. For the full text see: http://news.bbc.co.uk/2/hi/middle_east/3628069.stm (accessed 24 February 2015).
19. *Süddeutsche Zeitung*, 'Keine Verhandlungen mit Terroristen oder Schwerverbrechern', 15 April 2004. Online at: http://www.sueddeutsche.de/politik/bundesregierung-keine-verhandlungen-mit-terroristen-und-schwerverbrechern-1.439366 (accessed 24 February 2015).

References

Anderson, R. D. (2004) 'The causal power of metaphor. Cueing democratic identities in Russia and beyond', in F. A. Beer and C. de Landtsheer (eds), *Metaphorical World Politics*. East Lansing, MI: Michigan State University Press, pp. 91–108.

Aristotle (1982) *Poetics*. Oxford: Clarendon Press.

Bates, B. R. (2004) 'Audiences, metaphors, and the Persian Gulf War', *Communication Studies*, 55 (3): 447–63.

Beer, F. A. and de Landtsheer, C. (eds) (2004a) *Metaphorical World Politics*. East Lansing, MI: Michigan State University Press.

Beer, F. A. and de Landtsheer, C. (2004b) 'Metaphors, politics, and world politics', in F. A. Beer and C. de Landtsheer (eds), *Metaphorical World Politics*. East Lansing, MI: Michigan State University Press, pp. 5–52.

Black, M. (1979) 'How metaphors work: a reply to Donald Davidson', *Critical Inquiry*, 6 (1): 131–43.

Booth, W. C. (1978) 'Metaphor as rhetoric: the problem of evaluation', *Critical Inquiry*, 5 (1): 49–72.

Burke, K. (1945) *A Grammar of Motives*. Berkeley, CA: University of California Press.

Cameron, L. (1999) 'Operationalizing "metaphor" for applied linguistic research', in L. Cameron and G. Low (eds), *Researching and Applying Metaphor*. Cambridge: Cambridge University Press, pp. 3–38.

Campbell, D. (1998) *Writing Security: United States Foreign Policy and the Politics of Identity.* Minneapolis, MN: University of Minnesota Press.

Carver, T. and Pikalo, J. (eds) (2008) *Political Language and Metaphor: Interpreting and Changing the World.* London: Routledge.

Charteris-Black, J. (2003) 'Speaking with forked tongue: a comparative study of metaphor and metonymy in English and Malay phraseology', *Metaphor and Symbol*, 18 (4): 289–310.

Charteris-Black, J. (2004) *Corpus Approaches to Critical Metaphor Analysis.* Basingstoke: Palgrave Macmillan.

Charteris-Black, J. (2006) 'Britain as a container: immigration metaphors in the 2005 election campaign', *Discourse and Society*, 17 (5): 563–81.

Chilton, P. (1996a) *Security Metaphors: Cold War Discourse from Containment to Common House.* New York: Peter Lang.

Chilton, P. (1996b) 'The meaning of security', in F. A. Beer and R. Hariman (eds), *Post-Realism: The Rhetorical Turn in International Relations.* East Lansing, MI: Michigan State University Press, pp. 193–216.

Chilton, P. and Ilyin, M. (1993) 'Metaphor in political discourse: the case of the "Common European House"', *Discourse and Society*, 4 (1): 7–31.

Chilton, P. and Lakoff, G. (1999) 'Foreign policy by metaphor', in C. Schaffner and A. L. Wenden (eds), *Language and Peace.* Amsterdam: Harwood Academic, pp. 37–59.

Crelinsten, R. and Schmid, A. (1992) 'Western responses to terrorism: a twenty-five year balance sheet', *Terrorism and Political Violence*, 4 (4): 307–40.

Deignan, A. (2003) 'Metaphorical expressions and culture: an indirect link', *Metaphor and Symbol*, 18 (4): 255–71.

Diez, T. and Squire, V. (2008) 'Traditions of citizenship and the securitisation of migration in Germany and Britain', *Citizenship Studies*, 12 (6): 565–81.

Doty, R. L. (1993) 'Foreign policy as social construction: a post-positivist analysis of U.S. counterinsurgency policy in the Philippines', *International Studies Quarterly*, 37 (3): 297–320.

Drulak, P. (2005) *Metaphors and Creativity in International Politics*, Discourse Politics Identity Working Paper Series No. 3. Lancaster: Lancaster University Institute for Advanced Studies.

Drulak, P. (2006) 'Motion, container and equilibrium: metaphors in the discourse about European integration', *European Journal of International Relations*, 12 (4): 499–531.

Eco, U. (1994) *The Limits of Interpretation.* Bloomington, IN: Indiana University Press.

Edelman, M. (1971) *Politics as Symbolic Action.* Chicago: Markham.

Fairclough, N. (1992) *Discourse and Social Change.* Cambridge: Polity Press.

Gibbs, R. (1999) 'Researching metaphor', in L. Cameron and G. Low (eds), *Researching and Applying Metaphor.* Cambridge: Cambridge University Press, pp. 29–47.

Glucksberg, S. (2001) *Understanding Figurative Language: From Metaphor to Idiom.* Oxford: Oxford University Press.

Gozzi, R. (1999) *The Power of Metaphor in the Age of Electronic Media.* New York: Hampton Press.

Gunning, J. (2007) 'A case for critical terrorism studies', *Government and Opposition*, 43 (3): 363–93.

Hansen, L. (2006) *Security as Practice: Discourse Analysis and the Bosnian War.* London: Routledge.

Hartmann-Mahmud, L. (2002) 'War as metaphor', *Peace Review*, 14 (4): 427–32.

Hitzler, R. (1993) 'Verstehen: Alltagspraxis und wissenschaftliches Programm', in T. Jung and S. Muller-Doohm (eds)', *Wirklichkeit im Deutungsprozeß: Verstehen und Methoden in den Kultur- und Sozialwissenschaften.* Frankfurt am Main: Suhrkamp, pp. 223–40.

Hülsse, R. (2003) 'Sprache ist mehr als Argumentation. Zur wirklichkeitskonstituierenden Rolle von Metaphern', *Zeitschrift für Internationale Beziehungen*, 10 (2): 211–46.

Hülsse, R. (2006) 'Imagine the EU: the metaphorical construction of a supra-nationalist identity', *Journal of International Relations and Development*, 9 (4): 396–421.

Hülsse, R. and Spencer, A. (2008) 'The metaphor of terror: terrorism studies and the constructivist turn', *Security Dialogue*, 39 (6): 571–92.

Hyde-Price, A. (2003) 'Redefining its security role. Germany', in M. Buckley and R. Fawn (eds), *Global Responses to Terrorism. 9/11, Afghanistan and Beyond*. London: Routledge, pp. 101–12.

Jackson, R. (2005) *Writing the War on Terror*. Manchester: Manchester University Press.

Katzenstein, P. J. (2002a) 'Same war, different views: Germany, Japan, and the war on terrorism', *Current History*, 101 (659): 427–35.

Katzenstein, P. J. (2002b) *Sonderbare Sonderwege: Germany and 9/11*, AICGS/German-American Dialogue Working Paper Series, American Institute for Contemporary German Studies. Available at: http://www.aicgs.org/site/wp-content/uploads/2011/11/katzenstein.pdf.

Kornprobst, M., Pouliot, V., Shah, N. and Zaiotti, R. (eds) (2008) *Metaphors of Globalization: Mirrors, Magicians and Mutinies*. Basingstoke: Palgrave.

Kövecses, Z. (2002) *Metaphor. A Practical Introduction*. Oxford: Oxford University Press.

Lakoff, G. (1992) 'Metaphor and war: the metaphor system used to justify war in the Gulf', in M. Pütz (ed.), *Thirty Years of Linguistic Evolution*. Amsterdam: John Benjamin, pp. 463–81.

Lakoff, G. (1993) 'The contemporary theory of metaphor', in A. Ortony (ed.), *Metaphor and Thought*, 2nd edn. Cambridge: Cambridge University Press, pp. 202–51.

Lakoff, G. and Johnson, M. (1980) *Metaphors We Live By*. Chicago: University of Chicago Press.

Lazar, A. and Lazar, M. (2004) 'The discourse of the new world order: "out-casting" the double face of threat', *Discourse and Society*, 15 (2–3): 223–42.

Littlemore, J. (2003) 'The effect of cultural background on metaphor interpretation', *Metaphor and Symbol*, 18 (4): 273–88.

Llorente, M. A. (2002) 'Civilization versus barbarism', in J. Collins and R. Glover (eds), *Collateral Language. A User's Guide to America's New War*. New York: New York University Press, pp. 39–51.

Low, G. (1999) 'Validating metaphor research projects', in L. Cameron and G. Low (eds), *Researching and Applying Metaphor*. Cambridge: Cambridge University Press, pp. 48–65.

Lule, J. (2004) 'War and its metaphors: news language and the prelude to war in Iraq, 2003', *Journalism Studies*, 5 (2): 179–90.

Mahon, J. E. (1999) 'Getting your sources right. What Aristotle didn't say', in L. Cameron and G. Low (eds), *Researching and Applying Metaphor*. Cambridge: Cambridge University Press, pp. 69–80.

Mauer, V. (2007) 'Germany's counterterrorism policy', in D. Zimmermann and A. Wenger (eds), *How States Fight Terrorism. Policy Dynamics in the West*. London: Lynne Rienner, pp. 59–78.

Milliken, J. (1996) 'Metaphors of prestige and reputation in American foreign policy and American realism', in F. A. Beer and R. Hariman (eds), *Post-Realism: The Rhetorical Turn in International Relations*. East Lansing, MI: Michigan State University Press, pp. 217–38.

Milliken, J. (1999) 'The study of discourse in international relations: a critique of research and methods', *European Journal of International Relations*, 5 (2): 225–54.

Mio, J. S. (1997) 'Metaphor and politics', *Metaphor and Symbol*, 12 (2): 113–33.

Musolff, A. (2000) *Mirror Images of Europe: Metaphors in the Public Debate about Europe in Britain and Germany*. Munich: Iudicium.

Mutimer, D. (1994) *Reimagining Security: The Metaphors of Proliferation*, YCISS Occasional Paper 25. Toronto: York University Center for International and Strategic Studies.

Ortony, A. (1979) 'Metaphor: a multidimensional problem', in *Metaphor and Thought*. Cambridge: Cambridge University Press, pp. 1–16.

Oxford Dictionary of English (2005) *Oxford Dictionary of English*, 2nd edn revised. Oxford: Oxford University Press.

Paris, R. (2002) 'Kosovo and the metaphor war', *Political Science Quarterly*, 117 (3): 423–50.

Pragglejaz Group (2007) 'MIP: a method for identifying metaphorically used words in discourse', *Metaphor and Symbol*, 22 (1): 1–39.

Pronin, E., Kennedy, K. and Butsch, S. (2006) 'Bombing versus negotiating: how preferences for combating terrorism are affected by perceived terrorist rationality', *Basic and Applied Social Psychology*, 28 (4): 385–92.

Purcell, W. M. (1990) 'Tropes, transsumptio, assumptio, and the redirection of studies in metaphor', *Metaphor and Symbolic Activity*, 5 (1): 35–53.

Ricœur, P. (1978) *The Rule of Metaphor*. London: Routledge & Kegan Paul.

Ricœur, P. (1981) 'Metaphor and the central problem of hermeneutics', in J. Thompson (ed.), *Paul Ricoeur: Hermeneutics and the Human Sciences*. Cambridge: Cambridge University Press, pp. 165–81.

Santa Ana, O. (1999) '"Like an animal I was treated": anti-immigration metaphor in US public discourse', *Discourse and Society*, 10 (2): 191–224.

Sarbin, T. R. (2003) 'The metaphor-to-myth transformation with special reference to the "war on terrorism"', *Peace and Conflict: Journal of Peace Psychology*, 9 (2): 150–1.

Schmitt, R. (2005) 'Systematic metaphor analysis as a method of qualitative research', *Qualitative Report*, 10 (2): 358–94.

Schwarz-Friesel, M. and Kromminga, J. H. (eds) (forthcoming) *Metaphern der Gewalt vor und nach 9/11. Konzeptualisierungen von Terrorismus in den Medien*. Tübingen: Gunter Narr Verlag.

Sederberg, P. (1995) 'Conciliation as counter-terrorist strategy', *Journal of Peace Research*, 32 (3): 295–312.

Shimko, K. L. (1994) 'Metaphors and foreign policy decision making', *Political Psychology*, 15 (4): 655–71.

Simon, J. (1987) *Misperceiving the Terrorist Threat*, RAND Publication Series, R-3423-RC (June). Online at: http://www.rand.org/pubs/reports/2008/R3423.pdf.

Sontag, S. (1989) *Illness as a Metaphor and AIDS and Its Metaphors*. New York: Doubleday.

Spencer, A. (2010) *The Tabloid Terrorist. The Predicative Construction of New Terrorism in the Media*. Basingstoke: Palgrave.

Spencer, A. (2012) 'The social construction of terrorism: media, metaphors and policy implications', *Journal of International Relations and Development*, 15 (3): 393–419.

Thornborrow, J. (1993) 'Metaphors of security: a comparison of representation in defence discourse in post-Cold War France and Britain', *Discourse and Society*, 4 (1): 99–119.

Tonkiss, F. (1998) 'Analysing discourse', in C. Seale (ed.), *Researching Society and Culture*. London: Sage, pp. 245–60.

Vosniadou, S. and Ortony, A. (1989) 'Similarity and analogical reasoning: a synthesis', in S. Vosniadou and A. Ortony (eds), *Similarity and Analogical Reasoning*. New York: Cambridge University Press, pp. 1–17.

Zulaika, J. and Douglass, W. A. (1996) *Terror and Taboo. The Follies, Fables and Faces of Terrorism*. New York: Routledge.

8

TERRORISM

Knowledge, power, subjectivity

Verena Erlenbusch

I

Two months after I started university in 2001, two hijacked airplanes crashed into the World Trade Center in New York. This event not only resulted in the collapse of the Twin Towers and the death of three thousand people, but also led to massive legal and political transformations. It was no surprise that the courses offered in my majors, Political Science and Philosophy, bore titles such as 'Religious Fundamentalism and Terrorism,' 'Politics, Religion, and Violence,' 'State and Non-State Terrorism,' or 'Islamic Fundamentalism and Terrorism.' Much of the literature under examination in these courses suggested that, even though we were confronted with what was probably the decisive event of our lifetime, we were not witnessing a new form of political violence, but rather the latest episode in a long history of terrorism. On this view, the terrorists of 9/11 differed from ancient Zealots, medieval assassins, and Indian Thugs in weapon only. The nature of the perpetrators as well as their aims, motives, and tactics, however, are essentially identical.

But, I wondered, was it indeed possible to treat all these forms of violence as essentially identical? Did the immense differences in the responses to various forms of violence not indicate that we were, in fact, looking at different things? It seemed to me as though the equation of historically discrete instances of political violence betrayed a certain confusion as to what we actually mean when we talk about terrorism. As a consequence, I became interested in developing a way of thinking about terrorism that was more historically and contextually nuanced. For this purpose, I drew inspiration from the work of Ludwig Wittgenstein and Michel Foucault.

In his *Philosophical Investigations* (1953), Ludwig Wittgenstein notes that if one wanted to determine the meaning of the word 'think,' it would not be enough to observe oneself in the process of thinking. Assuming that 'what we observe will be what the word means' is, for Wittgenstein, 'as if without knowing how to play chess, I were to try and make out what the word "mate" meant by close observation of the last move of some game of chess' (Wittgenstein 2001: §316).

In this chapter, I aim to show that Wittgenstein's claim captures a common problem in terrorism research, and that in order to determine the meaning of the word 'terrorism' we have to extend our analysis beyond those behaviors that are today called terrorism. While much of the academic literature on terrorism claims to know the object of its research and defines it in terms of ostensibly universal features, it fails to recognize that these definitions merely reflect the last stage of a historical process. Scholars who study terrorism based on its current manifestations understand it no more than Wittgenstein's observer understands the meaning of the word 'mate.' Although they know something about the last move in the game, so to speak, they cannot be said to have knowledge about terrorism in any meaningful sense. They do not, in fact, know what they are studying.

Since this is a provocative claim, let me try to clarify what I mean by way of a concrete example. A significant number of books in the academic literature on terrorism profess to write, in the words of one author, the 'true history of terrorism' (Law 2009: 2). The works at issue usually proceed to give us a unified narrative about the history of terrorism 'from antiquity to al Qaeda,' variously locating the first examples of terrorism in Homer or ancient Judaea (Chaliand and Blin 2007; Laqueur 2001; Rapoport 1984, 1990; Sinclair 2004). While some scholars submit that 'there are few examples in the ancient world that would warrant inclusion in a history of the subject if we were limited by most of the modern definitions of the phenomenon,' they justify including certain forms of violence by positing that the ancients would have recognized features of what we today call terrorism in these acts (Law 2009: 11). Among the most cited early examples in the history of terrorism are the *sicarii*, an ancient religious sect who fought against the Roman occupation of Palestine in the first century CE. This classification is usually based on accounts of the Jewish-Roman historian Flavius Josephus. According to Josephus, the *sicarii* were robbers who got their name from their weapon, a small curved dagger called a *sica*. Referring to them by the Greek term for robbers, λησταί (*lestai*), Josephus is careful to explain that the word *sicarii* 'was the name for such robbers as had under their bosoms swords called Sicae'(Flavius Josephus 1987: 625).[1] For Josephus, in other words, the *sicarii* were robbers of a particular kind, namely those who could be distinguished from other robbers by the weapon they used. This reading is further supported by Josephus' observation that, after the apprehension of 'Eleazar the arch robber' and his followers, 'there sprang up another sort of robbers in Jerusalem, which were called *sicarii*' (Flavius Josephus 1987: 614).

To be sure, Josephus' description of the tactics of the *sicarii* at times conjures up the specter of modern-day terrorism. The *sicarii* 'slew men in the day time, and in the midst of the city; this they did chiefly at the festivals, when they mingled themselves among the multitude' (Flavius Josephus 1987: 614). The publicity and symbolism with which they carried out their actions is certainly reminiscent of today's carefully staged terrorist attacks. And the *sicarii*'s strategy to hide in the crowd after killing their enemies and become 'a part of those that had indignation against them; by which means they appeared persons of such reputation, that they could by no means be discovered' makes them seem like an early example of modern-day sleeper cells (Flavius Josephus 1987: 614). By interpreting their actions through the lens of our own categories, however, we fail to understand how the *sicarii* were understood at the time. Josephus describes them quite specifically as members of the genus 'robber' with the specific difference of carrying a small, crooked dagger – not as terrorists. And there is no reason for us to privilege our own categories over the ones used by the *sicarii*'s contemporaries. Calling them terrorists makes as little sense as calling Osama bin Laden a robber.

Not only did the concept terrorism not exist at the time of Josephus, but the concept robbery has clearly undergone significant transformation as well. It makes no sense to call bin Laden a robber, because our category robber has no application to someone plotting large-scale attacks that result, among other things, in the collapse of the World Trade Center and the deaths of 2,996 people. What it means to be a robber is determined in a particular context, and there is no reason to think it would be otherwise with regard to terrorism. The words 'terrorist' and 'robber' do not reveal anything about the things they name; they do not immediately refer us to their unchanging essence or a timeless truth. The word 'terrorism' is not just shorthand for a clearly defined set of actions whose precursors are readily identifiable in historical chronicles. Rather, it is a concept that synthesizes 'a heterogeneous set of discourses, institutions, architectural forms, regulatory decisions, laws, administrative measures, scientific statements, philosophical, moral, and philanthropic propositions – in short, the said as much as the unsaid' (Foucault 1980: 195). Its definition is purely conventional and, therefore, variable.

Having the concept terrorism presupposes a certain rationality, and it is this rationality which creates the conditions under which statements about terrorism are meaningful and comprehensible.[2] Because concepts acquire their meaning in a specific context, Arnold Davidson rightly emphasizes that the 'automatic and immediate application of concepts, as though concepts have no temporality … allows, and often requires, us to draw misleading analogies and inferences that derive from a historically inappropriate and conceptually untenable perspective' (Davidson 2004b: 41). To avoid the misrepresentation of historical facts and further obfuscation of an already difficult concept, we must pay attention to the historical emergence of terrorism as part of a historical-political rationality and then examine the categories through which we experience and make sense of it. As Ian Hacking argues, 'one would require a history of the words in their sites in order to comprehend what the concept was' (Hacking 2004b: 68).

II

The most instructive model for this kind of analysis has been put forward by Michel Foucault. In his 1982/83 lecture series *The Government of Self and Others*, Foucault offers a retrospective of sorts in which he describes his general project as a history of thought. Distinguishing his histories of madness, disease, criminality, and sexuality from a 'history of knowledge undertaken in terms of an index of truth' and a 'history of ideologies undertaken by reference to a criterion of reality,' Foucault notes that the history of thought is concerned with an analysis of experiences which constitute our present (Foucault 2011: 310).

Rather than asking whether or not a discourse actually speaks the truth, or why it might fail to do so, the history of thought comprises three operations that dovetail with the archaeological, genealogical, and ethical axes of Foucault's work.[3] First, Foucault's history of thought is concerned with practices that constitute the conditions of existence of bodies of knowledge. More specifically, it seeks to describe the rules that make statements about things true or false. Second, it examines power, which may be understood in terms of the mechanisms, norms, and techniques that make use of knowledge to manage and control the behavior of individuals. And third, it examines what kind of subject one can be in a context shaped by particular forms of knowledge and certain relations of power. The history of thought, Foucault urges, should be applied to 'any discourse which claims to be a discourse of truth and to assert its truth as a norm' (Foucault 2011: 310). It is a productive approach to all those phenomena that play out alongside the axes of knowledge, power, and subjectification. And terrorism is one of the most important experiences through which bodies of knowledge, norms of behavior, and possible subject positions are constituted today.

In the area of knowledge, there is an ever-growing body of scientific literature on terrorism. Today, numerous academic journals and conferences as well as an incalculable number of books are dedicated to the accumulation of knowledge about terrorism. While philosophers are concerned with conceptual and moral aspects of terrorism, the social sciences employ empirical methods to determine the constitutive features of terrorism in order to identify terrorist individuals and behaviors and inform counter-terrorist policies. The problem with most of this scholarship is its reliance on habitual conceptions of terrorism, which results in ideological bias, an anachronistic treatment of historical cases of violence, and a seriously inadequate understanding of terrorism.[4] Despite its shortcomings, the knowledge produced by these studies forms the basis of counter-terrorist laws and policies. Collaborative efforts between terrorism experts, law enforcement, and policy-makers reinforce dangerously vague ideas about terrorism, which serve as a justification for dismantling legal norms; justifying state violence and aggressive war; expanding imperial power in the name of freedom, security, and the empowerment of (Muslim) women; detaining and torturing terrorist suspects; suspending basic constitutional rights and liberties; militarizing airports; implementing massive surveillance programs; and intensifying border security.

We have learned from Foucault that the link between knowledge and power as well as the network of power relations cannot be understood if power is reduced to oppression and domination. To be sure, there might be cases in which an executive order can be tracked all the way down to its concrete effects on a particular terrorist suspect. And it could plausibly be argued that the actions of Lynndie England and other soldiers in Abu Ghraib were demonstrations of power as domination. But it is impossible to determine which one government official is responsible for this system in which soldiers, government officials, and private security contractors have the power to interrogate, harass, torture, humiliate, and detain people indefinitely without charge or trial. Understanding terrorism means understanding the practices that make possible and, indeed, require certain conceptions of terrorism.

Knowledge about terrorism and the practices connected with it also creates modes of subjectivity that did not exist earlier. While there were violent people who attacked innocent civilians for political purposes before there was a concept of terrorism, they were not recognized and treated as terrorists until there was a way of classifying them. The concept of terrorism brings into existence an entire system in which individuals have to find their place as potential terrorists, terrorist suspects, actual terrorists, politicians who sponsor terrorists, civilians who are afraid of terrorism, soldiers who fight terrorists, journalists who report on terrorism, or academics who study terrorism. Yet not all subject positions can be occupied by everyone. Take, for example, the case of Omar al-Omari, a Jordanian-American who lost his job at the Ohio Department of Public Safety in 2010 after a terrorism expert at a training seminar for the Columbus Division of Police identified him as a terrorist suspect. Apparently unaware of Omari's position as the leader of an internationally recognized Muslim outreach program, the instructor claimed that Omari had links to the Muslim Brotherhood, Hamas, and al-Qaeda. When state officials started an investigation, Omari lost his job – not because he could be linked to any terrorist organization, but because he had made a minor mistake on his job application form (Temple-Raston 2011). Compare Omari's story to the discursive portrayal of Anders Behring Breivik, who committed several bombings and a mass shooting in Norway in 2011. Immediately after the attacks and without information about the identity of the bomber, the media reported they were acts of terrorism committed by fundamentalist jihadis and al-Qaeda. When it became evident that the culprit was a right-wing extremist, the rhetoric changed from terrorism to descriptions of the violence as shootings and bombings. Even though Breivik was convicted of committing a terrorist act, he was generally portrayed as a mass killer, a shooter, a gunman, or a right-wing fanatic who, some commentators even suggested, had legitimate grievances (Bawer 2011).[5] The examples of Omari and Breivik illustrate the ways in which normative descriptions of terrorism bring into being the terrorist as a form of subjectivity that marks some people as terrorists when they have not committed terrorist acts, but are not applied to others even when their involvement in terrorist acts is established by a court of law.

This selective attribution of the terrorism label largely functions on the basis of racial and religious stereotypes and creates a general sense of fear of populations with certain ethnic or religious backgrounds. This conception of terrorist subjectivity is supported by ostensibly objective knowledge produced by academic discourses about terrorism, which also inform counter-terrorist policies. The history of thought enables us to unravel the reciprocal relationship between knowledge, power, and subjectivity in experiences of terrorism.

III

It might be objected that instead of engaging in detailed historical research to unpack the concept terrorism, we simply ought to be more careful in how we use the terrorism label. A history of thought, in other words, cannot achieve anything that could not be achieved by a reliable definition of terrorism, responsibly applied. Yet, the search for a definition in terms of necessary and sufficient conditions of terrorism and fail-safe criteria to identify terrorists is misguided. While I do not deny that definitions of terrorism can be useful in certain circumstances, it is important to remember that definitions are stipulated and do not tell us much about the things they name. A legal definition of terrorism, for instance, might be useful in specifying the legal status of actions included in the definition and determining permissible responses, but it does not refer us to the nature of terrorism. If we wish to understand terrorism, then we must recognize that it is the effect of diverse practices and a complex history. It is not the last move in a game but the latest move in a long series governed by complicated rules. If we want to know what the word 'terrorism' means, we have to examine how the concept is used and identify the rules that determine what can and cannot be said about terrorism, who can and cannot be a terrorist, and what can and cannot be done to terrorists.

Instead of attempting to define terrorism in terms of necessary and sufficient conditions, an approach modeled on Foucault's history of thought seeks to discover what can be said about terrorism if we reject the notion of a stable and universal, naturally or historically given essence. This view makes terrorism an unstable concept that means different things in different contexts. In linguistic terms, we might say that the meaning of the word 'terrorism' changes depending on the discursive and non-discursive conditions in which it is used, even though the same word is used at different points in time and in various social and political circumstances. 'Terrorism' and 'terrorism' are homonyms when they are used in different contexts, because we cannot be sure the word means the same thing in all cases. Moreover, the specific ways and contexts in which the word 'terrorism' is used determine the effects that can be produced. For example, reading about terrorism in the newspaper might scare us, while putting someone's name on a terrorist watchlist makes it possible to detain, interrogate, or even torture them. Together, discursive and non-discursive practices constitute the object of analysis of a history of thought, which examines a set of statements in which the word 'terrorism' appears and particular experiences of things which are described as 'terrorism.'

Rather than asking what terrorism is and why someone might have engaged in terrorism, we must investigate what exactly was said and done. The identification of certain behaviors as terrorism on the basis of current definitions is therefore replaced with a 'rigorous description of the statements themselves' in order to examine the historical, social, political, cultural, ideological, and epistemological conditions of existence of the concept of terrorism (Foucault 1998: 284). An analysis of terrorism in terms of a history of thought substitutes historical description for causal explanation.

It might be objected that a historical description of statements does not add to our understanding of terrorism because it merely records particular statements that have been made about terrorism. All that can be said about terrorism, the argument goes, is what has already been said. While I would argue that historical descriptions of singular events do not allow for generalizations about terrorism, it is possible to observe patterns and regularities in the relations into which the concept terrorism enters with other concepts. Only a comprehensive and meticulous analysis of a 'set of materials that were deposited in the course of time in the form of signs, traces, institutions, practices, works, and so on' enables us to discover a wider framework of references within which terrorism acquires its meaning (Foucault 1998: 281). For instance, the evaluation of violence as just or unjust, legitimate or illegitimate, furthering or threatening national security takes place against a background of more general conceptions of justice, legitimacy, and security. These conceptions are themselves determined by hegemonic political rationalities. As a consequence, changes in ideological commitments result in a transformation of the concept of terrorism. Terrorism can thus be understood as the name given to variable discursive and non-discursive practices whose meaning is determined within a network of concepts, ideologies, interests, and rationalities. It appears as an apparatus (*dispositif*) that 'at a given historical moment has as its major function the response to an urgency' (Foucault 1980: 195). The history of thought allows us to account for the ways in which the word 'terrorism' takes on new meanings and new functions depending on the various contexts and purposes in and for which it becomes useful.

IV

In order to flesh out the methodological claims discussed in the previous section, let us look at the different ways republicans and liberals used the word 'terrorism' during the French Revolution. This example will highlight the correlation between wider political rationalities and competing concepts of terrorism over a brief period of time.

When Robespierre took power in 1793, he articulated his political program in opposition to the liberal principles of universal rights and the rule of law. In a famous speech, Robespierre laid out the constitutive elements of Jacobin republicanism:

> If the mainspring of popular government in peacetime is virtue, the mainspring of popular government in revolution is virtue and terror both: virtue, without which terror is disastrous; terror, without which virtue is powerless. Terror is nothing but prompt, severe, inflexible justice; it is therefore an emanation of virtue; it is not so much a specific principle as a consequence of the general principle of democracy applied to the homeland's most pressing needs. (Robespierre 2007a: 115)

While Robespierre regarded virtue as the source of political authority under normal conditions, in exceptional circumstances virtue had to manifest itself as terror. In a revolutionary situation that sought to topple the monarchy and establish a republic, terror was necessary as a means to institutionalize virtue and free the people. Revolutionary violence, he claimed, 'is supported by the holiest of all laws: the salvation of the people; by the most indisputable of all entitlements: necessity,' and it ought to be continued by constitutional government, whose goal is 'to preserve the Republic' (Robespierre 2007b: 99–100). For Robespierre, in other words, violence was legitimate if it served the common good.

For Robespierre's opponents, the Republican conception of the common good was ideological and dogmatic. They contended that terror was necessary to create an atmosphere of insecurity and suspicion to make the people abide by the Jacobins' rules. It was this arbitrary and unlimited violence that the liberals identified with terrorism. On 28 August 1794, a month after Robespierre's execution, Jean Lambert Tallien, a leading member of the moderates, addressed the National Convention and laid out the principles of a government committed to freedom and justice. He argued that 'even a temporary tyranny cannot be included among the means of establishing liberty' (Tallien 1847: 613).[6] Such tyranny 'consists in threatening *people*, in threatening them always and for everything, in threatening them with the most cruel things the imagination can conceive' (Tallien 1847: 613). Tallien maintained that the government of terror can only function 'by threatening with constantly renewed and ever growing excess; by threatening every kind of action, and even inaction; by threatening against all kinds of evidence and without a shadow of evidence; by threatening with the always striking aspect of absolute power and unbridled fear' (Tallien 1847: 613). Because it relies on absolute, arbitrary, unlimited, and concentrated power, tyranny cannot be restricted to 'suspicious classes without affecting the rest' for there cannot be 'security for some where there is no justice for all, where one prejudges actions by people, and not people by actions' (Tallien 1847: 613). The justice of the Jacobins, Tallien maintained, was a 'justice of cannibals' that did not judge but murder (Tallien 1847: 615). While fear of the laws 'can be increased according to need,' terror is 'not susceptible to either more or less' (Tallien 1847: 613). 'Either terror must be everywhere,' Tallien claimed, 'or it is nowhere' (Tallien 1847: 613). Since, for the liberals, the 'system [of terror] has been that of Robespierre', the execution of Robespierre amounted to nothing less than the seal of victory over the Jacobin Reign of Terror. For 'once terrorism has stopped for a moment to terrify, it can only be terrified itself' (Tallien 1847: 614).

Tallien's description of the Jacobin system as terrorism was initially taken up by journalists, pundits, and politicians of all stripes. While Gracchus Babeuf, an early socialist and fiery supporter of the revolution, used his *Journal de la Liberté de la Presse* to defend the Jacobin quest for equality, he condemned the means of achieving it as 'the government of blood, the government of Robespierre, the tyranny of Robespierre, the despotism of the committees, and all the subsequent atrocities, the guillotining, the shootings, the drownings, oppression, despair, all forms of squalor, deprivation and misery' (Babeuf 1966a: 4). Babeuf hoped that Robespierre's execution and the establishment of a new government would lead to the restoration of the rights and liberties granted by the constitution of 1789 and which had been curtailed by the Jacobins under the pretext of their idea of freedom.

In an effort to replace Jacobin republicanism with the rule of law, the liberals argued that violence was only justifiable for the preservation of the law. The immediate consequence was an eruption of law-preserving violence against anyone who was opposed to laws supported by the liberals. While Tallien had initially defined terrorism as Robespierre's system, sustained by terror and fear, the liberals now strategically conjured up the specter of terrorism to denounce political opposition as an attempt to return to the bloody excesses of the Jacobin terror. As a consequence, allegations of terrorism were extended to the radical left, aristocrats, and royalists alike.

When the liberals began to turn their political purges into mass liquidations, they were soon accused of using terrorism as a 'trompe-l'œil,' a sham that allowed them to secure their power (Brunot 1937: 654). Early on, Babeuf criticized the Thermidorians for presenting themselves as champions of public liberty while at the same time unleashing excessive violence against everyone who was opposed to their principles. A month after the first publication of his journal, he openly attacked Tallien and his followers. Taking Tallien's definition of terrorism at face value, Babeuf argued that the Thermidorians were terrorists by their own standards and that Tallien, the 'terrorist from Bordeaux' (Babeuf 1966c: 306), had to be 'guillotined … like a terrorist, too … a drinker of blood, a destroyer, an incendiary' (Babeuf 1966c: 332).

When Babeuf's subversive use of the term failed to gain political traction, he argued that terrorism had, in fact, become just another word for patriotism. The word 'terrorist,' Babeuf argued, was 'synonymous with patriot and friend of the principles' (Babeuf 1966b: 304). In other words, he accepted the Thermidorian accusation and endowed it with a positive valence. If the term terrorism referred to the demand for freedom, real democratic government, legitimate violence, and justice for the people, then terrorism appeared to be the appropriate and legitimate means against those who stood in the way of freedom and justice.

Eventually, Babeuf was arrested for promoting revolutionary opposition and declared 'an outlaw' (Babeuf 1966d: 159). Before he even appeared in court, Babeuf knew the liberals had already condemned him. Trials in partisan courts were not the only means by which the government hoped to eliminate political opponents. On 21 July 1795, the *Moniteur Universel* reported that 'the assassins of the counter-revolutionary regime have stabbed those whom they call terrorists in the prisons, in the streets, even in their homes, and the men without passion assure that more than one good citizen has died in these massacres' (Panckoucke 1847: 258). Allegations of terrorism led to exile, arrest, and confinement to the dungeons, 'to rotten straw, to the most despicable darkness, to the horror of having to exist for a number of months in this subterranean place where the floor was covered a foot deep in putrid and infected water' (Babeuf 1966e: 159). The liberals succeeded in asserting an understanding of terrorism that combined definition with condemnation. Whoever was identified as a terrorist was at the same time pronounced guilty. There was no law and no predetermined sentence for terrorism; instead of dealing with terrorism by making it illegal, the government strategically suspended the law with regard to those individuals identified as terrorists. The legal void into which terrorists descended meant that neither the terrorist nor the government was subject to the law: the terrorist lost any legal status and protection, while the state was unbound by legal restraints on the use of violence.

Within a short period of time, the ideological disputes of the French Revolution engendered at least four different concepts of terrorism: as the name for the system of Robespierre, an umbrella term for all opponents of the liberal rule of law, an accusation against the liberals themselves, and an affirmative endonym adopted by radical revolutionaries. A close examination of any one of these concepts would not give us an accurate understanding of how the concept of terrorism actually functioned in this historical context. By casting a wider net and describing the statements that deploy the term as well as the relationships into which the word 'terrorism' enters with other concepts such as justice, freedom, legitimacy, or the common good, we can develop a more nuanced account of the meaning of terrorism and the practices of power it made possible at the time.

V

As the example of the French Revolution shows, any detailed analysis of terrorism that includes a range of historical and political contexts will reveal the various ways in which concepts of terrorism function in at the intersection of knowledge, power, and subjectification. Yet not even a complete study of terrorism in the mode of what Foucault calls a history of thought would solve the problem of terrorism.

In the first place, a complete history of thought is practically impossible. Not only are the concept of terrorism, the statements that use it, and the practices it engenders subject to change, but the material in question can always be re-examined according to a different periodization and in relation to different frameworks of evaluating violent behavior. As Foucault points out, the 'description will be different then … In one sense, description is infinite, therefore; in another, it is closed, insofar as it tends to establish the theoretical model of accounting for the relations that exist between the discourses studied' (Foucault 1998: 284).

Moreover, a history of thought with regard to terrorism can neither prevent the problematic use of the terrorism label, nor end violence. The aim of such a project is to uncover 'the accidents, the minute deviations – or conversely, the complete reversals – the errors, the false appraisals, and the faulty calculations' that have given the concept of terrorism the meaning it has today (Foucault 1991: 81). Showing that terrorism has a variable and contingent history allows us to undercut the determinism of ahistorical and essentialist accounts of terrorism and develop more productive ways of thinking about violence.

Notes

1. I am following Whiston's standard translation of Josephus, which renders the Greek λησταί as robber. Many scholars have suggested bandit as a more adequate translation. While the etymology and legal history of this term is interesting and highly relevant for a comparative study of violence, it suffices to note for the purpose of this chapter that, whether robbers or bandits, the *sicarii* were not terrorists. For a legal history of banditry and robbery as well as an outstanding account of banditry in the Roman Empire, the interested reader is referred to (Jackson 1970; Shaw 1984).
2. While I am not able to develop sufficiently the notion of rationality in the context of this chapter, I shall note that I am particularly interested in the political rationalities under-pinning conceptions of terrorism. I follow Thomas Lemke's characterization of political rationality as 'an element of government itself which helps to create a discursive field in which exercising power is rational' (see Lemke 2002). On theoretical elaborations on the notions of styles of reasoning and mentalities, which are close to my understanding of rationality here, see Hacking (2004a), Davidson 2004a), and LeGoff (1985).
3. On the periodization of Foucault's work see Dreyfus and Rabinow (1983), Golder and Fitzpatrick (2010), Flynn (2010), and Hacking (2004b).
4. For a more substantial critique of the academic literature on terrorism see Erlenbusch (2013).
5. For a concise retort to this line of argument see Lentin and Titley (2011).
6. All translations from the French original of the material used in this section are mine.

References

Babeuf, G. (1966a) 'Le Tribun Du Peuple, Ou Le Défenseur Des Droits de l'Homme. No. 34,' in *Le Tribun Du Peuple, Ou Le Défenseur Des Droits de l'Homme, An III – An IV*. Milan: Galli Thierry, pp. 1–52.

Babeuf, G. (1966b) 'Le Tribun Du Peuple, Ou Le Défenseur Des Droits de l'Homme; En Continuation Du Journal de La Liberté de La Presse. No. 30,' in *Journal de La Liberté de La Presse, An II – An III*. Milan: Galli Thierry.

Babeuf, G. (1966c) 'Le Tribun Du Peuple, Ou Le Défenseur Des Droits de l'Homme; En Continuation Du Journal de La Liberté de La Presse. No. 32,' in *Journal de La Liberté de La Presse, An II – An III*. Milan: Galli Thierry, pp. 323–38.

Babeuf, G. (1966d) 'Le Tribun Du Peuple, Ou Le Défenseur Des Droits de l'Homme. No. 40,' in *Le Tribun Du Peuple, Ou Le Défenseur Des Droits de l'Homme, An III – An IV*. Milan: Galli Thierry, pp. 213–67.

Babeuf, G. (1966e) 'Le Tribun Du Peuple, Ou Le Défenseur Des Droits de l'Homme. No. 38,' in *Le Tribun Du Peuple, Ou Le Défenseur Des Droits de l'Homme, An III – An IV*. Milan: Galli Thierry, pp. 149–78.

Bawer, B. (2011) 'Inside the mind of the Oslo murderer,' *Wall Street Journal*, 25 July, Second Opinion. Online at: http://online.wsj.com/article/SB10001424053111190399990457646 5801154130960.html?mod=googlenews_wsj (accessed 8 November 2013).

Brunot, F. (1937) *Histoire de la langue française des origines à 1900. Tome IX, Deuxième partie, La Révolution et l'Empire. Les événements, les institutions et la langue*. Paris: A. Colin.

Chaliand, G. and Blin, A. (eds) (2007) *The History of Terrorism: From Antiquity to Al Qaeda*. Berkeley and Los Angeles, CA: University of California Press.

Davidson, A. I. (2004a) 'Styles of reasoning: from the history of art to the epistemology of science,' in *The Emergence of Sexuality Historical Epistemology and the Formation of Concepts*. Cambridge, MA and London: Harvard University Press, pp. 125–41.

Davidson, A. I. (2004b) *The Emergence of Sexuality Historical Epistemology and the Formation of Concepts*. Cambridge, MA and London: Harvard University Press.

Dreyfus, H. L. and Rabinow, P. (eds) (1983) *Michel Foucault: Beyond Structuralism and Hermeneutics*. Chicago: University of Chicago Press.

Erlenbusch, V. (2013) 'How (not) to study terrorism,' *Critical Review of International Social and Political Philosophy*, 17 (4): 1–22.

Flavius Josephus (1987) 'The wars of the Jews,' in *The Works of Josephus*. Peabody, MA: Hendrickson, pp. 543–772.

Flynn, T. R. (2010) *Sartre, Foucault, and Historical Reason, Volume Two: A Poststructuralist Mapping of History*. Chicago: University of Chicago Press.

Foucault, M. (1980) 'The Confession of the Flesh,' in C. Gordon (ed.), *Power/Knowledge: Selected Interviews and Other Writings, 1972–1977*. New York: Random House, pp. 194–228.

Foucault, M. (1991) 'Nietzsche, genealogy, history,' in P. Rabinow (ed.), *The Foucault Reader*. London: Pantheon Books, pp. 76–100.

Foucault, M. (1998) 'On the ways of writing history,' in J. Faubion (ed.), *Michel Foucault: Aesthetics, Method, and Epistemology*. New York: New Press, pp. 279–95.

Foucault, M. (2010) *The Birth of Biopolitics: Lectures at the Collège de France, 1978–1979*. New York: Picador.

Foucault, M. (2011) *The Government of Self and Others: Lectures at the College de France, 1982–1983*, ed. A. I. Davidson, trans. G. Burchell. New York: Picador.

Golder, B. and Fitzpatrick, P. (eds) (2010) *Foucault and Law*. New York: Ashgate.

Hacking, I. (2004a) '"Style" for historians and philosophers,' in I. Hacking, *Historical Ontology*. Cambridge, MA: Harvard University Press, pp. 178–99.

Hacking, I. (2004b) *Historical Ontology*. Cambridge, MA: Harvard University Press.

Jackson, B. S. (1970) 'Some comparative legal history: robbery and brigandage,' *Georgia Journal of International and Comparative Law*, 1: 45.

Laqueur, W. (2001) *A History of Terrorism*. New Brunswick, NJ: Transaction Publishers.

Law, R. (2009) *Terrorism: A History*. Cambridge: Polity Press.

LeGoff, J. (1985) 'Mentalities: a history of ambiguities,' in P. Nora and J. LeGoff (eds), *Constructing the Past: Essays in Historical Methodology*. Cambridge: Cambridge University Press, pp. 166–80.

Lemke, T. (2002) 'Foucault, governmentality, and critique,' *Rethinking Marxism*, 14 (3): 49–64.

Lentin, A. and Titley, G. (2011) 'Anders Behring Breivik had no legitimate grievance,' *Guardian*, 26 July. Online at: http://www.theguardian.com/commentisfree/2011/jul/26/anders-behring-breivik-multicultural-failure (accessed 8 November 2013).

Panckoucke, C. J. (ed.) (1847) 'Gazette Nationale Ou Le Moniteur Universel N° 303 (21 Juillet 1795),' in *Réimpression de L'ancien Moniteur: Seule Histoire Authentique et Inaltérée de La Révolution Française Dupuis La Réunion Des États-généraux Jusqu'au Consulat (mai 1789–novembre 1799): Avec Des Notes Explicatives*. Paris: Plon Frères, pp. 257–9.

Rapoport, D. C. (1984) 'Fear and trembling: terrorism in three religious traditions,' *American Political Science Review*, 78 (3): 658–77.

Rapoport, D. C. (1990) 'Religion and terror: thugs, assassins, and zealots,' in C. W. Kegley Jr (ed.), *International Terrorism: Characteristics, Causes, Controls*. New York: St. Martin's Press, pp. 146–57.

Robespierre, M. (2007a) 'On the principles of political morality that should guide the national convention in the domestic administration of the Republic,' in S. Žižek (ed.), *Robespierre. Virtue and Terror*. London and New York: Verso, pp. 108–25.

Robespierre, M. (2007b), 'On the principles of revolutionary government,' in S. Žižek (ed.), *Robespierre. Virtue and Terror*. London and New York: Verso, pp. 98–107.

Shaw, B. (1984) 'Bandits in the Roman Empire,' *Past and Present*, 105: 3–52.

Sinclair, A. (2004) *An Anatomy of Terror: A History of Terrorism*. London: Pan Macmillan.

Tallien, J. L. (1847) 'Convention Nationale,' in C. J. Panckoucke (ed.), *Gazette Nationale N° 343 (3. VIII 1794)*. Paris: Plon Frères, pp. 612–16.

Temple-Raston, D. (2011) 'Terror training casts pall over Muslim employee,' *NPR.org*. Online at: http://www.npr.org/2011/07/18/137712352/terrorism-training-casts-pall-over-muslim-employee (accessed 7 November 2013).

Wittgenstein, L. (2001) *Philosophical Investigations*, trans. by G. E. M. Anscombe. Malden, MA and Oxford: Blackwell.

Postcolonialism/ Decolonialism

9

'WE ARE NOT THE TERRORISTS!'

Using a reflexive postcolonial
methodology in the West Bank
of the Palestinian Territories

Caitlin Ryan

Introduction

When passing through Checkpoint 300, the checkpoint that controls access from
Bethlehem into Jerusalem, it is easy to see how Palestinians are constructed as 'The
Other' – 'the other' who are feared and thus 'the other' who can be subjected to
extreme security practices that often strip them of their dignity and their humanity.
The queues in the checkpoint reach epic proportions particularly in the mornings,
as well as on Christian and Muslim Holy Days. Soldiers patrol on catwalks above the
queues, and special locking turnstiles let one or two Palestinians at a time through
to the X-ray machine and metal detector. The strain is obvious on the faces of the
Palestinians waiting to cross. It is apparent that people are doing their best to keep
their composure during the whole process.

I observed the way Palestinians are framed as the dangerous 'other' throughout
my entire fieldwork process, both while living and traveling through the West Bank,
and from the concerns raised by people who asked if I was 'scared of the terrorists'
when they learned I was going to Palestine, or who reacted to my return by asking
'Weren't you scared of the terrorists?!' My motivation to go to the occupied West
Bank was driven by inherent discomfort with the prevailing international perception that the Palestinian 'other' is not to be trusted, taken seriously, or valued, because
she/he is a 'terrorist.' When I left for the West Bank I carried a research question
aimed at exploring how Palestinian women had experienced the Israeli occupation
and then reacted to it with violence. I wanted to know how experiences of daily life
under occupation had led some Palestinian women to the violent response of carrying out a suicide bombing/martyrdom operation, and I also wanted to know how
women in the occupied West Bank viewed this violence.

Perhaps unsurprisingly, I returned from the occupied West Bank carrying a different research question. From my conversations with Palestinian women, and my

travels through checkpoints and demonstrations and kitchens and women's groups, I came to understand how violent responses to the occupation are but a small element in the tapestry of women's resistance, and that focusing only on these small elements of violence would only contribute to the association of 'Palestinian' with 'terrorist.' This chapter engages with the methodologies that informed my field research, underpinned by critical reflexivity on how my own positionality and methodological choices resulted in obtaining the data. Before discussing fieldwork, I will explore how postcolonialism helped shape and determine my approach to questions of subjectivity and resistance in the occupied Palestinian territories.

A debt to Fanon and Said

Postcolonial approaches to political violence have challenged the possibility that 'terrorist' could ever be used as a 'neutral' term. This legacy draws from Franz Fanon, who argued that the logic and execution of colonialism was inherently a violent process, and the colonist only understood a language of violence, and that therefore the response of the colonized would necessarily be violent as well (Fanon 1963). 'Colonialism is not a machine capable of thinking, a body endowed with reason. It is naked violence, and only gives in when confronted with greater violence' (Fanon 1963: 23). He goes on to argue that 'The work of the colonized is to imagine every possible method for annihilating the colonist' (Fanon 1963: 50). Fanon's advocating of violence as a means to challenge colonization represents a remarkable element of postcolonialism, not necessarily because he is encouraging violence, but because of the way he frames this encouragement in relation to the violence of colonization. In framing colonization as a process imbued with violence he contextualizes the response of those subject to colonization. I should clarify that I am not advocating the use of violence by invoking Fanon in relation to Palestinian violence. Rather, the methodology for this research project drew inspiration from Fanon's insistence that the relationship between the colonist and the colonized is inherently a relationship of violence. As such, examining Palestinian people's violent resistance to occupation without examining the violence inherent to the processes of occupation would leave gaping holes, just as examining the violent uprisings of Algerians against French rule without examining the historical violence of the French colonization of Algeria would result in an incomplete picture.

Here also I must qualify how and why I draw an association between postcolonialism and the Israeli/Palestinian conflict, an association which I am sure may cause some readers to flinch. Throughout my project, I examined how elements of the Israeli occupation formed Palestinians as subjects, and in turn how they resisted. In addition to the obvious lineage to Foucault and other postmodern theory, such an aim also links back to Fanon. For Fanon, the colonized subject exists because it is the coloniser who 'made' them subjects. This is of course not to say that people in Algeria did not exist before French rule, but rather that their subject identities, how they are seen and framed and subjectified, is a product of their relationship to the colonizer. 'It is the colonist who fabricated and who continues to fabricate the colonized subject' (Fanon 1963: 2). We can also reference Du Bois here for what he can tell us about the formation of 'the other.' For Du Bois, 'the black man is a person who must ride Jim Crow in Georgia' (Du Bois 2002: 153). One is not riding in the Jim Crow section of the train because one is Black, but rather one is Black because they are riding Jim Crow (Olson 2004: 22). In relation to Palestinians, the Israeli occupation of the Palestinian territories forms the subject status of Palestinians as a population who can legitimately be occupied, and the different treatment accorded to Palestinians is in part what forms them as subjects in this way. To apply the logic of Du Bois to Palestinians, the Palestinian is the one detained at the checkpoint, thereby being established as a Palestinian (other). The value of Fanon's postcolonialism for field research in the Palestinian territories is the critical evaluation of the relationship between the Israeli occupation and Palestinians, the imbalances of power between them and how Palestinians are formed and framed as subjects as a result (Chowdhry and Nair 2004).

Finally, one cannot speak of doing research inspired by postcolonialism in the Palestinian territories without speaking of Said. Of course, Said speaks to the above discussion of the creation of the subject, arguing that Orientalism arose as a means of justifying colonialism by framing the inhabitants of 'the Orient' in contrasting terms to the inhabitants of 'the West.' 'Yet what gave the Oriental's world intelligibility and identity was not the result of his own efforts, but rather the whole complex series of knowledgeable manipulations by which the Orient was identified by the West' (Said 2003: 40). Said is concerned with how Orientalism as a way of thinking was able to justify and support colonialism by constructing 'The Oriental' as the other – in framing the inhabitants of the Middle East as the antithesis of everything we are in 'The West' we can justify all kinds of actions against them, supported by our Orientalist knowledge that we are their opposites. Such a mentality is rife in traditional approaches to terrorism research (Chalk 2003; Hoffman 1992; Laqueur 2003). My project in Palestine and the methodology used in the field research for it is inspired by the aim of postcolonialism to disentangle that which we in the West falsely take as 'given' knowledge about the lives of Palestinians, in order to start to take apart the 'knowledge' that equates them with terrorism without trying to understand the daily reality of life under occupation.

Field research logistics and basic statistics

I undertook field research for my PhD in the West Bank of the Palestinian territories for six weeks between December 2011 and January 2012. My research goals were to speak with Palestinian women to collect narratives of experiences of subjectification and resistance, trying to understand the connections between the violence of the Israeli occupation and Palestinian violent resistance. Conducting my field research in the West Bank of the occupied Palestinian territories (oPt) was the most rewarding, engaging and enlightening aspect of my PhD. Planning the trip and thinking about ethical and methodological challenges before departing was the most stressful. In the stages of applying for ethical approval, adapting a field research methodology, and thinking through logistics, I kept a reflexive journal to document aspects of the trip I was thinking through and how my feelings about my planned research had an impact on the types of plans I was making. I continued the reflexive journal for the duration of my time in the field, and it adds valuable insight to how I encountered and approached methodological, ethical, and emotional issues and how those issues may have affected the outcome of my research (Sylvester *et al.* 2011). Excluding a reflection on the effects of emotion on my research would have resulted in silencing and marginalizing an indispensable element of my research project.

Over the course of my field research I interviewed 18 individual Palestinian women and three non-governmental organizations (NGOs), two of them counseling centers and one a prisoner's rights advocate, Addameer. I also had a meeting with one of the Gender Officers at the East Jerusalem branch of the United Nations Refugee Works Agency (UNRWA) and went on two tours of troubled locations in the West Bank with the NGOs, one to the Jordan Valley with the Israeli Committee Against House Demolitions and one to Hebron with the Palestinian peace center Wi'am.

The 18 individual women I interviewed all had a variety of 'identities.' Each individual woman can be described in numerous ways, depending upon which 'categorizations' are used to examine them. If one examines them through a lens of religion, six of the women were Christian and twelve were Muslim. If looking through the lens of occupation, eight worked in their own homes and ten were either retired or still working outside the home. Of those who worked outside the home, occupations included community activist, shop owner, teacher, UN employee, Palestinian Authority minister, lawyer, and militant. However, those who worked in the home often expressed how they brought income into the house through activities such as tailoring, embroidery, or other handicrafts. Many of the stories women shared with me included a discussion of how they negotiated several identities between the formal and informal economies. One could also examine the participants through a lens of age, wherein some of the women were young and even unmarried, many had young children and others had grandchildren. Not all of the women lived in similar settings – some came from very small villages (less than 500 people), others came from cities or large towns, and two came from refugee camps.

All of these identities were intermingled, and each of my participants was unique in their circumstances, the only real commonality between them being that they all self-identified as being Palestinian. This demonstrates the importance of examining individual elements of the occupation, as women with different identities and coming from different areas have differing experiences of the occupation and subsequently different ideas about resistance to it. As my diverse 'research sample' illustrates, my aim is to explore the varied ways women in Palestine experience oppression and resistance, and how these experiences might challenge our perceptions of Palestinian women, the occupation, and resistance to it, be it violent or not. This analysis reflects the theoretical underpinning of postcolonialism insofar as I aimed to challenge pre-conceptions and stereotypes of Palestinian women as the 'other' – a woman who cannot be understood by 'us' in the West.

I utilized a 'snowball' method for my sampling. At the end of each interview and with the help of my translator I asked each woman if she could suggest someone else with whom I could speak. This was advantageous in Palestinian society because the pervasive Israeli security apparatus has resulted in a need for individuals and families to be especially protective of their identities and security. Therefore, using a snowball method allowed me to tell potential participants that their friend 'X' had given me their contact details, thereby utilizing indigenous networks and methods of communication. Furthermore, my translator was a retired school-teacher who was very involved in her local community. She was able to assist with this snowball method by using her acquaintances to acquire more contacts and request interviews. I also relied on the assistance of two 'fixers.' The first was an Israeli woman who is very active in Palestinian social justice issues. She was positively invaluable to moving my research along – as well as giving me the name of a woman whom I later interviewed, she gave the contact details of a Palestinian man who often works closely with internationals facilitating contact between them and local Palestinians. He introduced me to one of my participants, and after I interviewed her, she was able to help me to 'snowball' to a further four participants. Therefore the Israeli woman was able to connect me to six participants through snowball sampling.

I undertook my field research because I wanted to include narratives from Palestinian women about their own lives. Narratives of daily-lived experience are essential within postcolonial and other critical approaches to 'terrorism' studies because of their power to expose and insurrect subjugated knowledges, and for the capability of narratives to destabilize Orientalist assumptions about daily life. Narratives of daily life can help make experiences of occupation and resistance 'intelligible' to us in ways that other methods cannot. While I went to Palestine with my research questions in mind, I wanted to conduct 'interviews' with as little prompting and questioning from me as possible. My choice of a narrative approach to experiences of subjectification and resistance was informed by a study conducted by Stern (2006), wherein a narrative approach to Guatemalan women's experiences of (in)security was employed. Stern argues that: 'The spoken story must also therefore be seen as inscribing, not only the narrative, but also the self/ subject as character in the narrative, and the narrator. Furthermore, the act of narrating occurs in a particular moment which crucially informs the story told' (Stern 2006: 184). Further, a narrative approach is aligned with values of postcolonial research because it privileges the ways Palestinian women choose to reflect on their own experiences. My aim was to encourage women to speak about anything that they thought was important for me to know about life as a woman in Palestine, how they had experienced the occupation and how they enacted resistance.

I began each interview by introducing myself and explaining my project and then asking the women to tell me stories from their lives. For many of the interviews, the explanation of my project alone was sufficient to get a long narrative from the women illustrating how their lives have been impacted by the Israeli occupation and how and why they are challenging that occupation. At times this approach led them to explain things that I never would have asked about on my own but which were very interesting and helpful. There were also difficulties with this approach, which will be explored in the reflective section of this chapter.

Before my arrival in Palestine I was in contact with a local NGO. They were extremely helpful in aiding me in my search for a translator. They arranged for me to meet a member of their women's group, named Jadwa,[1] who agreed to translate for me, and she was absolutely instrumental in my field research. When I still knew no one in the West Bank, she arranged for many of my interviews. She would then accompany me to the houses of the women she'd arranged to talk to and act as a translator. The issue of language is one of critical importance to my methodology. While it caused a few of the problems I encountered (discussed in the next section) I was able to effectively communicate with my participants and record their stories despite the language barriers. Of the 18 interviews, nine were conducted exclusively in Arabic.[2] A further three interviews were conducted in a mix of Arabic and English. Jadwa was translating the Arabic in these interviews for me. The participants in these interviews knew English and wanted to practice their language skills by speaking to me in English, but they also requested that someone be there to translate if they did not know something. The final six interviews were conducted in English. These interviews were not conducted in Arabic because the women themselves expressed to me that there was no need for me to bring a translator.

Reflecting on this field research

This section is based upon data from the reflective journal I kept during my field research. There is supporting literature claiming that reflective journals are valuable methodological tools to help researchers document and explore the challenges faced, goals met, and emotions experienced during field research and how those experiences shape and affect the methodological process (Malacrida 2007; Mauthner and Doucet 2003). Reflexivity on my methodology and issues I encountered during field research helps me to better understand why and how I got the data I did, and how changes to my approach could have given me different data. Furthermore, it allows me to think about how I had some of my own underlying assumptions about Palestinian women conditioned by Orientalist thinking. Reflexivity also provides me with the opportunity to assess to what degree I achieved my research goals and the role that ethical considerations had on my research.

Communication issues

Some of my first experiences in Palestine involved attending various 'women's groups' in and around Bethlehem. Several organizations in Bethlehem host weekly meetings for women, providing the women with an opportunity to engage in cultural activities, explore issues of faith, or to socialize with one another. Attending these meetings was a valuable experience for me because it greatly enhanced my understanding of Palestinian culture. These meetings were also an opportunity for me to meet with the women whom I would later interview, allowing them to become more familiar with me. I learned more about the social norms and expectations of women while peeling and chopping five kilos of onions and then sharing a traditional Palestinian meal with thirty-plus women then I ever could have from reading any book and I absorbed many facets of Palestinian culture during such meetings. One of the most valuable observations I made helped me to understand a difficulty I later experienced with Jadwa, my translator. Almost as soon as I set foot amidst a group of Palestinian women I observed that it is extremely rare for only one woman to speak at once. The manner of sharing stories is far more cacophonous, with numerous women, all speaking at once, over the top of one another. Even though I couldn't understand the Arabic being spoken, I could understand that people were engaging in very animated, lively, and perhaps dissonant discussions. To me, as an outsider, it seemed extremely chaotic, and my perception of these situations was that everyone wanted to be part of the conversation at the same time.

Soon after these experiences I began to perceive a possible problem with the translation during some of my interviews. I first noticed the issue during the interviews where the woman we were interviewing wanted to speak English. During the three interviews where both English and Arabic were spoken, it was almost as though Jadwa did not have a job to do. She was also familiar with two of the three women in these situations, and these three interviews were full of intervention from Jadwa. My initial feelings were of frustration, annoyance, and fear that my research process was failing. I did not know how to approach Jadwa with the issue – as she was much older than me I was extremely unsure and worried about how to explain my critique without offending her. The more I reflected on the problem, the more I came to realize that this 'interference' in the interviews may have been an aspect of Palestinian culture I had not carefully considered, and that perhaps Jadwa perceived the interviews where predominately English was being spoken as a three-way conversation rather than a time for one woman to share a narrative with me. After a great deal of stress and anxiety on my part, I decided not to speak with Jadwa about it, and these three interviews, all in close succession, were the only ones that involved a great deal of 'interference.' The difficulties I had were reflected in my reflective journal during the time I realized there was an issue, and it was helpful for me to reflect on my experiences observing groups of women as I thought about the issue with translation. Now, upon further reflection, I realize that I should have been more direct when I met Jadwa for the first time, focusing on how important it was to my research process that she only translate as directly as possible.

Despite the difficulty I had in communicating to Jadwa that I needed her to translate the interviews rather than to engage in the conversation, I rarely found it difficult to speak with the women, even when the topic was violence. The exception was when I interviewed a young woman who had spent time in prison for providing assistance to a suicide bomber/martyr by accompanying him to his target.

The young woman was very helpful and kind during our interview, but I struggled to ask her questions after she gave her narrative. In my reflexive journal I wrote that:

> I am really, really regretting not asking her this question during the interview. It popped into my head at some point, but I felt really strange asking her questions somehow. I felt less comfortable around her, not because of what she'd done, but because she had to spend so long in prison. I can't explain it, but of all the women, I was most worried of offending her by asking her an insensitive question. (Author's reflexive journal, 14 January 2012)

Upon further reflection, I think my unease about offending this research participant in some ways reflects that even despite my attention to using a reflexive postcolonial method, and my aim of destabilizing Orientalist perceptions of Palestinian women, I still had pre-existing assumptions about women who had been involved in political violence because I was preoccupied with offending her rather than treating her as I treated my other research participants. Even now this reflection is difficult for me to grapple with, and I think it illustrates how the researcher who takes reflexivity and destabilizing existing Orientalist assumptions seriously often finds herself struggling with herself.

Cultural immersion as research

Overall, as well as helping me to understand the cultural differences in communication, taking part in activities with Palestinian women was a wonderful addition to my field research. As well as taking part in structured activities with organizations, I was living with a Palestinian family. The family was Christian, so I experienced the traditions and preparations for Christmas. I garnered an even better understanding of women's roles in Palestinian society and how cooperation among women is central to daily life through observing and helping my Palestinian 'host mother' as she undertook the mammoth task of preparing food and her home for a stream of visitors that continued for three weeks. One of the most memorable experiences was preparing the Christmas cookies, a task that involved the help of no less than eight friends and relatives. Taking part in this work helped me to understand the importance of cooperation among Palestinian women and further demonstrated the dynamics of communication. Living with a Palestinian family in the West Bank gave me a much more engaging experience of some of the ways Palestinian women experience daily life. For example, when the water supply was turned off and all the water in the tanks had been used, a frequent occurrence in the West Bank where water is ultimately controlled by Israel, I was able to see how my host mother managed her house without water in the taps for three days. This method of research is support by Mies' claim that feminist research takes part 'directly within life's processes' (Mies, cited in Tickner 2006: 29). By taking part directly in the living situation of Palestinians and being involved in women's activities I feel I was able to employ participant observation as part of a critical ethnography of life under occupation.

My nationality and my passport set me apart from the Palestinians I lived with every day insomuch as it determined the treatment I received at checkpoints, it determined that I could leave at the end of my trip, and it determined that I could fly out of Ben Gurion Airport instead of having to go out through Jordan like any West Bank Palestinian who takes a flight. Using participant observation to understand life under occupation does not change the subject status of the researcher, but it does allow a vantage point that facilitates the researcher being better able to see what daily life is like. As such, my research for the day did not finish when I finished an interview, but continued as I participated in daily life with my Palestinian host family. This also contributes to the aim of destabilizing Orientalist knowledge because writing about daily life in the occupied territories destabilizes knowledges that associate Palestinians with terrorism.

Problems with the narrative approach

Upon reflection I can also understand some of the shortfalls of my approach to interviewing. At times the narrative approach went well and women shared things that I never would have thought to ask about, but at other times leaving the interview format so open-ended and unstructured posed difficulties. I often did not have sufficient questions prepared for the times when an open-ended approach to interviews did not get respondents to start talking.

As a result of conducting most of interviews in the homes (or offices) of the women many of the interviews were relaxed and natural, and most of the women needed very little prodding from me to share their stories. In all but one of the interviews I was in the room only with women and young children. Based on my reflexive journal I think that being in the setting of women's homes in particular allowed for the women, and therefore me, to be more comfortable, in part, perhaps, because they could treat me as a guest. In their home environment women could also more thoroughly engage in the traditional and infamous Palestinian hospitality. I was initially concerned that women who could not afford to treat me to tea and sweets would put undue strain on their budgets. However, after participant observation in settings where Palestinians gathered together, and after reflection, I now feel that serving me tea, coffee or sweets was a way for women to enact agency and demonstrate their pride and determination. Engaging in culturally intelligible acts of hospitality can be seen as a way that my respondents exercised power in the interviews.

Upon reflection, I feel as though being explicit in my own position allowed the women I spoke to see me as a human with emotions and opinions rather than a researcher who was only interested in data. During and after interviews the women often asked me explicitly what I thought of their situation, of the conflict, or the United States' role in perpetuating the Israeli occupation. I was always completely forthright when I was asked of my opinion. I was also aware of how important it was that I make my own nationality clear. I was often presented or framed as an 'Irish' researcher because I had come to Palestine from an Irish university and I live in Ireland. However, I am a national of the United States. This information is extremely relevant to Palestinians, as the official US government policies have almost always favored Israel.[3] Given that my time in Palestine was limited, I hope that my approach of being open with my position helped with rapport building and resulted in more open conversations between my participants and myself. The excerpt below from my reflective journal illustrates how I experienced my own position after interviewing a woman whose son was killed by an Israeli settler:

> I am so grateful to even be here in Palestine. My country has culpability in everything that has happened here, including the death of this young boy. And yet everyone welcomes me. They ask me where I'm from, and then they say 'Welcome.' And they tell me their stories. They trust me with their stories. Honestly, I don't feel worthy. (Author's reflexive journal, 17 December 2011)

Role of emotions

Emotions affected my research far more in the preparation phases prior to my departure to Palestine than they did after I arrived. Prior to leaving I was extremely worried, particularly about the safety of my translator and research participants, as well as being worried about being deported. After beginning my field research my emotions were shelved much of the time. There were certain interviews where I did experience emotional difficulty because of the types of stories that were being told[4] and I know that in those situations where women were sharing very traumatic and sad stories I was less inclined to ask them further questions. I had mentally prepared myself for hearing sad stories so these were not a shock; however, I was unprepared for how angry I grew to feel every time I traveled through the West Bank and saw settlements, checkpoints, and soldiers.

My research participants also often spoke of their anger over the situation in the occupied territories and their treatment as Palestinians. The last woman I interviewed told me about how it was particularly when she was denied her humanity or treated without dignity that she would grow exceptionally angry. She told me that dehumanization happens every day, and she explained her reaction to being dehumanized or humiliated.

> That's the thing that I can't, I don't have an answer for it, I can't answer for it, I can't handle it, I'm SO frustrated, I'm SO angry and I feel that I can actually commit a crime at that moment. That person was humiliating me, I feel, so many times I have this feeling that I could actually kill this person, if I had the chance. ('Samaah,' interview 18, 2012, Al Walaja)

For 'Samaah' as well as many of my other research participants, the relationship between Palestinians and the Israeli state was one of violence insomuch as the occupation was sustained through violence. 'Samaah's reaction of anger to the violence of the occupation was triggered when the occupation treated her as though she was not a human. This clearly relates to how Fanon conceptualizes colonization as a process which forms the colonized as subjects who can be dehumanized, and similarly how Fanon saw resistance to the colonizer as infusing in the colonized 'a new humanity' (Fanon 1963: 2). Upon reflection, my own anger can also be related to how I saw Palestinians framed as 'the other' and treated as less than human. Despite the sadness and anger I sometimes felt, most of my feelings were positive, and my research was certainly bolstered every time a woman (or anyone) expressed to me how much hope they had for the future. Overall, my mental state and my negotiation of emotion was not as difficult as I had anticipated, most of which I attribute to the positive mental attitude of almost every Palestinian I met.

Conclusion

While my methodology may not fit into the mold of 'traditional' international relations methods, my research goals were inherently to challenge the dominant picture that is painted of Palestinians by such traditional methods in international relations. Especially since the failure of the 1993 Oslo Accords and after September 11th, Palestinians are portrayed as being terrorists out to destroy Israel and all Israelis, or as being tied to a wider 'Global Islamic Jihad' (Chalk 2003; Laqueur 2003).

By starting from my ethnographic observations of daily-lived experiences and using narrative interviews I gained insight into how the occupation is experienced by women and how they expressed their roles in resistance. While my position in regards to the issue is by no means objective, I have explicitly accounted for that position and I truly feel as though it helped me gain access to insights I never would have gotten had I placed myself as an objective international researcher. Furthermore, living with a Palestinian family in the West Bank enhanced my research in ways that would have been impossible to achieve had I lived anywhere else during my stay.

Said wrote: 'All knowledge that is about human society is historical knowledge. This is not to say that facts or data are nonexistent, but that facts get their importance from what is made of them in interpretation' (Said 1997: 162). To me, this means that a researcher concerned with challenging the status quo of 'terrorism' studies needs to understand how particular 'knowledges' came about and how those knowledges are products of imbalances of power between 'us' and 'the other.' In order to challenge the association between 'Palestinian' and 'terrorist' it was crucial that I take a narrative and reflexive approach to my research in order to challenge Orientalist knowledge about Palestinians and the occupation.

Notes

1. All names have been changed.
2. Of these, Jadwa translated for five. My field research coincided with the holiday season for the Christian families in and around Bethlehem, among them Jadwa. As a result, she was often very busy with her own family and so I sometimes needed to find other translators. The remaining four interviews were translated by three other people (one woman translated two interviews for me).

3. While I was in Palestine, Republican presidential candidate Newt Gingrich made the statement that 'Palestinians are an invented people.' This comment sparked a lot of discussion with Palestinians when we talked about my national origins and the government of my country.
4. Interviews 3 and 6 were particularly difficult.

References

Chalk, P. (2003) *Non-Military Security and Global Order: The Impact of Extremism, Violence and Chaos on National and International Secuity.* London: Macmillan.

Chowdhry, G. and Nair, S. (2004) *Power, Postcolonialism and International Relations: Reading Race, Gender and Class.* London: Routledge.

Du Bois, W. (2002) *From Dusk to Dawn: An Essay Toward an Autobiography of a Race Concept.* London: Transaction Publishers.

Fanon, F. (1963) *Wretched of The Earth.* New York: Grove Press.

Hoffman, B. (1992) 'Current research on terrorism and low-intensity conflict,' *Studies In Conflict and Terrorism,* 15 (1): 25–37.

Laqueur, W. (2003) *No End to War: Terrorism in the Twenty-First Century.* London: Continuum.

Malacrida, C. (2007) 'Reflexive journaling on emotional topics: ethical issues for team researchers,' *Qualitative Health Research,* 17 (10): 1329–39.

Mauthner, N. and Doucet, A. (2003) 'Reflexive accounts and accounts of reflexivity in qualitative data analysis,' *Sociology,* 37 (3): 413–31.

Olson, J. (2004) *The Abolition of White Democracy.* Minneapolis, MN: University of Minnesota Press.

Said, E. (1997) *Covering Islam.* London: Vintage.

Said, E. (2003) *Orientalism.* London: Penguin Books.

Stern, M. (2006) 'Racisim, sexism, classism and much more: reading security-identity in marginalised sites,' in B. Ackerly, M. Stern, and J. True (eds), *Feminist Methodologies for International Relations.* Cambridge: Cambridge University Press.

Sylvester, C., Marshall, S., Mackenzie, M., Saedi, S., Turcotte, H., Parashar, S., and Stoberg, L. (2011) 'The forum: emotion and the feminist researcher,' *International Studies Review,* 13 (4): 687–708.

Tickner, J. A. (2006) 'Feminism meets international relations: some methodological issues,' in B. Ackerly, M. Stern, and J. True (eds), *Feminist Methodologies for International Relations.* Cambridge: Cambridge University Press.

PART 6
Feminism

10

MARGINALITY AS A FEMINIST RESEARCH METHOD IN TERRORISM AND COUNTER-TERRORISM STUDIES

Katherine E. Brown

Introduction

Marginality emerged as a sociological concept in the 1930s and was used to refer to those 'living and sharing intimately in the cultural life and traditions of two distinct people' (Park 1928: 892). Therefore, while it is a 'condition' inferring lack of power and poverty, it is distinct from exclusion or conceptualising as 'outside' as it implies a more connected relationship to centres of power (significantly: Wardwell 1952; Bock 1967). The marginalised are also considered hybridised identities, they are those 'who must live in, yet are excluded from, the dominant cultural order' (Ortner 1996: 181). For example, women in academia are often positioned marginally: academia is just another organisation where no woman can forget she's in a man's world – in other words that the main text is socially, politically and culturally constructed as male and supporting male privilege (Soloman 1985: xix). Gendered differential and hierarchical patterns of participation persist over the years and across universities and countries, with Acker and Armenti (2004: 23) concluding: 'All the signs pointed to women having had to struggle to achieve recognition.' Yet although women are under-represented in senior academic and administrative positions (Priola 2007; Wynarczyk 2010), in high-status disciplines (Bebbington 2002), in prestigious institutions (Hearn 2001) and in research assessment exercises (Corbyn 2009), their presence as 'good citizens' in departments and emphasis on teaching keeps universities productive. Women's ability to squeeze onto the page (but not the main text) of higher education is the story upon which the myth of progress and meritocracy in universities is narrated into existence (Berkovitch *et al.* 2012). Thus the margins are perilous zones, with inhabitants easily ignored, their journeys to the centre hindered, and they are easily erased because it is an unequal power relationship between the margins and the main text/core. This frequent travelling to the core allows greater access but with no structural power within it means the margins are also radical sites of possibility: a subversive location from which to challenge and reshape the main text. As Aoki argues 'probing [of the main text] does not come easily to a person flowing within the mainstream … It comes more readily to one who lives at the margins' (1983: 325).

Applying the insights of marginality to terrorism and counter-terrorism research reveals that marginality can be seen as a condition, as a journey and as a subversive space informing not only the object of our research, but also how we research and why we research. Terrorism itself is a contested object of research, with debates surrounding its definition absorbing many a volume. In this chapter, I broadly define terrorism and provide examples from related feminist research on conflict/violence scenarios in order to outline possibilities for critical terrorism research.

Conditions of marginality: what to research?

Feminist research into terrorism and counter-terrorism frequently begins with the assumption that that which is excluded, scribbled out in the margins, tells us more about what is understood than that which is included in the final edit. By considering women's position in terrorism and counter-terrorism, it is possible to see more on the page of international relations.

The first step towards this is to begin by asking the first feminist question 'Where are the women?' Women are often presumed to be in marginal positions in terrorist groups, their numbers and visibility are often less than those of men, but there are also the questions why and how they are placed there. For example, Megan Mackenzie (2009) looking at the disarmament, demobilisation and reconciliation (DDR) process in Sierra Leone finds that women's experiences as combatants are excluded and denied. As a result they are not given appropriate relief from the state or aid agencies working to facilitate peace. Similarly Sandra MacEvoy (2009) focuses her research on the Loyalist paramilitary women of Northern Ireland. By doing so she is able to reveal how, despite their activism and violence during the Troubles, they are excluded from the peace process. She reveals class, gender and social connections of terrorism that impact on the peace process that are otherwise dismissed. Thus we see in the exclusion of the margins in the consideration of terrorism how women's lives are systematically written out of public discourses and ideologies of security and politics (Hirschmann 1989). As Cynthia Enloe writes, mainstream terrorism studies only take the powerful into account because it 'presumes a priori that margins, silences and bottom rungs are so naturally marginal, silent and far from power that exactly how they are kept there could not be of interest to the reasoning, reasonable explainer' (1996: 188). For example, Colvin explores Meinhof's writings and through this she questions the 'fallen angel' (pacifist activist and mother corrupted by the men in her life) or 'intellectually pure' idealist (unwilling to accept the realities of East German communism) roles in which others have cast her. Colvin shows that by placing Meinhof in these categories, previous analysis place her 'marginally' in the RAF's development and actions. This occurs despite her name being used to describe the group – 'the Baader-Meinhof gang'. Colvin, however, suggests that Meinhof had a greater role to play in formulating the acts of terrorism than previously acknowledged. A similar challenge exists in recognising the agency of female suicide bombers: they tend to leave no archive or record of their own and my own work shows how their actions become understood in the main text as the responsibility of men (Brown 2011; Sjoberg and Gentry 2007). Even those involved in the process may not shed light on their marginality. Samira Jassim's video confessional of her recruitment of over eighty women in Iraq for the purposes of suicide-bombing missions reveals very little about the women's desires or motivations – rather it focuses on the men of al-Qaeda and what they did. As a result her 'confessional' ultimately displaces the agency and power of women in the group (Deylami Shirin 2013: 189–90). Indeed, while there are increasing references to the 'growing significance' and numerical rise of women's suicide bombing, this is frequently presented as a marginal and desperate tactical device used by terrorist groups (Brown 2010). But by questioning violent women's marginality, researchers are able to challenge attempts by men of terrorist groups to deny their agency when they claim that women's participation is merely a reaction to state agencies rather than a consequence of women's actions and influence. In doing so this method encourages us to take seriously how the marginal might know their condition (Spivak 1988; Guha 1983). For example, Colvin (2009) finds new revelations in West German terrorism by exploring seriously the writings of Ulrike Meinhof, rather than relying on the stories others have told of her. In studying her work it is shown that Meinhof conceptualised and thought through the relationships between language and violence in a way that pre-empts the linguistic turn in 'terrorism studies'. Implicitly Colvin is suggesting that Meinhof's works should be considered as 'expert' as those of Che Guevara or Mao. Here we can see how the field of 'terrorism' also prioritises men's writings and experiences of terrorism over those of women. Thus we see in these few feminist examples not only 'who' or what is in the margins, but also challenges to what those margins and the main text look like holistically and how the margins are filled.

However, feminist approaches grounded in marginality note that it is not just that women are marginalised, but also that they refuse to stay or acknowledge their marginality. In Pakistan women of the Red Mosque escalated religious militancy through violence, kidnapping and assault, beyond what was initially expected of the men of the group. They extended the grounds for violence and widened the range of individuals targeted, transforming the claims of the group who had to respond/react to their actions. There are also women who shape conflict and terrorist politics through their own groups. Asiya Andrabi, a prominent devout Muslim activist in Kashmir, leads the Dukhtaran-e-Millat (Daughters of Faith), an all-women's group often referred to as a 'soft terror outfit' in Kashmir (Parashar 2010: 439). Her group is explicitly and overtly religious in its nature, and believes that Jihad is the only way Islamic values can be imposed in Kashmir and the Indian state rejected. The Daughters of Faith have targeted unveiled women by throwing paint on them and vandalized cinemas and beauty parlours, arguing that they promote corruption and decadence that are dangerous to women and Kashmir (2010: 439). By targeting the spaces and places of women's lives as well as those of men, they extend the geography of terrorism and blur the public-private distinction (Mustapha *et al.* 2013). Furthermore, taking marginality rather than exclusion as a starting point enables feminists to show where feminism and gender have been influential in 'terrorism' discourses and practices. 'The War on Terror' has generated new global priorities and structures and we can also see that feminism(s)/feminist ideas have been coopted in neoliberal global policy-making and for military interventions (Eisenstein 2009; Squires 2007; Rai and Waylen 2008). There is now an 'ngo-isation' and huge demand for gender experts, and ideas of feminism have been appropriated by organisations keen to put into practice gender change for security, development and governance (Zalewski and Runyan 2013: 299). This has led to recognition that certain types of 'feminism' are facilitated, especially those that reinforce existing imperial global power politics (Abu Lughod 2002; Ferguson 2005). Kinsella (2005) argues in relation to the UN Security Council Resolution 1325 on Women and Peace and Armed Conflict that although women are recognised as combatants and perpetrators of violence, the gendered binary of protected civilian/protector combatant remains unchallenged. In *A Decade Lost* Huckerby and Fakih (2012), however, chart the failures to consider the negative impact on women, as women, of global counter-terrorism measures. Furthermore the continual need to 'prove' and count women's participation in violence renders their violence as 'exceptional' and in need of explanation, whereas male participation is treated as normal (Shepherd 2008; Enloe 2006). Furthermore, although women are seen to be involved in conflict, as McEvoy (2009) notes, it is only women who are 'neutral' or involved in peace movements that are included in formal post-conflict activities (see also Shepherd 2011). This affirms Cynthia Weber's argument that whenever feminism threatens to spill over the boundaries within which the discipline and practice of international relations has sought to confine it (such as minimising women's role in conflict and terrorism), the mainstream creates new ones or seeks to reimpose them (by casting women in particular limiting roles and ascribing their agency to men) (Weber 1994: 38). What these feminist examples demonstrate is how, by starting from the margins, terrorism studies can move beyond the spectacle of violence and reveal the entire page. We also show the 'travelling' and 'traversing' central to the concept of marginality, which distinguishes it from framing research around exclusion/inclusion binaries.

Marginality does not simply refer to the object of research, but also the artefacts and data sets used by feminists engaging in critical terrorism studies. Grounding research in an awareness of marginality also means taking seriously the discarded and the dismissed research material. For example, Sara Särmä (2012), working on fears of nuclear terrorism and rogue terrorism, developed 'junk feminism' as a way for explaining her approach. She argues that the 'junk' of the Internet, media outlets and governments reveals as much about the issues as the official reporting and expert or elite sources. Furthermore, the 'junk' material she finds relates to the official stories and can become mainstream, and vice versa. Her work is also highly 'visual' and draws on her own montages of 'nuclear' order/disorder. The role of 'visuality' in critical terrorism studies, introduces previously 'marginal' artefacts to the core of research and practice. The refusal of the US government to circulate a photo of Osama bin Laden's dead body and the circulation of pictures of torture taken in Abu Ghraib are only the most recent examples of how myths and narratives of security, terror and violence are visually constructed (Heck and Schlag 2013: 893–4). Åhäll also uncovers myths of motherhood and agency in British 'war on terror' culture by looking at a British TV series *Britz*, with a blending of machine and human, manipulating images of femininity and womanhood that 'leave one cold' and 'still removed from the reality of why a woman would chose this path' (Gentry 2012: 81; Åhäll 2012). Åhäll argues that most research focuses on the written word, and instead she engages with 'mass culture' because it is how meanings are made. Jill Gibbon's work also operates within the margins and marginality of war and terrorism as she draws undercover not in 'war zones' as conventionally understood but in the 'margins' of war: arms fairs, arms company dinners and their AGMs (Gibbon 2011, 2014). She writes:

> With few ties to any state, they sell to both sides of disputes, unstable governments, and repressive regimes. Most of these deals take place in arms fairs – trade shows for military equipment. Here, bombs, drones, tanks and guns are promoted like luxury goods. Hostesses give away show catalogues, sweets and condoms. Products are promoted for each political moment – heavy arsenal for the war on terror, 'less lethal' weaponry for the Arab Spring. New lines are launched with spectacular displays – a fashion show alongside racks of missiles, a string quartet on the back of a military truck. And between the vast bombs, tables are laid with champagne and pretzels. (Gibbon 2014)

Her art and writings of the margins, in a marginal form, reveal the connections between sex, money and terror. But she does this through 'caricature' which is deliberately exaggerated, a manual practice, and necessarily subjective. She shows that this is a 'practice-based' approach offering a different kind of knowledge through the artefacts she smuggles in and out of war zones (her sketch books) to that traditionally valued by academia (Gibbon 2010). This knowledge is garnered through the interaction between the observer's mind and body, as a sensory experience, with the observed, and rejects a mind-body dualism of rationalism. Here we see that the margins are of a different texture to the text of the main body. Working with the material of the margins also encourages feminists of critical terrorism studies to be grounded in reflexive research practices.

Marginal journeys: everyday researching

This reflexive approach means that feminist methods, and feminist research, are often located in the margins and from positions of disciplinary homelessness (Kronsell 2005; Sylvester 1994, 2002; Enloe 1996). The process of research is not only of accessing the data or entering the field, but also how that data travels in our lives and across lives.

Christina Masters (2009), in her work on Jessica Lynch and Lynndie England, asks us to consider the connections across difference, and ask after 'that which appears at the margins of the text, at the edges of the screen, on the borders of the photograph' (2009: 35). She asks for us not to consider the 'real' story, or the 'real' woman, but asks instead that we 'traverse' and read the limits of representations (rather than effecting better representations) (2009: 34). She asks us to see the women cast out of the stories told about Abu Ghraib, the female detainees, the Iraqi women 'barricaded in their homes' and the US servicewomen who have been sexually assaulted and raped by their colleagues (Eisenstein 2004). Masters argues that some women are seemingly 'present' as subjects, while simultaneously cast as absent from the political realm, as marginal to it. Instead, violence against these women is marginalised in order to protect the state and to minimise reprisal attacks (2009: 43). Here the prioritisation of state security is revealed as research and data travels from Iraq to the USA. Claudia Brunner also questions the ways in which the marginalised are reproduced in IR as they travel to academic, journalist and policy-makers' desks. She finds in writings on terrorism, and women's participation in it, how 'the secular cosmopolitan West is constructed in opposition to a ubiquitous, threatening, orientalized patriarchy' (Brunner 2007b: 958, 969). Here Muslim women's actions outside of the West 'travel' and are reinterpreted in the West as the 'irrational Other'. As Masters seeks to do, and asks others to do in their research, feminist analysis should aim to travel and traverse data and not remain static in the readings offered of them.

My own research considers how Muslim women 'traverse' across the security landscapes before them. Considering the daily insecurities of an elite but minority group of Muslim women (those studying at British universities) derived from terrorism-counter-terrorism policies and discourses, my work shows how Muslim women's insecurities are marginalised in the pursuit of an ever-expanding and intrusive 'war on terror' (Brown and Saeed forthcoming). These women are assumed to be connected to 'radicalization'. Perpetually 'at risk' of succumbing to it because of their faith, they are presented as in need of 'saving'. Yet the very place in which they might be 'saved', the university, because of its presumed embodiment of liberal values, is increasingly securitised and their presence on campuses justifies recasting higher education as a 'risky' location where Muslims may be radicalised. Like Jawahara K. Saidullah, who traces her own identity as a Muslim woman through her experiences of war and dislocation, explains: 'I was a suspect, a violent terrorist, even in my own eyes. This is what the outside world told me' (2006: 190). Aware of this, the women challenged dominant ideas of radicalization, of 'moderate Islam' and of activism, generating new meanings and shifting the boundaries of their terms in order to relocate themselves in public discourses. This shows how categories of terrorism move beyond simple binaries in the margins and take on what Tyrer (2010) calls 'degrees of alterity'. However despite their attempts to blur categories in their daily lives and transcend their assumed vulnerability, the women found they could not overcome the 'securitising' discourses about/around them. It is ultimately the 'White man' who decides what is an acceptable or unacceptable Muslim, the 'white man' who determines who are tolerated 'at given places under given conditions, in a given ghetto, while at other points simply erased' (Tyrer 2010: 105). Instead of trading 'truths' about terrorism, addressing terrorism from the margins asks us to consider the different modes of travel, or to highlight the different stories possible from our research.

Thus in traversing our data, we are also called on to reflect the stories and outcomes of our research. Parashar (2012) and others lament the elitist nature of feminist and academic writing, and she demands an 'activist' feminism that connects with the world. Pentinnen argues on behalf of the IR scholar as not only someone who reflects and represents the pains of the world, but as someone who is in active engagement with the world. In other words, we do not only write about the world out there, but we create the world through our writing. As a result, she argues, we should transport our research with a 'heartfelt' joy. She suggests that by only discussing trauma, violence and destruction we minimise human potentiality and therefore writers should seek the marginal positions in war: love, laughter and life (2013; see also Pentinnen and Brown 2013). Emotions are everywhere in world politics (Crawford 2000: 119) yet they are frequently erased in mainstream analysis – including feminist research (Sylvester 2011). MacKenzie titles her forum piece 'Their Personal Is Political, Not Mine' (Sylvester 2011) where she questions the erasure of emotions in fieldwork. In my own reflective work I have questioned the role of the body in these emotions, how the body feels and reacts in creating 'knowledge' in doing. This is a different form of knowledge, a craft-based knowledge becoming of a 'reflective practitioner'. It is a form of knowledge that I have written out of my writings for publication because publication depends instead upon the creation of 'stick figures' of fieldwork and field research (MacKenzie, in Sylvester 2011). In contrast, a feminist analysis from the margins embraces emotions, and indeed 'feeling the pain' of others, that is empathy, becomes an important part of 'being' and 'meaning making' of the world (Sylvester 2002; Sjoberg 2006). The statement in June 2002 of Cherie Booth, the Prime Minister's wife, that she could understand 'how decent Palestinians became terrorists' (cited in Walker 2011: 385) was widely commented upon and criticised by supporters of the British state and its anti-terrorism laws because it was a powerful act of empathetic cooperation and human connectedness. It was not an unproblematic speech-act, neither was it a 'perfect' act. She could speak and be heard when Palestinians could not *because* she was the wife of the Prime Minister and a QC. The power of her emotions are noticeably louder to effect/affect global politics than those of Palestinian women.

This question of silencing is quite apparent in the entire research process. As reflexive practitioners of research feminists cannot assume our marginality as women (they tend to be but are not exclusively women); rather researchers are multiply positioned vis-à-vis their research (Ackerly and True 2010). Sontag (2003) discusses the violence 'we' (feminists) do in our quest to sympathise with the marginalised, and our neoliberal imperative to act (Žižek, 2009) and publish. Zalewski and

Runyan (2013: 298) ask whether Western feminists have lingered too long on the notions of 'good' or innocent' feminist to be able to effectively cut through the undergrowth of sympathy or empathy and so instead prefer to maintain a coherent and central 'ethical feminist' self. For example, although figured as a moral, innocent antiracist response, intersectionality is arguably as much about presenting an ethical white feminist self as it is understanding the complexity of the experience of the racialised Other (Srivastava 2005: 33, 44). As Chela Sandoval writes in the *Methodology of the Oppressed* 'any "liberation" or social movement eventually becomes destined to repeat the oppressive authoritarianism from which it is attempting to free itself, and become trapped inside a drive for truth that ends only in producing its own brand of dominations' (2000: 59). As Gentry asks 'how much of it [academic feminist work] is simply riding the wave of an academic trend that has become akin to a pop-phenomenon? … How does academic knowledge-bearing contribute to the heft of marginalization?' (2012: 81). Yet as Parashar (2012) and I (Brown 2013) debated in a brief blog exchange in 2013, the failure of 'Western feminism' to stand in solidarity with other feminists and women comes at its own costs. This exchange revealed the shifting margins, their liminality and perilous nature. Indeed as Bouteldja (2010) argues: 'Why should you, white women, have the privilege of solidarity? You are also battered, raped, you are also subject to men's violence, you are also underpaid, despised, your bodies are also instrumentalized …' Applying these insights explicitly to terrorism and counter-terrorism studies encourages us to consider the negative gendered impacts of counter-terrorism, as well as that of terrorism. It means recognising as well the constraints on western academics to 'speak' and research in light of current counter-terrorism legislation (Brown and Saeed forthcoming). However it also encourages us to consider the academies' reproduction in terrorism and counter-terrorism knowledge.

The subversive category

Terrorism and counter-terrorism studies, along with the discipline of international relations more generally, has been lambasted for its prioritisation of state security, for its continual self-justification as 'useful' knowledge to state counter-terrorism agents (Tickner 2006; Jackson 2007). Tickner (2006) argues that with this comes an erosion of academic freedom and free spaces for academic critique. Giroux (2003, 2008), Armitage (2005) and Der Derian (2009) have made similar points about the militarisation of universities. However, at the same time, higher education and 'the university' is also criticised for being 'distant' from the policy world and being 'located in ivory towers'. Tickner (2006) also says that academics are watching from the 'sidelines' the development of a new empire. While she criticises our 'sidelined' and marginalised position I propose here, that it is not always an imposed nor powerless position. There is the possibility to relocate to the margins via a process of 'contentious objection' (Colley *et al.* 2007). Some theorists argue that by being deliberately situated between two groups – liminality – marginality enables a positive and unique perspective, namely 'the knowledge and insight of the insider with the critical attitude of the outsider' (Stonequist 1937: 54–5). Collins (1986: 529, cited in Gilbert 2004: 5) puts it: 'When you have mastered the dominant discourse but are still able to stand apart from it (in the margin), you are in the best most informed position to critique it.' This reconceptualises marginality as subversive and to be an academic is also to offer more than technical or problem-solving knowledge but to seek emancipatory knowledge (Cox 1981; Habermas 1971).

Unlike other approaches to terrorism and counter-terrorism, a focus on marginality doesn't seek to 'fix it' but accepts it as open-ended while at the same time clearly acknowledging power over what are and who determines the dominant expressions of terrorism research (in other words the main body). Jessica West studying the Chechen 'Black Widows' (2004/5) argues that feminists should embrace their position at the margins of the discipline, as it provides opportunities to destabilise hierarchies and exclusions upon which 'IR'/terrorism studies is based. She argues feminist scholarship should resist attempts to create a 'hegemonic femininity'. For her marginality is a site of resistance. Gibbon also does this in her art; she 'reverses the gaze' of surveillance in the war on terror (2010). She offers resistance to state power from the margins, and is only able to do so because she is located there.

However, marginality is more than just a place for resistance. bell hooks sees marginality (when not imposed) offering 'radical possibility'. This line of thinking is following on from Foucault (1977), in particular his work on the logic of unreason and discussions of madness, which enable us to see how marginalisation can have positive values and be a site of pleasure and pain. This is because existing on the margins enables individuals to see things differently because they are not so invested in the dominant discourses or bound by its conventions. In other words, the process of escaping from the narrow confinement of the professional main text to the margins furthers access to creativity. In some ways feminist responses to their disciplinary and institutional marginality are examples of this. In particular, I would like to highlight the strategies of 'homesteading' and 'empathetic cooperation' (Sylvester 1994, 2002; Kronsell 2002). Homesteading, per Sylvester, is a mechanism for expansion and radical openness rather than serving to confine and bound. Premised on the notion of empathetic cooperation, homesteading 'entails recognising that certain spaces have been marked out as homes for certain bodies, activities and talents and not for others, and it entails taking seriously the possibilities to homestead those turf-bound homes with the knowledges gleaned from infidels at the fences' (Sylvester 1994: 2). Homesteading enables a process of reconfiguring subject statuses 'in ways that open up rather than fencing in terrains of meaning, identity, and place' (Sylvester 1994: 2). Kronsell applies and develops this thinking. Beginning by noting women's homelessness in defence and military institutions and in academia (2002, 2005), she develops a method for studying their silences and absences. Homesteading, she argues, is about making a home for oneself in order to go beyond and surpass the life of contradictions and anxieties that characterises homelessness. She argues 'studying such homelessness means in practice that the researcher has to work with what is not contained within the text, what is "written between the lines"' (2002: 283). The resonance 'homesteading' has with hooks' ideas of marginality as a site of radical possibility is clear although it is perhaps more static than the concept of marginality. This begins the 'new worlds' that (hooks 1990) invites us to create and engage with.

Conclusion

Parashar asks 'whether feminism is "feminism" if it does not speak "of" and "within" the margins?' (2009: 252). First, to research within and of the margins is to recognise that marginalia are literally of a different 'texture' to the main body, but nevertheless frame the main text. Second to research is to be constantly travelling to and from the margins, and that there are various routes, which bring emotions, experiences and awareness. This is necessarily a different form of knowledge-bearing and relies on the 'craft' knowledge of the feminist researcher. Finally to research using marginality as your method offers the potential to be productive, and that even under conditions of terror marginality can be a place of resistance.

References

Abu Lughod, L. (2002) 'Do Muslim women need saving? Do Muslim women really need saving? Anthropological reflections on cultural relativism and its others', *American Anthropologist*, 104 (3): 783–90.

Acker, S. and Armenti, C. (2004) 'Sleepless in academia', *Gender and Education*, 16 (1): 3–24.

Ackerly, B. and True, J. (2010) *Doing Feminist Research in Political and Social Science*. New York: Palgrave Macmillan.

Åhäll, L. (2012) 'Motherhood, myth and gendered agency in political violence', *International Feminist Journal of Politics*, 14 (1): 103–20.

Aoki, T.T. (1983) 'Observation: experiencing ethnicity as a Japanese Canadian teacher: reflections on a personal curriculum', *Curriculum Inquiry*, 13 (3): 321–35.

Armitage, J. (2005) 'Beyond hypermodern militarized knowledge factories', *Review of Education, Pedagogy, and Cultural Studies*, 27 (3): 219–39.

Bebbington, D. (2002) 'Women in science, engineering and technology: a review of the issues', *Higher Education Quarterly*, 56: 360–75.

Berkovitch, N., Waldman, A. and Yanay, N. (2012) 'The politics of (in)visibility: on the blind spots of women's discrimination in the academy', *Culture and Organization*, 18 (3): 251–75.

Bock, E.W. (1967) 'The female clergy: a case of professional marginality', *American Journal of Sociology*, 72 (5): 531–9.

Boutledja, H. (2010) *White Women and the Privilege of Solidarity*, 4th International Congress of Islamic Feminism, Madrid. Online at: http://www.decolonialtranslation.com/english/white-women-and-the-priviledge-of-solidarity.html.

Brown, K. E. (2010) 'Contesting the securitization of British Muslims: citizenship and resistance', *Interventions: International Journal of Post-Colonial Studies*, 12 (2): 171–82

Brown, K. E. (2011) 'Blinded by the explosion? Security and resistance in Muslim women's suicide terrorism', in L. Sjoberg and C. Gentry (eds), *Women in Global Terrorism*. Athens, GA: University of Georgia Press, pp. 194–226.

Brown, K. E. (2013) 'Perfect feminism, a response to Swati Parashar', *Gender in Global Governance Net-work*. Online at: http://genderinglobalgovernancenet-work.net/comment/perfect-feminism-a-response-to-swati-parashar/.

Brown, K. E. and Saeed, T. (forthcoming) 'Radicalisation and counter-radicalisation at British universities: encounters and alternatives', *Journal of Ethnic and Racial Studies*.

Brunner, C. (2007a) 'Discourse-occidentalism-intersectionality: approaching knowledge on suicide bombing', *Political Perspectives*, 1 (2): 1–25.

Brunner, C. (2007b) 'Occidentalism meets the female suicide bomber: a critical reflection on recent terrorism debates, a review essay', *Signs*, 32 (4): 957–72.

Colley, H., David, J. and Diment, K. (2007) 'Unbecoming teachers: towards a more dynamic notion of professional participation', *Journal of Education Policy*, 22 (2): 173–93.

Colvin, S. (2009) *Ulrike Meinhof and West German Terrorism: Language, Violence and Identity*. New York: Camden House.

Corbyn, Z. (2009) 'Unequal opportunities in final RAE', *Times Higher Education*, 17 September. Online at: http://www.timeshighereducation.co.uk/story.asp?storycode=408202.

Cox, R. (1981) 'Social forces, states and world orders: beyond international relations theory', *Millennium*, 10 (2): 126–55.

Crawford, N. C. (2000) 'The passion of world politics: propositions on emotion and emotional relationships', *International Security*, 24 (4): 116–56.

Der Derian, J. (2009) *Virtuous War: Mapping the Military-Industrial Media-Entertainment Network*, 2nd edn. New York: Routledge.

Deylami Shirin, S. (2013) Saving the Enemy, *International Feminist Journal of Politics*, 15 (2): 177–94.

Eisenstein, H. (2009) *Feminism Seduced: How Global Elites Use Women's Labor and Ideas to Exploit the World*. Boulder, CO: Paradigm.

Eisenstein, Z. (2004) 'Sexual humiliation, gender confusion and the horrors of Abu Ghraib', *Women's Human Right's Net*. Online at: http://frodo.ucsc.edu/~jthomp/EH_Eisenstein_SexualHumiliation.pdf (accessed 12 February 2014).

Enloe, C. (1996) 'Margins, silences and bottom rungs: how to overcome the underestimation of power in international relations', in K. Booth, S. Smith and M. Zalewski (eds), *International Theory: Positivism and Beyond*. Cambridge: Cambridge University Press, pp. 186–202.

Enloe, C. (2006) 'Foreword', in K. Hunt and K. Rygiel (eds), *(En)gendering the War on Terror: War Stories and Camouflaged Politics*. Burlington, VT: Ashgate, pp. vii–x.

Ferguson, M. L. (2005) '"W" stands for women: feminism and security rhetoric in the post-9/11 Bush administration', *Politics and Gender*, 1: 9–38.

Foucault, M. (1977) *Discipline and Punish: The Birth of the Prison*, trans. Alan Sheridan. London: Penguin Books.

Gentry, C. E. (2012) 'Thinking about women, violence, and agency', *International Feminist Journal of Politics*, 14 (1): 79–82.

Gibbon, J. (2010) *The Art of Infiltration*. Online at: http://www.inter-disciplinary.net/wp-content/uploads/2010/04/gibbonpaper.pdf.

Gibbon, J. (2011) 'Counter-Terror Expo', *Peace News*. Online at: http://peacenews.info/blog/6443/counter-terror-expo.

Gibbon, J. (2014) *Full Spectrum Combat*. Online at: http://www.jillgibbon.co.uk.

Gilbert, J. (2004) *Performing Marginality: Humour, Gender and Cultural Critique*. Detroit, MI: Wayne State University Press.

Giroux, H. A. (2003) 'Public pedagogy and resistance: notes on a critical theory of educational struggle', *Educational Philosophy and Theory*, 35 (1): 5–16.

Giroux, H. A. (2008) 'The militarization of US higher education after 9/11', *Theory, Culture and Society*, 25 (5): 56–82.

Guha, R. (1983) 'The prose of counter-insurgency', in R. Guha (ed.), *Subaltern Studies: Writings on South Asian History and Society*, Vol. 2. Delhi: Oxford University Press.

Habermas, J. (1971) *Knowledge and Human Interests*, trans. Jeremy J. Shapiro. London: Heinemann.

Hearn, J. (2001) 'Academia, management and men: making the connections, exploring the implications', in A. Brooks and A. Mackinnon (eds), *Gender and the Restructured University*. Buckingham: SRHE.

Heck, A. and Schlag, G. (2013) 'Securitizing images: the female body and the war in Afghanistan', *European Journal of International Relations*, 19 (4): 891–913.

Hirshmann, N. (1989) 'Freedom, recognition and obligation: a feminist approach to political theory', *American Political Science Review*, 83 (4): 1227–44.

hooks, b. (1994) *Teaching to Transgress: Education as the Practice of Freedom*. London: Routledge.

Huckerby, J. and Fakih, L. (2012). *A Decade Lost: Locating Gender in U.S. Counter-terrorism*, Center for Human Rights and Global Justice. Online at: http://chrgj.org/wp-content/uploads/2012/07/locatinggender.pdf (accessed 12 April 2015).

Kinsella, H. (2005) 'Securing the civilian: sex and gender in the laws of war', in M. Barnett and B. Duvall (eds), *Power in Global Governance*. Cambridge: Cambridge University Press, pp. 249–72.

Kronsell, A. (2002) 'Homeless in academia: homesteading as a strategy for change in a world of hegemonic masculinity', in J. A. Degeorgio-Lutz (ed.), *Women in Higher Education: Empowering Change*. Westport, CT: Praeger, pp. 37–56.

Kronsell, A. (2005) 'Methods for studying silence: gender analysis in institutions of hegemonic masculinity', in B. Ackerley, M. Stern and J. True (eds), *Feminist Methodologies for International Relations*. Cambridge: Cambridge University Press, pp. 108–28.

McEvoy, S. (2009) 'Loyalist women paramilitaries in Northern Ireland: beginning a feminist conversation about conflict resolution', *Security Studies*, 18 (2): 262–86.

MacKenzie, M. (2009) 'Securitization and desecuritization: female soldiers and the reconstruction of women in post-conflict Sierra Leone', *Security Studies*, 18 (2): 241–61.

Masters, C. (2009) 'Femina sacra: the "war on/of terror", women and the feminine', *Security Dialogue*, 40 (1): 29–49.

Mustapha, D., Brown, K. and Tillotson, M. (2013) 'Antipode to terror: spaces of performative politics', *Antipode*, 45 (5): 1110–27.

Ortner, S. (1996) *Making Gender: The Politics and Erotics of Culture*. Boston: Beacon Press.

Parahsar, S. (2009) 'Feminist international relations and women militants: case studies from Sri Lanka and Kashmir', *Cambridge Review of International Affairs*, 22 (2): 235–56.

Parashar, S. (2010) 'The sacred and the sacrilegious: exploring women's "politics" and "agency" in radical religious movements in South Asia', *Totalitarian Movements and Political Religions*, 11 (3): 435–55.

Parashar, S. (2012) 'The silent feminism', *Gender in Global Governance Net-work*. Online at: http://genderinglobalgovernancenet-work.net/comment/the-silent-feminism/.

Park, R. E. (1928) 'Human migration and the marginal man', *American Journal of Sociology*, 33 (6): 881–93.

Pentinnen, E. (2013) *Joy and International Relations: A New Methodology*. Basingstoke: Routledge.

Pentinnen, E. and Brown, K. (2013) 'Conversation piece: "a 'sucking chest wound' is nature's way of telling you to slow down …": humour and laughter in war time', *Journal of Critical Studies on Security*, 1 (1): 124–6.

Priola, V. (2007) 'Being female doing gender. Narratives of women in education management', *Gender and Education*, 19 (1): 21–40.

Rai, S. and Waylen, G. (eds) (2008) *Global Governance: Feminist Perspectives*. London: Palgrave Macmillan.

Ruddick, S. (1989) *Maternal Thinking: Towards a Politics of Peace*. New York: Houghton-Mifflin.

Saidullah, J. K. (2006) 'War stories', in S. Husain (ed.), *Voices of Resistance: Muslim Women on War, Faith, and Sexuality*. Emeryville, CA: Seal, pp. 187–95.

Sandoval, C. (2000) *Methodology of the Oppressed*. Minneapolis, MN: University of Minnesota Press.

Särmä, S. (2012) 'Feminist interdisciplinarity and gendered parodies of nuclear Iran', in A. Pami, M. Sami, and H.Vilho (eds), *Global and Regional Problems: Towards an Interdisciplinary Study*. Farnham: Ashgate, pp. 151–70.

Sattherwaite, M. and Huckerby, J. *A Decade Lost*.

Shepherd, L. (2008) *Gender, Violence and Security*. London: Zed Books.

Shepherd, L. (2011) 'Sex, security and superhero(in)es: from 1325 to 1820 and beyond', *International Feminist Journal of Politics*, 13 (4): 504–21.

Sjoberg, L. (2006) 'Gendered realities of the immunity principle: why gender analysis needs feminism', *International Studies Quarterly*, 50: 889–910.

Sjoberg, L. and Gentry, K. (2007) *Mothers, Monsters, Whores*. London: Zed Press.

Solomon, B. M. (1985) *In the Company of Educated Women: A History of Women and Higher Education in America*. New Haven, CT: Yale University Press.

Sontag, S. (2003) *Regarding the Pain of Others*. New York: Farrar, Straus & Giroux.

Spivak, G. C. (1988) 'Can the subaltern speak?', in C. Nelson and L. Grossberg (eds), *Marxism and the Interpretation of Culture*. Urbana, IL: University of Illinois Press, pp. 271–313.

Squires, J. (2007) *The New Politics of Gender Equality*. Basingstoke: Palgrave Macmillan.

Srivastava, S. (2005) '"You're calling me a racist?": the moral and emotional regulation of antiracism and feminism', *Signs: Journal of Women in Culture and Society*, 31 (1): 29–62.

Stonequist, E. (1937) *The Marginal Man*. New York: Russel & Russel.

Sylvester, C. (1994) *Feminist Theory and International Relations*. Cambridge: Cambridge University Press.

Sylvester, C. (2002) *Feminist International Relations: An Unfinished Journey*. Cambridge: Cambridge University Press.

Sylvester, C. (2011) 'The forum: emotion and the feminist IR researcher', *International Studies Quarterly*, 13: 687–708.

Tickner, J. A. (2006) 'On the frontlines or sidelines of knowledge and power? Feminist practices of responsible scholarship', *International Studies Review*, 8 (3): 383–95.

Tyrer, D. (2010) '"Flooding the embankments": race, bio-politics and sovereignty', in S. Sayyid and A. Vakil (eds), *Thinking Through Islamophobia: Global Perspectives*. London: Hurst, pp. 93–110.

Walker, C. (2011) *Terrorism and the Law*. Oxford: Oxford University Press.

Wardwell, W. I. (1952) 'A marginal professional role: the chiropractor', *Social Forces*, 30 (3): 339–48.

Weber, C. (1994) 'Good girls, little girls, and bad girls: male paranoia in Robert Keohane's critique of feminist international relations', *Millennium – Journal of International Studies*, 23: 337–49.

West, J. (2004–5) 'Feminist IR and the case of the "black widows": reproducing gender divisions', *Innovations*, 5. Online at: http://www.askus.ucalgary.ca/innovations/files/innovations/Inv2005spr-2.pdf (accessed 14 February 2014).

Wynarczyk, P. (2010) 'Still hitting the ceiling', *ESRC Society Now*, Issue 6, updated 5 March 2010). Online at: http://www.esrc.ac.uk/ESRCInfoCentre/about/CI/CP/societynow/issue6/ceiling.aspx.

Zalewski, M. and Runyan, A. S. (2013) 'Taking feminist violence seriously in feminist international relations', *International Feminist Journal of Politics*, 15 (3): 293–313.

Žižek, S. (2009) *Violence: Six Sideways Reflections*. London: Profile Books.

11

TALKING ABOUT REVOLUTION

Ex-militant testimony and conditions of 'tell-ability'

Charlotte Heath-Kelly

Introduction

I clearly remember the moment when a critical methodology became necessary for my PhD research. I had just completed two of my final interviews with ex-militants from the Italian leftist struggle of the 1970s and 1980s. I was sitting by the river Tiber feeling like something crucially important had just happened to me – something that I couldn't quite put into words. Having interviewed ex-militants from the 1950s anti-colonial struggle in Cyprus the previous year, I had expected a similar type of discourse about joining militant struggles from those I spoke to in Italy. And yet there had been a profound difference in the method and content of their delivery. So I decided to sit by the river, smoking hand-rolled cigarettes, until I could fathom and express in words what had been so startlingly different about those interviews. The river was peaceful and the sun was perfectly warm, but my head felt like chaos. Something important had happened which would escape me forever if I didn't sit, relax and let it return in a verbalised and processed form. I couldn't 'find words' for several hours. Something striking had happened which I couldn't express. Why did language desert me so suddenly? How could it disappear at the point where it was most needed? After all, isn't language a tool – ever-ready for its deployment onto the world?

My inability to comprehend the importance of those interviews was actually closely linked to the methodological sea change in the project. They fed into each other. Language, I slowly realised, had been a problem for each interviewee. The past they had tried to access was not easily accessible, and not easily verbalised, despite speaking in their mother-tongues with a translator present for my benefit. And sitting by the river, I realised a profound difference in the ways that Italian interviewees spoke about the past from those I had interviewed in Cyprus. Originally I had been working on an exploration of the ways in which people came to join clandestine revolutionary groups through the influences of ideas and networks. After I sat by the river that day, I realised that each story and interview actually pointed to the retrospective constitution of those processes through discourse and power. The profound differences in 'talking about revolution' between the contexts of Italy and Cyprus came to replace the previous focus of the project. The project could never truly explore the forward trajectory of persons into militant organisations, as had been intended; instead the stories I had been told by interviewees pointed to the importance of retrospective constitution through narrative.

How do we explain who we are and the things we have done, and how are these narratives situated within contemporary arrangements of power? How do we explain the 'tell-ability' of certain stories, and the incommunicability of others? To rework the thesis in this direction, I realised I would need to shift to a critical methodology.

Before I explain this shift towards a critical methodology, and how I justified the use of feminist narrative approaches while situating them in broader poststructuralist theory, I will briefly outline the conclusions I reached while pondering my PhD thesis on that fateful day. (Although, this is also a retrospective constitution of those moments of course!) I came to realise that revolutionary moments are particularly important windows onto broader political processes which constitute authority. Revolutionary struggles overturn systems of knowledge and rule so that others may take their place. 'Politics', in Žižek's reading, refers to institutional efforts to obscure the heritage of law, politics and authority in contestation. Through retroactive legitimation, politics forgets that things could have been otherwise and retroactively posits its own causes when trying to account for the past. Politics retroactively invents its own foundations. In Žižek's account, the time of politics 'runs backwards' through this compulsion to evacuate traces of alternative paths, and to leave indicators which seem to point towards the inevitability of the present order (Žižek 1991: 201–2). To maintain the facade of a foundation for authority, politics retroactively reorganises the past and reconstitutes its origins backwards to absorb and conceal the traumatic gaps within language, subjectivity and the relationship to the sovereign (Žižek 1991: 203). It is here, perhaps, that ex-militant testimonies of revolutionary violence become so crucial to investigations of politics and authority. Politics cannot allow forms of remembering which expose this traumatic kernel that belies the foundation of authority. Certain things have to be silenced for the performance of coherent foundations.

The performance of one 'symbolic order' becomes discredited and vanishes during a revolution, before another such order is instated. This new constellation of ideas then narrates the course of history so that it ignores the 'gap' in the production of reality where such systems were overturned. This re-consolidation of political authority renders some protagonists as heroes, who narrate post-conflict history to suggest that they were always destined to overcome injustice, whereas others are subjected to the identities of 'terrorists' or 'enemies'. When these despised figures leave prison, they encounter histories of their struggles which they cannot recognise and bear no relation to their own recollections. So how should we talk about revolutionary struggles, given their retrospective constitution and the lacunas which permeate their histories? What can ex-militant testimonies from successful and failed revolutions teach us about the political constitution of authority and foundations through retrospective narration?

This chapter will draw from my doctoral research into the armed campaigns waged to overturn British colonial rule in Cyprus and against the neoliberal trajectory of postwar Italian politics. It discusses the use of tools from poststructuralist and feminist methodologies which enabled an exploration of the conditions which structure ex-militant testimony. Using interviews with fighters from the *EOKA* organisation on Cyprus and ex-militants from the Italian leftist groups of the 1970s and 1980s, the chapter reflects on the political situation of testimony – which renders some things tell-able and others unspeakable. In short, when I sat by the river that fateful day, my thesis moved from being an investigation of the journeys taken *into* radical groups to an exploration of the *retrospective* construction and narration of those journeys, one which challenged the ability of knowledge to ever access an unreconstructed moment in the past.

Why a critical method?

As my transition towards the use of critical methodology occurred late in my PhD, I will begin with the 'why' of this question before describing how I utilised critical thinkers and narrative methods to explore the retrospective solidification of meaning and history after militant struggles. Why did I need to shift towards a critical method?

When sitting on the riverbank in Rome, I had slowly realised some profound differences between the ways militant struggle had been described by protagonists from Italy and Cyprus. In the situation of Cyprus, where interviewees spoke of their participation in a somewhat successful[1] armed struggle in the 1950s against the British Empire for national self-determination, only one interviewee made a brief reference to his imperfect access to the past. His name was Spyros Stephou, and he presented a profoundly contrasting perspective to the other interviews I had carried out in Cyprus. The other ex-*EOKA* fighters had answered confidently and banished all hints of ambiguity from their testimonies. In style, Spyros' narrative was closer to that used by Italian interviewees from the leftist struggle of the 1970s and 1980s, who regularly bemoaned their loss of language in a context of defeat and their struggles to understand the past. In Cyprus, Spyros was the only ex-militant to hint that the past might not be easily accessible to present-day interpretation and contemporary language. He had regaled me over biscuits and Earl Grey tea with tales of smuggling explosives into Famagusta port and destroying freighters. But at the end of our interview he stated that he couldn't entirely explain his reasons for joining the *EOKA* organisation. He said:

> Sometimes my answers were not clear because I am personally confused also about what make me enter *EOKA*, and what make me insisting – I don't know! If I cannot explain that very clearly, how should I expect you to understand! (Stephou, quoted in Heath-Kelly 2013: 144)

Spyros had made some indications throughout our conversation that he did not have exact answers to questions about his participation in the *EOKA* struggle, but he had always previously resolved these lacunas by invoking the 'spirit of freedom' and 'Hellenic identity' which drove the fighters to struggle against the British Empire. However, his admission of imperfect access to the past, quoted above, was a striking moment of clarity. It destabilised his retrospective narration of nationalist drivers for the struggle and for his motivation to join. Furthermore, it also provided a profound contrast with the narratives given by other *EOKA* fighters. In all the other interviews I conducted with ex-fighters in Cyprus, a solid chronological narrative had been presented about the exact causes and exact motivations of the struggle – down to historical events and legacies which pre-dated the interviewees by decades or centuries. This history of the *EOKA* organisation had been almost perfectly embedded within the foundational narrative of the Republic of Cyprus, appearing as solid, uncontestable factual history through the testimonies of most interviewees, but Spyros' comments exposed a fragility to this narration of the past by momentarily stepping outside the frame. He cannot account for the factors which caused him to join the organisation. He questions the reading of history which suggests that nationalist feelings compelled all right-thinking Greek-Cypriot males to participate in the struggle for national union with Greece.

Sitting on the riverbank in Rome, after my interviews with Italian ex-militants, I remembered another curious feature of my conversations with *EOKA* fighters and their repetition of the historical narrative of conflict which centralises a powerful Hellenic identity. These conversations began with the clarification of the purpose of the interview and with the checking of interviewees names and ranks in *EOKA*, but after these initial points our conversations would turn to the question 'how did you join *EOKA*?' After the response, this introductory query would then be followed by 'why did you join *EOKA*?' This sequence of questions was intended to supplement the more mechanical detail of finding an entry point into the organisation with motivational detail. It often did not function well. On many occasions interviewees would not perceive the difference between the questions of 'how' and 'why' and would voice queries.

I found these perceptions of repetition quite interesting, as they occurred despite the phrasing of the questions in Cypriot-Greek by fluent translators. The difference between the 'how' and 'why' questions was often not perceived and was questioned. On reflection, I believe that these queries may reflect the embedding (and cross-pollination) of personal stories within the foundational myth of Cyprus. The dominant chronological account of the transition of colonial Cyprus into a republic has apparently absorbed the scope of 'why' questions within its determination of the sufficient causes of the rebellion. As such, these 'why' questions became indistinguishable from accounts of 'how' the struggle started. 'Why' has become obvious. Ex-militants were often unprepared to answer the 'why' question in Cyprus, as the struggle always goes unquestioned. Interviewees often did not have answers to draw upon about *why* they joined the organisation and would take a few moments to think before answering. However, those who regularly give interviews for Cypriot television and newspapers (I am mostly aware of these dimensions thanks to my translators) did not skip a beat in connecting 'why' questions to the situation of colonial Cyprus as slavery. Renos Kyriakides, who had been a prominent district leader in *EOKA*, engaged in the following exchange with me:

> *Me:* Why did you join *EOKA*?
>
> *Renos Kyriakides:* [without a pause] I was a slave of the British. Do you understand it when I say I was a slave? I was not a free man; I could do nothing without the permission of my master – the English. And I had the chance to study in the University of Greece. When I went there I enjoyed a free life, I could make a comparison between the free life – and the life of a slave. And I said it's better to be killed than to be slave. And this was the belief of all Cypriots at those times. And all of us fight either to be free, or to be dead.
>
> *(Kyriakides, quoted in Heath-Kelly 2013: 128)*

Most interviewees would ponder for a while before indicating that Hellenic destiny or the force of self-determination caused them to join the struggle, but Renos jumped straight in with the answer. Both Renos' immediate reference to the force of freedom and the difficulties experienced by others when distinguishing between 'why' and 'how' point to the stability of the past as narrated in the Republic of Cyprus. Renos, like other media-savvy members of *EOKA* Veterans Associations, did not skip a beat in locating the correct answer from the foundational myth. Ex-militants with less experience of interviews took a few moments to consider why they joined *EOKA*. It seemed as if this question was unfamiliar to them, as if no one had asked them 'why' before. The 'past' has been successfully managed in ways that make questions about 'why' unfamiliar and odd.

So unlike the position of Italian ex-militants, many *EOKA* fighters were not used to reflecting on the reasons for their participation. The dominant historical narrative already explains the course of the struggle and the events which provoked it. This stability of narrative has also forged a certain type of association between interviewees and their pasts – one where continuous identities are assumed. By this I mean that *EOKA* interviewees (except Spyros) did not engage in problematisations of their access to their pasts, or their understandings of their past conduct, but instead posited implicit association between their subjectivities of then and now. They continued to speak *in the name of* an *EOKA* militant without qualification.

Sitting on the banks of the river Tiber in Rome, I suddenly realised the importance of the contrast with the Italian testimonies I had collected from ex-militants of *Brigatte Rosse*, *Prima Linea* and other organisations of the tumultuous 1970s. While only one *EOKA* fighter made note of how he found it hard to account for his past actions, most Italian militants were profoundly concerned with shifts in their identities and finding explanations for their past conduct. In various ways, every Italian interviewee encountered a profound struggle when trying to narrate the past – something completely different from the context in Cyprus. Interviewees were either forced to deploy hours of chronology to attempt to explain their participation in militant groups (undermining their own efforts to communicate a clear story in the process), or dissociated themselves from the past and spoke about themselves as people with shifting identities, or heavily protested the structures of politics which simplified and condemned their struggle to an identification as 'terrorism'.

Taken alone, the length of interviews in Italy (which far exceeded the duration of interviews with victorious militants in Cyprus) also speaks to a struggle experienced by ex-militants in narrating the past in the context of the present – it has become somewhat unspeakable. This unspeakability and troubled access to the past was expressed by ex-militants in different ways. For example, Nadia Mantovani, who participated in the early years of the *Brigate Rosse* campaign, wrote me a letter after our three-and-a-half-hour interview to continue our conversation. She mentioned the frequent, unsatisfying attempts she had made to understand her past by stating:

> The purpose of this letter is to get back in touch, as well as to provide me with the opportunity to reflect, for the nth time, on bits and pieces of my life which I now often feel very far from everyday life. (Mantovani, quoted in Heath-Kelly 2013: 91–2)

Compared to the appropriation of authoritative narrator-position in most *EOKA* testimony, where ex-militants felt comfortable to speak in the name of the organisation still within the identity of a liberation fighter, this is a very different position for the speaker. Such invocations of a distance between ex-militants and the past through references to an inability to render it were a repeated feature of Italian testimonies. Many interviewees asserted that a gap exists between history as they remember it, history as it is publicly remembered and their linguistic capacity to contest the political reconstitution of the past. Such problematisations of language and history powerfully asserted that institutions had been able to discursively disconnect Italy from aspects of its past and, in so doing, hinder ex-militants' own access to their histories. Interviewees were very clear about these features of post-conflict Italy. The consolidation of Italian neoliberal politics has been performed through repeatedly narrating the defeat of the militant organisations, the continuing suppression of the alternative trajectory they offered, while simultaneously consolidating a postwar Italian identity which fetishises the anti-Nazi Resistance as nationalist (rather than socialist).

To return to Žižek, politics is founded upon the erasure of alternative trajectories. Often my discussions with Italian ex-militants would turn towards the connection between power and popular memory, given their explicit assertions of this continuing suppression of history for political purposes. For example, Sergio Segio, a founder of the *Prima Linea* militant organisation, stated that:

> Right now in Italy, sometimes they talk about armed struggle without mentioning what happened before. And those very same people who wanted to establish fascism again in Italy are back in power. And they have interests in high places. They have interests in showing these movements like monsters, as if they had woken up one morning and had arms with them and decided to

be violent. You cannot just start from the end and read the last chapter, you have to read all the book. (Segio, quoted in Heath-Kelly 2013: 92)

On other occasions, the claim that Italian politics excludes militants and rewrites history was made in a more subtle manner. For example, Susanna Ronconi focused more on the changes in cultural context that render the period inaccessible than deliberate strategies on the part of the Italian state. She stated:

It's difficult to understand that time, because back at that time you would really think in revolutionary terms [...] When now we talk about that period, we use terms that have no meaning [...] We have to use words that nowadays have no sense anymore, no meaning, it's really difficult, sometimes it's difficult for me to talk about this – because in that time it was absolutely obvious to us the world revolution, the world to change in a drastic way, the society, the state, and so on. And it was something obvious, in the cultural context. (Ronconi, quoted in Heath-Kelly 2013: 92)

This rewriting of history and/or the unspeakability of Italian testimonies compounded a difficulty for ex-militants to maintain authoritative speaking positions. Unlike ex-*EOKA* fighters from Cyprus who continued to speak in the name of the organisation, Italian ex-militants were consistently troubled by a need to explain the reasons for their conduct and even to dissociate themselves from it by asserting shifts in their identities. They contextualised their narratives of history within descriptions of a gap between their memories and history as it is publicly performed.

And suddenly, on the riverbank, the importance of political context and of winning and losing your revolutionary struggle became clear. The resetting of political reality during conflict compels those who fought losing battles to continually account for their reasons for doing so, but allows victorious militants to claim stable subjectivities across the pre-conflict and post-conflict eras. Those who 'win' do not need to explain 'why'. Conversely, those who 'lose' are not only imprisoned and tortured, but also continually subjectified as terrorists in the post-conflict era. They cannot speak. They lose the tools of language.

And I realised that talking about revolution opens windows onto political power and its constitution of the tell-able.

Which critical method?

To account for the radically different styles of testimony from interviews with Cypriot and Italian ex-militants, I required a critical method which could appropriately highlight the connections between language and power, while also enabling me to point to revolutions as integral, foundational moments in the retrospective constitution of authority. Revolutions are narrated as if political authority was always-already present, through the medium of stories about impending heroes and villains who are read backwards in time.

The method relied upon in my research was based upon a comparison of the testimonies from each conflict in the style of feminist narrative analysis, but the 'methodology' was drawn from a much wider range of critical scholars who have problematised the connections between power, history and language – such as Foucault, Benjamin, Žižek and Derrida. To begin with the method of investigation: the testimonies of interviewees were situated within explorations of the post-conflict contexts which influenced their 'tell-ability', to borrow Molly Andrews' phrase (2007). Andrews' work on narrative and political change highlights the situation of dominant histories in structures of power and explores the possibility for opening other ways of thinking and knowing through counter-narratives of political experience. But she simultaneously highlights that narrative research is more ambiguous than other forms of qualitative methodology. Narrative research, she states in an edited volume, 'offers no automatic starting or finishing points' and 'clear accounts of how to analyse the data, as found for instance in grounded theory and in Interpretive Phenomenological Analysis, are rare' (Squire *et al.* 2008: 1). There are no epistemologically agreed rules, like in discourse analysis. And yet the salience and importance of narrative research lies in its ability to bring counter-narratives into meaningful conversation with other discourses and to enable us to reflect upon practical examples of 'tell-ability' and silence and the connections between language and power. Furthermore, drawing from trajectories of poststructuralism and literary criticism in the social sciences, narrative research allows the researcher to avoid overly agentic framings of the storyteller as the gatekeeper of narrative meaning. Instead the storyteller and the society are also 'told' through the story and its silences (Squire *et al.* 2008: 3).

Using this approach, I was able to situate ex-militants within the discursive conditions of their political environments and look at the formations of language and meaning which rendered them as storytellers, while also constituting some tales as tell-able and others unspeakable. Among other things, this approach enabled me to focus on the situation of interviewee testimonies in post-conflict politics, and the ways in which 'winning' and 'losing' revolutionary struggles affects tell-ability.

When examining the lingering politics of historic conflicts, victory and defeat are points of importance. How do victory and defeat affect the tell-ability of ex-militant testimony? In one sense, we can know the presence of victory or defeat through the practices performed upon ex-militants in the post-conflict scenario. For example, are they tortured and/or imprisoned? But this is not the whole story. Victory can also be identified through narrative authority – the ability to perform a story without difficulty, to communicate something when the relationship between signifier and signified remains relatively undisturbed. Even though Cypriot *EOKA* fighters did not achieve every political goal of their organisation, we can understand them to have been victorious over the British Empire because they can tell their stories. They were not radically betrayed by language like the Italian interviewees who often confessed to sensing a profound gap between their histories and the means with which they could be expressed.

Victory and defeat are not objective categories then, but perhaps also reflect the situation of 'truth' and memory. When the ability to effectively perform a narrative of conflict is lost, we might identify defeat. As Elaine Scarry's conception of war argues, conflict is produced by the presence of two narratives which effectively de-realise each other and violent struggle functions to resolve this competition for legibility (Scarry 1985). Conflict ends when one party can successfully enforce a symbolic regime. A decisive moment occurred in both struggles where they became legible in one way but not the other. Victory, in Cyprus, can be conceived as the relatively stable harmony between signifier and signified – the hermeneutical hori-zon reset after the conflict to narrate the irrepressible force of Hellenic nationalism. Contrastingly, the defeat of the Italian groups can be conceived through the ren-dering of their narratives as unspeakable in the terms of public discourse, and the difficulties in expression experienced by ex-militants.

While using Andrews' narrative methodology to situate interviews within their respective political contexts, I also deployed a broader methodology drawn from the work of prominent philosophers who have problematised the relationship between language and power. I was to find many critical scholars whose ideas could help me to situate the narratives of ex-militants and to explain how victory, defeat and tell-ability are interrelated. In using the ideas of these thinkers, I became able to read interviewee statements as reflections upon the politicality of violence – where histories of conflict provide foundations for the performance of political authority and sovereignty.

While international relations has embraced the reductionist Clausewitzian for-mula that 'war is the continuation of politics by other means', a host of critical scholars have critiqued this instrumental reading of politics and violence. Many have argued that the popularity of the instrumental conception of violence (whereby it is conceptualised as a means to an end) is derived not from its reflection of the world, but rather from its central position within liberal philosophy. In liberal thought and practice, violence is considered to be abolished from the polity and the use of force is instead reconceived as the 'keeping of order' or security. Trajectories of thought within Marxism, feminism and poststructuralism have critiqued this assumption as a liberal fallacy which conceals the continuing perpetuation of vio-lence within the economic and disciplinary practices of politics. Here I was to find thinkers who could help me to conceptualise the interrelation of violence and power and to situate revolutions and their tell-ability within practices of politics such as the invention of foundations for authority.

Crucially important to this was Walter Benjamin's seminal 1921 contribution to the debate about violence and politics entitled 'Critique of Violence' ('Zur Kritik der Gewalt' in the original German). Reflecting upon Georges Sorel's earlier defence of the violent proletarian strike, Benjamin meditated upon the dynamic between law and violence where authority is ultimately grounded not in 'right' (as is maintained) but in the violent founding moment of political authority. Utilising the double-meaning of 'Gewalt' as both 'power' and 'violence', Benjamin argues that it is not possible to separate violence from law. Violence is bound up in the law, and is either law-making or law-preserving (Benjamin 1996: 287). It either defends the body which makes law or it overturns that regime to implement its own law. Accordingly, all law, however remote it may seem from its origins and from the forces which maintain it, is latent violence. As Anthony Auerbach has expressed this tautological circularity:

> It is violence itself which decides what violence is justifiable for what ends. (Auerbach 2007)

Interestingly, for our discussion of violence as more than the empty Clausewitzian instrument, Benjamin also invoked the language of means and ends. Beginning with a categorisation of violence as means, he progresses to deconstruct the means/ends relationship by contending that the ends never escape the means – law is founded upon violence, subsumed within violence and cannot move beyond this founding in violence. As a result, it does not make sense to talk about means and ends when discussing violence and politics. They overlap. The power which guarantees any legal contract is of violent origin, even if violence is not introduced into the contract itself (Benjamin 1996: 288). The supposed foundations of political authority are illusions. In this critique of the liberal separation between politics and violence, Benjamin shreds any distinctions between the spheres. Invoking the image of the liberal parliament, a tactic later deployed within Schmitt's anti-liberal writings, he mocked the short-term democratic memory found in parliaments which deny their roots in violence:

> When the consciousness of this latent presence of violence in a legal institution disappears, the institution falls into decay. In our time, parliaments provide an example of this. They offer the familiar, woeful spectacle because they have not remained conscious of the revolutionary forces to which they owe their existence […] They lack the sense that lawmaking violence is represented by themselves. (1996: 288)

With reference to Benjamin's destruction of liberal claims to the suspension of violence, it becomes possible to reformulate the Clausewitzian formula. Given the wonderful ambiguity of the term 'Gewalt', which signifies both political authority and violence, it becomes possible to rework Clausewitz's maxim such that Gewalt is the continuation of Gewalt by other means.

Building upon Benjamin's assertion that violence is either law-making or law-protecting, and Derrida's later appropriations of Benjamin (1990), my research was able to interrogate the functionality of militant and law-protecting violence. I became able to speak of the importance of revolutionary struggles as windows onto broader processes of political constitution and legitimation. The importance of these violent revolutionary struggles is that they point to the undoing, and foundation, of political authority. Through militant struggles to overturn a regime, we can glimpse the subsequent retroactive processes of legitimation which invent authority. A close inspection of militant violence and its subsequent tell-ability can help us to expose the constitution of illusory foundations for political authority and the other histories which are silenced to give the appearance of coherence to the dominant narrative.

Conclusion: getting messy

By way of conclusion, I would like to return to the riverbank. My methodology for the project was never that methodical. It shifted dramatically, ended up embracing the free structure of Andrews' narrative approach and then read the results through a combination of poststructuralist theories. But this slightly haphazard approach is probably closer to how life actually works than a nailed-down, tight methodological structure could ever approximate. Life is messy, my adoption of these methods was messy, and I have produced research which reflects upon the messiness of post-conflict contexts and the rendering of tell-ability.

It was only by sitting by a riverbank and dedicating myself to hearing the unobvious, to identifying the slight silences between sentences, by paying attention to the forms of speech that I would have otherwise ignored, that I was able to produce something that I am proud of. Of course, not everyone will like it. But I am convinced that critical methodologies enable one to go beyond the 'proof of facts' and to engage with mess and difficulty. In doing so, they can be quite messy in themselves. But who is scared of a little mess? Isn't mess what life and research are all about?

Note

1. The *EOKA* organisation fought against the imperial possession of Cyprus between 1955 and 1960. After the London Agreements of 1959, Cyprus became an independent (yet troubled) state. The level of *EOKA*'s success as an organisation is deeply contested because, while the British Empire was removed, the primary aim of the group (national union with Greece) was not achieved. Furthermore, ex-militants sometimes recounted the struggle as a failure due to the bi-communal organisation of the independent constitution which, they opine, led to later civil disturbances between Greek and Turkish Cypriots and the eventual occupation of Northern Cyprus by Turkey (for more detail on this fraught issue, see: Heath-Kelly 2013). However, by 'somewhat successful' I am referring to the freedom and levels of political participation enjoyed by ex-*EOKA* fighters after their struggle concluded. Unlike ex-militants from my Italian case study, they were not imprisoned or demonised as 'terrorists' by the political community they attempted to represent. They also enjoyed an ability to narrate their own history rather than needing to contest a dominant interpretation.

References

Andrews, M. (2007) *Shaping History: Narratives of Political Change*. Cambridge: Cambridge University Press.

Auerbach, A. (2007) *Remarks on Walter Benjamin's Critique of Violence*. Paper presented to the seminar 'After 1968', Jan van Eyck Academie. Online at: http://aauerbach.info/research/urban/benjamin_violence.html (last accessed 14 January 2013).

Benjamin, W. (1996 [1921]) 'Critique of violence', in M. Bullock and M. W. Jennings (eds), *Selected Writings: Volume* 1: 1913–1926. Cambridge, MA: Harvard University Press, pp. 236–52.

Derrida, J. (1990) 'Force of law: the mystical foundation of authority', *Cardozo Law Review*, 11 (5–6): 919–1045.

Heath-Kelly, C. (2013) *Politics of Violence: Militancy, International Politics, Killing in the Name.* Abingdon: Routledge.

Scarry, E. (1985) *The Body in Pain: The Making and Unmaking of the World.* Oxford: Oxford University Press.

Squire, C., Andrews, M. and Tamboukou, M. (2008) 'Introduction: what is narrative research', in M. Andrews, C. Squire and M. Tamboukou (eds), *Doing Narrative Research.* London: Sage, pp. 1–21.

Žižek, S. (1991) *For They Know Not What They Do: Enjoyment as a Political Factor.* London: Verso.

PART 7

Visual Analysis

12

VISUALIZING OTHERS

A conversation with Cynthia Weber on films and visuality in the 'war on terror'

Priya Dixit[1]

If someone is asked to describe the world around them, almost all the time they will do so in visual terms. 'This is what I see'... 'Looking at the house over there ...', 'Examining this further, I ...' Of course, this assumes the person is physically capable of seeing but it remains the case that of all the senses, the eyes and looking is often centralized in descriptions. The language of visuality has saturated our relationship with life in general and terrorism in particular. While looking might be one of the most common human actions in general scholarship on terrorism, visual methods are still making inroads. Sarah Pink describes 'visual methods' as:

> The use of visual images and technologies such as video, film, photography, art, drawing and sculpture in qualitative social research to both produce and represent knowledge. This includes using the visual as a documenting tool to produce visual records, in interviews to elicit comments from informants, in participant observation to research ways of seeing and understanding, analysing visual and material culture and using visual media to represent the findings of such research. (Pink 2006)

Thus visual methods direct attention to a study of the visual aspects of the world or to how (and to what ends and by whom) the world is visualized. In the context of terrorism and the 'war on terror,' research on visualization has examined various visual media, including TV shows, films, photographs, video games, online texts, and so on. Researchers have also produced visual media on various aspects of the 'war on terror'.

With regard to films, there have been two main ways in which films have been studied in the 'war on terror.' One, scholars have examined various films and visual media such as TV shows, documentaries, etc. in order to note depictions of security and insecurity, how the 'war on terror' is understood, how 'terrorism' is deployed in such media and the ways in which 'self' (usually the US or 'the West') and others (usually people of color) are constituted. The other way in which film is related to a study of terror(ism) and the impacts of the 'war on terror' has been through the making of various films about political violence, terrorism, and their impacts. In international relations (IR), too, more than one film about the effects of the 'war on terror' have been produced. These films – such as James der Derian's *Human Terrain* and Cynthia Weber's *I Am an American* – were made in response to the 'war on terror' or as illustrations or critiques of how people's lives in the 'war on terror' are played out. This chapter focuses on this second aspect of films, visual culture, and the 'war on terror,' and outlines the way in which IR scholar and activist Dr Cynthia Weber has produced and utilized film in her own research.

The interview process: hearing, listening, looking, seeing

It was on the afternoon of 23 March 2013 that I walked into Virginia Tech's Graduate Life Center to interview Dr Weber. She was the keynote speaker for the Alliance of Social, Political, Ethical, and Cultural Thought (ASPECT) conference on 'Border Crossings: Transnationality, Citizenship, and Identity in Theory and Practice.' The previous evening, I had attended a film showing of her film *I Am an American*. The film consists of a series of short films, all of which focus on one person or a couple. Each short film or segment starts with claim 'I am an American' made by the person and then proceeds to outline how and why they think they are a US American. During the showing of the film at Virginia Tech, a memorable moment there was when the film ended and the floor was opened up for questions – there was a long silence before numerous hands shot up.

Conference sessions were winding down in the afternoon of the 23rd. I walked into the building and one of the people asked if I was a graduate student who was visiting for the conference. I should mention I had on a T-shirt with a cartoon cat on it, jeans and yellow sneakers. I had been running late and hadn't had time to go home first – between the choice of being late to interview Dr Weber and 'proper' (or more formal) clothes, the latter had to be sacrificed. Here, we can comment on what a 'graduate student' might look like – this was the graduate center, there was a conference on and I was there. In terms of visuality, clothes, attitude (I tend to be somewhat nervous in general and especially then when I thought I was running late and had an important interview lined up), and place mattered in constituting a specific kind of 'subject' – that of the graduate student. This, of course, is an everyday illustration of how looking entails evaluation and categorization – a person becomes a specific kind of person; an issue is portrayed as a particular kind of issue in the process of being visualized. Studying a topic through visual methods directs our attention to these kinds of evaluative and categorization practices and to questions such as 'who gets to look?' 'who sees and is seen (and how)?' and 'whose categories matter?' (in terms of leading to 'general definitions'). I went to the room where Dr Weber was a discussant on a panel. Before this, we had communicated over emails as we set up the interview and, like many other IR people, I had read her work since my undergraduate days but I had never met her in person.

She was surrounded by people and I hesitated in going forward. She saw me hovering, asked if I were Priya (a benefit of having a name that remains fairly uncommon in IR circles, I guess), and excused herself from the people around her. As we walked along the corridors trying to find a good place for our conversation. I remember apologizing for taking her away from other students and faculty and her replying that it was fine. She asked me how long I had been there, what I did, etc. – this worked to calm my nervousness. In terms of an interview experience, this was one of the easiest and yet one of the more stressful. I kept telling myself that it was sheer cheek to ask such 'simple questions' (you shall see what I asked) to someone who had such extensive experience doing interviews. We found ourselves in a classroom, sat facing each other and began talking. I didn't take handwritten notes – I can barely read my own writing. Someone looking at us would have seen an almost empty classroom (though there were a couple of people towards the back of the room), trays of food lined up in the front (remnants from a reception that had occurred earlier) and semi-frequent interruptions by various people who saw Dr Weber and wanted to talk with her (I'd closed the door but there was a window from which people could see inside). I had told Dr Weber my questions would take 10–15 minutes at most; we ended up talking for almost an hour. The main topic of our conversation was, of course, visuality and visual methods – film – in understanding the effects and impacts of the 'war on terror' on questions of citizenship and belonging.

Characters seem a complete whole. Nobody is. (Cynthia Weber, 2013)

This sums up the main theme of visuality and visual methods (and interpretive research more generally). The notion that 'we' see others in their fullness and completeness is both a product of how people and issues are framed visually, especially in media and films, and also of how our language is accustomed to writing and making sense in terms of complete-ness. As Weber reminded me during our conversation, we never see the whole-ness of any character that is interviewed or presented on screen (or on paper/sound/etc.). And yet, due to editing and framing, most characters might seem complete. It seems as though we saw them in their entirety. A narrative or a framing in which 'we' only see part of a story or some of a character is often described as incomplete or quirky. Two points can be made here: one, completeness is a construction – both of our expectations of what we should read or see but also of the writer and film-maker who is building a particular narrative; two, by recognizing the incompleteness of how characters are presented on screen (for the purposes of this chapter), we can ask how did this issue or person become presented in this way? In what other way(s) could they have been presented? Thus a recognition of the power of visualizing and presenting images on screen is tied to a recognition of their instability and lack of wholeness, making us able to disaggregate what seems to be complete and ask questions about power relations, interests, and social hierarchies which lead to specific depictions of characters and issues. Visibility is a system of meaning-making practices, one which includes certain ways of seeing but also excludes others. By recognizing the incomplete-ness of characters that are filmed and presented on film, the structures of visualizing others can be questioned and dismantled, if need be.

On using film

In Weber's words, 'films can do a range of things that texts cannot do or can rarely do.' They provide an immediacy and a visuality while being more accessible. They are disciplinary interventions but also interventions into daily life and how 'we' understand the world. Weber explained that she made *I Am an American* in response to a television Public Service Announcement (PSA) which had an affective quality and moved people to tears. The advertisement aired soon after 9/11 and responses to it included feelings of patriotism and being moved by the depictions on screen. Weber says:

> I wanted to respond to it [the advertisement] because while it choked me up it also made me angry because I could see the kinds of exclusion that it was creating ... while I knew I could write about it a journal article as a response, I knew this was not going to have the same affective impact as the PSA, and it would also only reach those within the academy. So, I wanted to respond to this PSA in a way that made a political intervention – in a way that was also not just a disciplinary intervention but that was a disciplinary intervention as well.

Weber quoted James Der Derian as another scholar who uses films for disciplinary and political intervention. Films thus allow for depicting different emotions and images than texts do and also open up spaces for discussions that are often closed off in texts. Furthermore, Weber hoped that her films go 'some small way to authorizing other people to do film as research' and named Michael Shapiro, Tim Luke, and others as pioneers of using film in IR. Finally, using film was part of a dream that she had had:

> I had been working writing a textbook about film and I'd described how films worked and, as I was writing that book, I was doing a mini film studies course for myself figuring out how film worked and becoming more aware of how cameras moved and how shots were edited ... editing, it's been my fantasy ever since I was a teenager to be a film editor and when everything went digital, I was like: Oh I can do this!

On film (not) as method

Weber pointed out that film is not a method but is both a technique and an output of a research project. So, the 'how to do research?' question can be answered with 'film' and so can the 'what is the result/outcome of this research?' question:

> [Film] has to be informed by the same kinds of things that inform any kind of research project. What is the research question? What is the theory that

informs it? How do I operationalize that theory? What are my case studies? Who are my interview subjects? What do those interviews do? So what? Why does this matter? What does it do for international relations or American studies or whatever it is?

Similar to all research, a set of skills is necessary to make films. Weber adds:

> [T]o generate that research project as film you need to ask lots and lots of technical questions about film-making itself: What is your story? Who are your characters? How do you tell a story visually and orally? Will you have a narrator? What will certain cuts do? There are all sorts of technical things … how will you use sound to make transitions? What is the narrative? What is the emotional arc?

Films, just like books, are *not* research methods for Weber. Both books and films require a set of skills and grammar but the grammar of films – techniques of narration, visualization, framing, and so on – are used to show objects, spaces and peoples and to be seen. Weber gives the example of her *I Am an American* project while discussing this:

> In a sense it's like saying a book is a research method – no – a book is not a research method, an article is not a research method. But you learn a whole set of skills to writing. Grammar. There is grammar to film-making. There are visual grammars and oral grammars and a lot of us respond primarily to three things: movement, color and sound. Now, if I'm writing a book or an article, I don't get any image movement. I don't get any color. Maybe I get some color photos … but usually I don't get any color, right? And I don't get any sound. So for me I find it was more interesting in my *I Am an American* project to take my research question – how do US Americans engage with their inalienable rights to life, liberty, and pursuit of happiness during times of crisis? – and to explore it filmically.
>
> So when I take a project like the *I am an American* project which allows me to use not just sound, color and movement but a whole range of editing techniques about the juxtaposition of images next to one another to raise questions … introductions … music tracks … there's all sorts of things one can do and when I try to write about it, I find that extraordinarily difficult. I almost feel like I'm bound and gagged … that I've lost all of these tools that I rely upon to tell a story.

For Weber, using film can give voice and agency not just to herself – as the film-maker – but also to the participants in her films:

> This work is more participatory … its aim is to raise critical questions in its viewers, even in its interview subjects. It's about crafting critical theories into public engagement.

On documentary film-making and choosing data

So far, films made in and by IR scholars have been documentaries regarding some aspect of the 'war on terror.' James Der Derian, with Michael and David Udris, directed *Human Terrain: War Becomes Academic* in 2010. This film portrayed the US Army's Human Terrain System (HTS) where academics embedded themselves with the military and worked to provide socio-cultural information about various contexts (mainly Iraq and Afghanistan) to the military.

Weber talks about her own experiences in filming documentaries – in addition to the *I Am an American* project, Weber has been filming short films on how people in the US have dealt with the recession and financial crisis. Here, she talks about documentary film-making in general, focusing on how documentaries are different to reality and include the outcomes of decisions made by the film-maker regarding subjects and narratives but also regarding how people and places are framed and the storyline developed. She gives the example of the fact-based film *Argo* where viewers in the United States thought that was actually what happened, that 'US people figured out the plan and rescued the American hostages from Iran,' and says this amazes and amuses her Canadian friends, who are aware of the role the Canadian government played in devising the plan to rescue the US hostages. Turning to documentaries, Weber says that while most viewers realize documentaries are not real, the way some documentaries are presented makes it seem as though they capture rather than create reality. Weber adds:

> A documentary film is not the truth. A documentary is the creative treatment of actuality. That's the classic definition of documentary.

Regarding whose point of view is then prioritized when visualizing others, Weber points out there is always more than one point of view in any documentary. However, the main one(s) are, of course, that of the film-maker and of the people depicted in the film. In the case of *I Am an American*, there were 13 short films, each focusing on one or two people. However, there is also the overall viewpoint of the film-maker (Weber) herself. Weber makes this clear:

> So you are looking at actual events. You are filming actual people. But you are doing it for your own point of view. When I made the *I Am an American* film, I made a decision about the way in which I was going to present my 'data' and my decision was I was going to present my 'data' from two points of view at the same time which film allows you to do. One is from the narrative point of view of the subject I was interviewing whoever it may be and also from my own point of view. I can tell those two stories at the same time. The interviewee will tell the story in their own words and I represent … I edit the story in such a way that they recognize it as their story. No one's ever said to me, 'You've misrepresented me.' They've all loved their films … I don't knowingly put any falsehoods in my films, but that doesn't make them 'true.' That makes them my creative treatment of particular actualities.

I don't want the film to be seen as *the* historical record but it is *one* historical record, told from various subjects' points of view. Fourteen subjective points of view – 13 from the characters themselves and one from me. Here's a story – let's see if we can make identification happen with the audience that leads them to ask critical questions.

Here, the data is the interview itself but also images, other photographs, etc. that are usually provided by the interviewee. Weber clarifies:

Where do these images comes from? Most of these come from the individuals themselves, whether they give me the images they made or they discuss images others made [talks of Abu Ghraib images which were part of one of the short films]. You have to always be aware of who your audience is and my audience is the US citizenry and they were aware of those images and they'd have been able to take that line [where one interviewee says Iraqis were just like him] and feel that line and that's why I put those images. But those are editing decisions. That's where my point of view comes in.

For Weber, creating a 'visual imaginary' is important – not all research participants have a visual imaginary that suits what the film-maker is trying to do and show in the film. Most of us are more used to watching films – consuming a visual imaginary – rather than making them. Therefore documentaries generally stitch together individuals and their narratives into a larger whole, making it all seem seamless while it is (obviously) not. The outcome – the film itself – is the result of a series of negotiations between Weber and those she films. It is the result of editing, narrative, and story decisions made by Weber, depending on her research interests, and her commitment to have interviewees recognize their stories in her films about them. Weber explains this process through the negotiations she has with her interviewees over the 'flag shot' and the 'I am an American' line in her films:

We collaborate on these. I suggest things, but my suggestions often very seldom are taken up by my interviewees. But it is a way to get them to think about what the flag shot and the 'I am an American' line are supposed to do, how they are supposed to represent that character's relationship to the US state in relation to their story and their crisis.

On the right to look

With regard to visualizing self and others, one of the key concerns is that of the 'right to look'. Who has this? Who should have it? How does it play out in our everyday activities but also in more formalized contexts such as a documentary film (for example)? These are questions not just about how to film people but about ethical decision-making – how are people shown? – and agency. It is important to recall that once a film is made and shown in public, the characters in it often do not get a chance to speak back or look back. Thus, filmmaking (and visualizing) constitutes certain types of subjects and places individuals in particular subject positions regarding the overall research topic or the issue depicted. Weber discusses this 'right to look':

> The first thing about right to look is that no one should presume they have the right to look. You have to ask permission to tell the sorts of stories I tell on film. You have to be truthful about what your project is to the best of your knowledge and how these representations will be used.

She added that there was no legal obligation to show somebody the film before it was released but that she believed there was an ethical obligation. In one case, a person she was filming broke down in distress on film, and she kept the camera rolling for a while. She discusses the implications of this here:

> The first rule of film-making is show it, don't say it. The second rule of film-making — maybe it's also the first rule — is you never turn your camera off. But I did because I couldn't bear this [person crying on film]. It's not like you don't have a relationship with the people you're filming. You meet these people, they tell you their stories. It's such an intimate space — this is why my stories are the way they are. It's helpful that I am just one person. They are telling *me*; they are trusting *me* not to betray that trust, to portray them sympathetically. So really the question in this case — as in every case — was 'Is this gratuitous looking?' I didn't have that impression from my interview subject who was crying — who was reliving how their experience broke them — when I was filming them. Indeed, quite the opposite. That person said, 'I'm glad you are doing this. Now the world can see … I want the world to see my story.' But it's one thing to be in the moment and give me permission, and it's another thing to see it on film.

So what did she do? She went back to the person she had filmed and showed the film to them. They loved it. She says, 'It is our responsibility to ensure that the person is comfortable being looked at in that way.'

These issues of the ethics of looking as well as the creation of an 'intimate space' when filming individuals and their stories are issues that become relevant in the production of visual images. Overall, Weber's claim that is it 'our responsibility' that the person who is being looked at (photographed and filmed — visualized) is comfortable with that gaze is something that is worth teasing out further: how will this 'comfort' be assessed? How will we know if the person is comfortable or not? But this is the responsibility of those who visualize others — to make each other comfortable with the gaze and to avoid trespassing on the intimacy that is created between the visualizer and the gazed upon. Is this always possible? No. But it remains an important consideration when filming others, especially if they are vulnerable and exposed on film.

On the suitability of film for portraying violence

Often, some aspects (and issues) of the 'war on terror' are more visualized than others. For example, while there were almost daily reports of bombings in various part of the Middle East in early 2014, there was often no accompanying photograph or film of the dead bodies. Death, in the 'war on terror' seems to be invisible and often kept out of sight of viewers in the United States. This is similar with regard to civilian deaths by unmanned aerial vehicles – we read about them but generally don't see the dead bodies. Other dead bodies – US soldiers, the hundreds of thousands dead in Syria, the many children who die daily due to preventable diseases, etc. – do not get visualized either. Visualization is tied to emotion – how we the viewers respond to the images depicted on screen. Weber discusses how film – and the act of filming – can decide who appears on the film and how. She points out the appearance of films to 'capture everything' even while the actual depiction is carefully planned and filmed. She says:

> I mean let's be clear here … film is used [in many different ways] … there are film cameras on drones and these are used to target people – that's a use of film. That's violent. Film is used in Hollywood to show an explosion from five different angles. Both of these are violent but there are different modes of distancing that occur in those spaces. And if I were to use film and not get permission to expose a character's raw emotion, that would [also] be violent. So, these are just three examples. There are innumerable examples.

Furthermore, she discusses how films can lead to different questions about the world that other media generally find it more difficult to raise and to a specific kind of emotional reaction on the part of the viewers:

> I think one of the things that film can do – it doesn't have to be film – the arts can do is that they can implant a question in a person in an affective way. They can move you to feel something which is different to how you would read a journal article or an academic book – it can be a novel. A novel can implant a question in you, implant a doubt. It can move you emotionally and move you to action. If you can produce short, visual images effectively, you can move people. The best moment for me last night was when the lights came on and no one had anything to say because they were moved. That kind of silence that was produced by the experience of watching the *I Am an American* film is the kind of silence where you can think differently maybe. Not everyone will but somebody might and maybe that will do something. I don't know any other medium where I can produce work and have that effect.

Thus questions of intimacy, distance, and different meanings of violence all emerge from thinking about the role of the film-maker and the film itself.

On using films to teach (about) IR

As one of the pioneers of using visual material to learn from and teach IR, Weber elaborated upon how the 'discipline of IR was founded on an identity crisis of "do we exist as a discrete discipline?"' and discussed how films and popular culture have been seen as part of the divide between high culture and low culture 'as if there is a division between the two.' She pointed out that using visual media and placing class materials online is now encouraged and that it has become easier to use visual media in teaching. However, she added the place and the construction of the student body matters in terms of how receptive students are to the use of films and visual materials in teaching. She explains her film has been used for teaching and describes how she herself uses visual materials in her classes:

> The short films for *I Am an American* are on the website www.iamanamerican-project.com, and they are used for teaching. Indeed, that is in part what I created it for – for teaching as one form of public engagement, of engaging with students who are and will go on to be crucial members of various publics. There are strategies [to teach using visual materials]. I teach a class in Britain called 'The United States in the World' – this could be a foreign policy or a geopolitics course but I teach it as: How does the US imagine itself in the world? How is the image of the United States created by US cultural artefacts, and what do these cultural artefacts do? We look at things like the architecture of US embassy buildings. We look at specific debates and texts within IR. I use a lot of podcasts and I take students through an understanding of diplomacy from traditional to cyberdiplomacy. It's not about: Let me show a film so I don't have to teach today. It's about teaching students to critically analyze visual media. How does a film imagine the US in the world, for example?

When asked about the difference between the film *I Am an American* and Weber's accompanying book, *I Am an American: Filming the Fear of Difference*, Weber claims there is a difference between writing and seeing (on film). There follows a discussion of one of the short films, that focuses on Ofelia Rivas (http://www.iamanamericanproject.com/project%20page.html), a member of the O'odham nation, and her feelings about being American. In the film, Ms Rivas' way of life is disrupted by surveillance and monitoring practices of the US state. It is a visceral moment, one which resonated with many of the viewers present at the Virginia Tech film screening on 22 March 2013. Weber explains the difference between writing and visualizing such events:

> If *I* just wrote these stories, I think they could be dismissed as oversentimentalized. But when you actually see a person struggling through their daily lives. I mean, it's her life. You can feel your way into her predicament. Those who are more artfully expressive with words can maybe do that through writing. I can do it with film.

Film as research: is it? (and who can do it?)

Unlike other types of qualitative methods, visual methods are relatively less used in IR. Film-making, especially, remains limited with only a handful of scholars making films. Weber, however, does not think that film-making and using visual methods are only available to those who are more experienced and thus able to take on risky tasks without having to worry about being penalized. Anyone can make films – it needs dedication and a lot of practice. She says:

> There are different rewards and risks. I'm never someone who has fit in, and I'll never be someone who fits in. That 'outsider' position is helpful in my work, maybe especially in my film-making … You have to do what you feel passionately about. It took me a long time to get competent at making films, at combining that passion with visual techniques. I didn't have the skills. I made crap films for a very long time. That was actually refreshing – it felt good to be really terrible at something, because it meant I had a lot to learn. That's a nice thing to feel in the middle of your career. So I just kept making films until I learned more about what makes a good film. It's about editing, about production. You have to have a research question to make a good film.

Ironically, for Weber, her film-making isn't always recognized as 'academic research.' Weber explains:

> Academics do not always understand that film-making is research – that it is a way of investigating a research question and presenting your research results. That's annoying, both because this attitude discourages academics from making films *as* research and because it's much harder to make a film than it is to write a book, at least for me. For anyone, really, there are more steps required to make a good film than to write a good book, because you sort of write the 'book' as the paper edit of your film, and then you have to go on and make the film after that … Filming is intellectual and emotional. If you're not feeling what you are filming, you are never going to get that on film.

On the question of how film is research, Weber had this to say:

> The point of doing research is to grapple with problems but it's also to reach beyond the academy. To have an impact with what you do. If the intent of a particular project is public impact, you have to design that impact into your research from the beginning, and that's what this [film] was about for me. I was engaging with something that was very publicly impactful … I needed to explore it in those terms.
>
> I have 23 more films to make in the 'I am an American' project, and I am really excited about making them.

Conclusion

For Weber, the experience of film(ing) and making film is tied up with larger concerns about violence and how it is made sense of. Questions about inclusion – whose stories are included when saying 'I am an American' – and exclusion – who is left out – are key to how she understands research. Visual methods, therefore, can direct attention to the power relationships that underlie representations and help researchers question existing ways of seeing and representing.

Note

1. Interview with Dr Cynthia Weber, Virginia Tech, Blacksburg, 23 March 2013.

Reference

Pink, S. (2006) 'Visual methods', in V. Jupp (ed.), *The Sage Dictionary of Social Research Methods.* London: Sage.

13

FALLING BODIES

Confronting the iconography of terror

François Debrix

Fallen man

On 15 April 2013, at the finish of the annual Boston Marathon, two pressure cooker bombs were detonated within seconds of each other, leaving three people dead, and scores of runners, their family members, and spectators gravely injured. A few days later, a manhunt in the Boston area resulted in the death and arrest of the two immediate perpetrators, Tamerlan Tzarnaev (killed during a chase and shooting with the police) and Dzhokhar Tzarnaev (caught by the police and suffering from multiple wounds), two brothers originally from the Central Asian nation of Dagestan.[1] The Boston Marathon bombing quickly resurrected the specter of terrorism on US soil. Within a matter of minutes, US media drew connections between 'Terror at the Marathon' and the 9/11 attacks,[2] no matter how different these two events might have been in their execution, points of origin, and immediate effects.

Among the many images of the Boston Marathon bombing, one kept coming back over and over on TV screens, online, through social media, or in newspapers/ magazines a few days later: the image of one of the marathon runners, 78-year-old Bill Iffrig, forced to the ground by the blast within a few feet of the finish line, falling to his knees, and later helped across the line by marathon officials. This image was very powerful. It showed how fierce the bomb's blast had been, and how powerless human beings were in that precise instant. It also was quite graphic and potentially traumatic without, however, displaying gruesome injuries, dismembered bodies, or dead people. In its symbolism as well as its visual representation, this image of the Boston Marathon 'Fallen Man' (as some media networks and journalists called him[3]) was not without recalling two similarly tragic, awe-provoking, yet relatively 'clean' images from 9/11, images that also would be shown over and over: that of one of the planes impaling itself into one of the Twin Towers; and that of the towers collapsing in a cloud of dust, smoke, and debris. In those two infamous images from 9/11, no human beings were immediately visible (although other snapshots and films from 9/11 would show bodies jumping from the skyscrapers). In the Boston bombing episode, by contrast, human beings and bodies were back in the picture as the blast brought human victims to their knees, even if many of them, this time, would get up again.

The visual insistence on the Boston Marathon bombing's 'Fallen Man' is not innocent, incidental, or trivial. I want to argue here that the sight of fallen or falling bodies and, in some instances, the representational emphasis placed on the particular body parts that lead bodies to fall (reports liked to repeat that Bill Iffrig fell down because 'his knees buckled' from under him) have something to tell us about the status of the war on terror today, some 12 years or so after 9/11, and about the contemporary deployment of contemporary security politics and policies designed to 'keep us free from terror.' More broadly, I want to suggest that 'our' late Western modernity has become quite adept at dealing with falling or fallen bodies, at seeking them out, in fact, and at highlighting their presence and purpose – symbolic, aesthetic, political, moral – in societies allegedly always in need of security and moral reassurance. The falling bodies of hapless victims of terrorism in the West (like Bill Iffrig's in Boston); the fallen bodies of soldiers or government officials turned heroes when returning (some of them dead) from 'our' wars against terror in Iraq, Afghanistan, Libya, Pakistan, Somalia, and so on; the felled and often barely visible (although still seen thanks to online and digital media) killed and, sometimes, partially mutilated bodies of some of 'our' biggest villains and enemies (Saddam Hussein, Osama bin Laden, Muammar Gaddafi). These are ubiquitous sights of 'our' security politics and wars in the last decade. At some level, these images seem to tell us that, as the war on terror goes on, bodies slowly but surely are allowed back into the picture (again, we did not see many bodies in the 9/11 photos and videos, other than those of the rescuers, and we certainly were not allowed to see fallen bodies in the early years of the wars in Iraq and Afghanistan). Bodies do matter more and more, it appears, in the representations 'we' give or the stories 'we' want to tell about 'our' ongoing need for security in an always insecure world.

Fallen or falling bodies may now serve to humanize 'our' wars on terror and 'our' security politics, while continuing to dehumanize 'our' enemies. This is more or less how official and media discourses have tried to make sense of the Boston Marathon bombing's 'Fallen Man' images: resilience, courage, compassion, and collective moral uplifting in the face of terror, all centered around the sight of the body that falls but, sometimes, is propped up thanks to fellow human beings. This interpretation, comforting as it may be for 'us' to believe, is rather problematic. After all, the emphasis on some fallen or falling bodies, such as those mentioned above, should not blind us to the fact that there are many more fallen/falling bodies that we are still not allowed to see, think of, or, indeed, as Judith Butler intimates, grieve for.[4] Even the images of the dehumanized fallen bodies of our greatest enemies perform a similar task: the killed body of a terrorist or terrorizing figure seems to justify, after the fact, after the long wars and endless security operations and tracking missions, the fall of 'our' heroes (Western troops, above all), but also the invisibility of the hundreds of thousands of bodies that 'our' wars and security campaigns have forced to the ground, never to rise again.

Bringing the human back into the picture in the form of a body that is shown to be vulnerable to insecurity and terror is no guarantee that humanity is recognized or, at least, sought after in 'our' most common representations of terror and 'our' responses to it. In this essay, I want to show that the visual presence of the falling/fallen body in images/representations of the ongoing war on terror or, if you prefer, of 'our' endless crusade to fend off the evil of global insecurity, corresponds to a different logic, one for which humanity is mere afterthought. Indeed, I believe that the insistence on the image of the falling/fallen body is the assurance that the threat of terror/terrorism that anchors our contemporary politics of security will not go away and, thus, will remain productive of security policies and politics. Put differently, theories and practices of security must remain essential to the missions and workings of the Western state and state sovereignty because 'we' are repeatedly told that it is through them, and perhaps through them only, that 'Fallen Man' can stand up again.

We need to challenge the representational logic that links the moment/event of terror to the so-called humanity of 'Fallen Man.' 'Fallen Man' never falls naturally, normally, or inevitably in many of those representations of terror. 'Fallen Man' falls and, in some cases, never gets up because, as commentaries about the Boston Marathon bombing already suggested, specific body parts have been targeted. As these body parts are being hit, the unity of the body is challenged in the moment/event of terror captured by the image. The body loses its balance; it is toppled over. Knees no longer provide bodily stability. Limbs, in some cases, are torn apart. Faces are disfigured. Body parts and bits and pieces of things are all blown by the blast, merged together, unrecognizable, unidentifiable. If I am right that the iconography of the humanity of 'Fallen Man' is challenged by the presence and sight of body parts no longer serving the function of uniting the body or making it whole again, then different questions can be asked. For example, what if the sight of falling or fallen man matters, not because of the singular human body or being who drops to the ground and may or may not get up again, but because it reveals that contemporary security politics as well as the logic of terror it supposedly confronts can only conceive of the body as an amalgamation of parts or bits that can be dismantled, dismembered, or disseminated in some cases (for example, when looking at enemy or terrorist bodies) but never so when 'our' own human bodies and their assumed integrity/unity is at stake? What if the iconography of 'Fallen Man' counts primarily as a visual, narrative, or representational cover not only for what the war on terror and the contemporary politics of security do to bodies (fallen, falling, felled, or possibly fallible bodies, including sovereign bodies) and, indeed, to body parts, but also for the impossibility of the human(ized) body to stand up as one again, even 'our' Western body in need of security? These questions may well put us face to face with the 'vision of the unthinkable' or the idea of the 'unrepresentable,' as Jacques Rancière has put it.[5] But the allegedly unrepresentable becomes something, some vision, some event, that nonetheless demands to be dealt with and can no longer be deferred by allegories and iconographies of the humanity of the body. Before I touch upon these questions, the first section of this essay provides a critique of the role played by the image of the fallen/falling body in prevalent representations and interpretations of terror and security politics.

Falling for terror

The image of the falling/fallen body victimized by the act of terror is central to 'our' ways of understanding terror/terrorism, of dealing with the endless insecurity and fear brought on by it, of making sense of 'our' responses to terror attacks through war and various security strategies, and of keeping terror/terrorism alive. Thus the sight of the fallen body has become our late modern iconography of terror. Iconography, as Kristeva has explained, is primarily an invention found in medieval Christian faith that enables the image/representation of God.[6] It is, Kristeva adds, an 'economy of the visual' that ensures that the invisible or unrepresentable becomes visible or represented.[7] An icon 'inscribes' a transcendental idea or ideal into everyday life. Thus it also 'provides the conditions for the possibility of discourse on God' in this world.[8] The icon enables a 'space of representation,'[9] one that pushes the visible or the image towards the guaranteed presence of something or someone (a transcendent being, an essence) that is not materially evident and yet must order all of human life. As I will argue below, iconography always points to some kind of 'metaphysics of substance.'

As an iconography of terror, the image of 'Fallen Man' crystallizes what terror means for societies that have geared their politics of security to its prevention. This icon of terror serves as a reminder of what 'our' politics and policies stand for: resilience, perseverance, unity, victory, superiority, and, last but not least, a triumphant humanity. The ideals or values that we attach to those human sentiments and that, often, we deploy to justify 'our' wars, campaigns, strategies, policies, or measures – democracy, human rights, freedom, equality – are colorful excuses that seemingly justify 'our' quest for security in the face of endless terror threats. 'Fallen Man' as 'our' contemporary icon of terror also simplifies what is at stake in security politics, on a daily basis, at home and abroad, even if 'we' do not immediately understand it (it is, once again, the force of its 'visual economy'). Just as importantly, the glaring and glorious vision of 'Fallen Man' blinds us, too. Indeed, the iconography of terror hides as much as it illuminates. It occludes much of what takes place in the war on terror and in 'our' security operations. To start with, as I intimated above, it removes a lot of bodies, other fallen or falling bodies, from 'our' field of vision and domain of understanding.

But the image/icon of 'Fallen Man' has a pedagogical function, too. It teaches 'us,' citizens of the state/sovereign and subjects of security politics, how to behave in an age of terror and terrorism, what to expect in a security emergency, and what 'our' motivations, as human bodies, should be in a context of terror-induced generalized insecurity. 'Fallen Man' tells us that bodies will indeed fall, and that, perhaps, it is impossible *not* to fall when assaulted by terror. More crucially perhaps, it reveals that falling does not have to be a permanent condition (for 'us,' at least), that it may only be a painful, dramatic, and traumatic phase leading to recovery, response, retaliation, resilience, re-affirmation, possibly resurrection. All these concepts and beliefs were famously invoked by George W. Bush during his first address to the nation after the 9/11 attacks.[10] But they may be better allegorized by the icon of 'Fallen Man' today, whether it is in the image of Bill Iffrig getting up again to finish the marathon in Boston, or in the eulogies recalling the courage and abnegation of 'our' fallen troops whose dead (but supposedly not forgotten) bodies are returned to 'us' from the various hot zones of the war on terror.

Even if terror is what forces us to fall to the ground, even if terror is, as Adriana Cavarero suggests, a force that pushes us to flee,[11] terror always allows the body – at least, the surviving or resilient body – to come back, or to rise again, in one way or another. Contemporary security politics relies on this conditioned belief in human resilience, on this allegorized power to run away, perhaps, but only in order to better return, more united, and, possibly, more resolute and powerful. This, I think, is what the iconography of 'Fallen Man' tells 'us' as well. It explains that terror is a dynamic force or, again as Cavarero argues, that it has a movement or, in fact, *is* the very definition of movement. Yes, terror forces movement; it leaves us with no choice but to escape and run (thus, ironically perhaps, a marathon was always going to be a prime site for an iconography of terror). But terror enables a dynamic opening too, a physics of response and return. We run away, and we may well fall as we try to escape, but it is only to better regroup or restart. 'Our' contemporary security politics actively rely on this expectation to regroup, return, respond, and restart that, as Cavarero puts it, is part of the dynamics/physics of terror.[12] In fact, contemporary security politics is premised upon the expectation and anticipation that terror attacks and terrorist actions will occur and demand a response, often an already anticipated reaction. Even when an attack takes place, the techniques and technologies mobilized in the act of terror, innovative as they may appear to be, present security politics with an opportunity to reorganize itself, to rearrange its *dispositifs*, and indeed to resecuritize aspects of social life that were always potential targets of terror even if they had not been prioritized in previous security strategies or designs. Put differently, terror does not prevent security from deploying its modalities of action/operation. Rather, terror provides security with a chance to be reassessed, recalibrated, or redirected. In the process, terror also gives security systems new ways to reinvest bodies (soldiers, government officials, security forces, but also, and more crucially, the bodies of the state's citizens). This probably explains why, for many individuals working for the state's various security agencies today, dealing with terror/terrorism amounts to being involved in a constant play or game where guessing, anticipating, preempting, reacting, and retaliating are key. In other words, terror and security are part of the same motion, of the same physics of movement, of the same dynamic and fluid domain where falling, rising, falling again, and rising again (and so on) are normal occurrences.

It is such an acceptance of terror as part of the processes of everyday security (or, perhaps, the acceptance of security as part of everyday terror) that the iconography of 'Fallen Man' helps 'us' to understand. That 'Fallen Man' indeed falls should not and cannot prevent bodies from rising again and, more importantly perhaps, from stopping the course or movement of security politics. In fact, it is mainly through security politics, as we saw above, that human bodies are today enabled to get up and stand tall again. 'We' can get up and stand tall thanks to 'our' wars (that also make some of 'our' fallen bodies into the nation's heroes), thanks to 'our' security operations overseas (that ensure that the felled bodies of 'our' dehumanized enemies will never rise again), and thanks to an array of security and safety procedures and devices 'at home' (that guarantee that the vast majority of the state's or nation's human bodies will be ready to get up and move along even if an attack is to take place on home soil again).

Thus one could say that the politics of security in an age of terror has fallen/falling bodies as its primary object. This point should not only be taken to mean that both terror and security politics target bodies, individual and collective, through many of their operations and executions. It is undoubtedly the case, and many contemporary studies emphasizing the relevance of biopower/biopolitics in security configurations have covered much of this terrain.[13] But biopolitically informed perspectives may not be sufficient here (as I have suggested elsewhere[14]). To say that contemporary regimes of security have the icon of 'Fallen Man' as their main object also means that security politics and terror, together, as part of their endlessly dynamic encounter, want to make sure that any question regarding the unity or integrity of the body is not raised. That a body brought down to its knees by a terrorist bombing must get up and walk or run again (and live to tell about it), or that a body's disappearance as a result of an improvised explosive device must never be a vain loss, speaks to the ideas or values of human resilience, continuity, or unity that are expected of the human body in security politics and, even, in what security politics understands terror to be and do. Put differently, security politics and its understanding of what terror is and does to human bodies insists on maintaining a 'metaphysics of substance' at the very heart of both terror/terrorism and its security challenges.

Simply stated, the 'metaphysics of substance' guarantees that there is always an image of the human body, a representation of an embodied humanity, that can be found in both terror and security politics. As Elizabeth Povinelli explains, the metaphysics of substance has served to anchor the body to the idea of the unity or identity of being throughout Western modernity.[15] One could say that the metaphysics of substance goes back to Aristotle's discovery of 'social man' whereby the main characteristic of being alive and human is associated with the capacity of the human body to exhibit individual qualities that give it a political/social presence (or identity). Povinelli writes that substance, attached to a human body, reflects 'a hierarchy of being in which being has a primary sense (substance) and a secondary sense (qualities, quantities, relations, and modalities of substances).'[16] Thus each substance represents some being, or essence, yet each embodied substance also has fundamental characteristics derived from its primary being. For human beings, the primary substance is to live (zo), but this being/life is qualified as having or representing a humanity, which becomes essential to the meaning of having/being a human body (*bios*).[17] The quality of humanity, this metaphysics of substance, stipulates, demands, that beings and bodies (characterized as selves, subjects, individuals, agents, citizens, and so on) be prioritized as what or, rather, as who must be preserved, who must continue to live, and whose existence and bodily permanence cannot be questioned, let alone interrupted. The humanity in and of beings and bodies must be immutable. And moral, political, and cultural institutions must elevate it as such since it represents the primary (human) substance as the 'singular, stable, independent, and ultimate referent.' Thus humanity marks the presence of (indeed re-presents) 'an immovable and unmoving being.'[18]

The preserved unity or resilient continuity of the body of 'Fallen Man' (as an icon of terror) sustains the requirement in the contemporary politics of security and terror for the continued dominant presence of the metaphysics of substance. We may say that security politics represents 'our' last line of defense, not so much against terror per se, but rather against the loss or meaninglessness of the metaphysics of substance. To lose the metaphysics of substance would *not* be terrorizing since terror, as we saw above, does not really problematize the integrity of the body and humanity. Rather, to lose the metaphysics of substance would be what I would call horrifying. The horror (not the terror) provoked by the possible disappearance of the metaphysics of substance is something that is far more unbearable to the idea of humanity than the idea of terror. Whereas terror remains 'in line' with security, horror is what 'our' politics of security cannot confront and must representationally cast away. Yet, perhaps, such a horror is already announced in the targeting of and focus on body parts in the iconography of suffering and terror, something that the next section starts to explore.

A horrifying parody of terror

I want to turn to the relationship between the targeting of body parts and the confrontation with horror, a horror that may well be already on display in the image of terror. But to start to perceive the horror already at work in the sight of terror, we need to defamiliarize ourselves with the iconography of 'Fallen Man' and with the promises it appears to offer to political, moral, and cultural regimes of representation still dependent upon a metaphysics of substance. Here, I wish to introduce a deconstructive detour, one enabled by another vision of 'Fallen Man.' This deconstructive detour is provided by Don DeLillo's post-9/11 novel, *Falling Man*, which recounts the disjointedness of a few New Yorkers' lives in the days and months that followed the attacks of 11 September 2001.[19]

What DeLillo's novel provides is a counter-iconography of terror. In *Falling Man*, there is no humanity that responds or stands up again in the wake of the trauma. As 'Fallen Man' falls, and falls again, DeLillo's characters are faced with a blank screen, a void, a boundless and banal incomprehension. The survivors go on living their lives with the paralyzing images of the fallen (for example, those who jumped to their death from the burning Twin Towers), of the dead, and of those never-to-be-found-again forever engraved in daily routines, in one's sense of normalcy. DeLillo's fallen or falling bodies have a contagious effect. But instead of uplifting, reviving, or resurrecting, this counter-icon of 'Fallen Man' contaminates 'us' and condemns 'us' to a blunt realization: humanity is always 'beyond reach.' This is perhaps not so much what the 9/11 event reveals (for there is little place for 9/11 as an event in DeLillo's text). Rather, what the languishing hours, days, weeks, and months after 9/11 convey is that there is not and perhaps never was such a thing as a human community, human communication, or human communion organized and united against terror, or possibly 'evil,' or anything that causes harm to the human body. All there always ever was is an 'inoperative community,'[20] an incomplete or unfinished mode of communication among individual bodies and lives that, far from bearing witness to a metaphysic of substance, incarnates an existential or melancholic aimlessness, meaninglessness, and vulnerability.

Some passages from DeLillo's *Falling Man* poignantly illustrate this inoperativeness of the iconography of 'Fallen Man.' In the days that followed the 9/11 attacks, a stuntman/street performer simply referred to as 'Falling Man' had become famous for faking his own fall (and death) by jumping from tall structures in the city. The act typically took place in front of huge crowds of terrified New Yorkers who were left to wonder about the meaning (and apparent visual cruelty) of the performance. One afternoon, on one of her walks through the city, Lianne (one of the protagonists of the novel) comes upon what seems to be Falling Man. The following are excerpts from DeLillo's rendition of this encounter:

> It took a moment for him to come into view, upper body only, a man on the other side of the protective fence that bordered the tracks. He wasn't a track worker in a blaze orange vest. She saw that much. She saw him from the chest up … He seemed to be coming out of nowhere. There was no station stop here, no ticket office or platform for passengers, and she had no idea how he'd managed to gain access to the track area. White male, she thought. White shirt, dark jacket … The man had affixed the safety harness to the rail of the platform … She moved back. She moved the other way, backing into a building that stood on the corner. Then she looked around for someone, just to exchange a glance … She wished she could believe this was some kind of street theater, an absurdist drama that provokes onlookers to share a comic understanding of what is irrational in the great schemes of being or in the next small footstep … This was too near and deep, too personal. All she wanted to share was a look, catch someone's eye, see what herself was feeling. She did not think of walking away. He was right above her but she wasn't watching and wasn't walking away … Lianne tried to understand why he was here and not somewhere else. These were strictly local circumstances, people in windows, some kids in a schoolyard. Falling Man was known to appear among crowds or at sites where crowds might quickly form. Here was an old derelict rolling a wheel down the street. Here was a woman in a window, having to ask who he was … He stood balanced on the rail of the platform.

> The rail had a broad flat top and he stood there, blue suit, white shirt, blue tie, black shoes. He loomed over the sidewalk, legs spread slightly, arms out from his body and bent at the elbows, asymmetrically, man in fear, looking out of some deep pool of concentration into lost space, dead space.[21]

DeLillo's depiction of the scene at times seems to evoke the image or sensation of the planes bursting into the Twin Towers. Perhaps it can be read as an allegory for it, albeit one deprived of the meanings and categories 'we' have tried to attribute to the event, after the fact (attack on the homeland, America versus terror, the 'evil' of terrorism, US security threatened, war on terror justified, etc.). But Falling Man's act is a very strange allegory of terror and of its meanings for the US nation, American people, and the US government. The fall of Falling Man is carefully planned, stylishly performed, and meticulously choreographed. It may mimic the terror/terrorist attacks this way. But it also renders them commonplace (by reproducing the performance of falling/fallen bodies throughout the city). Perhaps it is the choreographed replay of the 9/11 images and story, the meanings 'we' are supposed to get out of this iconography of terror, that this Falling Man's fall/jump toward a suspension of both life and death (he does not die but his body remains lifelessly suspended) wishes to mimic. In this way, critically perhaps, it aims to achieve maximal effects of awe and incomprehension, not so much about the terror attacks themselves, but about the discourses and representations of them, the political and ideological justifications they enable, and their rationalizations.

As Lianne's bodily expressions betray, Falling Man does not provoke terror among the onlookers. Instead, Falling Man freezes the body of the spectator in horror. De Lillo continues:

> She slipped around the corner of the building. It was a senseless gesture of flight, adding only a couple of yards to the distance between them … She watched him, her shoulder jammed to the brick wall of the building. She did not think of turning and leaving … They all waited. But he did not fall. He stood poised on the rail for a full minute, then another … Then she began to understand … he wasn't here to perform for those at street level or in the high windows. He was situated where he was … waiting for a train to come, northbound, that is what he wanted, an audience in motion, passing scant yards from his standing figure … The man stared into the brickwork of the corner building but did not see it. There was blankness in his face, but deep, a kind of lost gaze … The train comes slamming through and he turns his head and looks into it (into his death by fire) and then brings his head back around and jumps … Jumps or falls. He keels forward, body rigid, and falls full-length, headfirst, drawing a rustle of awe from the schoolyard … She felt her body go limp. But the fall was not the worst of it. The jolting end of the fall left him upside-down, secured to the harness, twenty feet above the pavement. The jolt, the sort of midair impact and bounce, the recoil, and now the stillness, arms at his sides, one leg bent at the knee. There was something

awful about the stylized pose, body and limbs, his signature stroke ... She could have spoken to him but that was another plane of being, beyond reach.[22]

Lianne, De Lillo notes, attempts a half-hearted movement away from the scene, but she cannot walk or run away (to gather herself, to call the police, to ask for help). She is tethered to it. She cannot grasp what she is witnessing. But she also cannot prevent herself from staring at it (the 'absurdist drama,' the irrationality in 'the great schemes of being'). Falling Man does not seem to have any grand scheme either ('a blankness in his face' and 'kind of a lost gaze'), other than to fall/jump in front of an 'audience in motion' who may or may not be able to capture the act. In fact, falling in front of a moving audience may be the act's only objective: to force some of them to stop running, to block their movement/motion, to compel them *not* to get up by turning their backs to the moment/sight of trauma, to transform their terror into horror.

Falling Man is never presented to Lianne, and to the reader, as an entirely human form, as a human being, with a clear, perhaps recognizable, identity. Nothing about his appearance reveals human traits, or a unity/integrity about his body. Lianne can only describe him by the clothes he is wearing. His choreographed postures are those of a lifeless puppet, an automaton. His shape merges with the surroundings (the rail, the platform, the train, the 'lost and dead space' around). More tellingly perhaps, what appears to be his body is depicted as a loose collection of body parts: his 'upper body' is the only thing Lianne sees for a while; his legs, arms, and elbows are displayed 'asymmetrically,' his face is blank, his limbs are jolted and evoke an 'awful stylized pose.' Faced with this amalgamation of parts, Lianne's body too is rendered purposeless, almost lifeless: she wants to walk away but cannot; she hopes to catch someone else's eyes or 'share a look' to see 'what she is feeling,' but does not manage to do so; she could have tried to speak to him but that was always 'beyond reach.' She, like Falling Man, becomes completely anonymous. Falling Man's body fragmentation and its resistance to identity, human unity/integrity, and indeed substance seem to proliferate similar effects to other bodies and forms around. This is also why Falling Man's performance is *not* about offering an allegory of terror. Rather, I would argue that Falling Man – the stylized performance, the dismembered and upside-down dangling body, and the novel's narrative itself – is a vision of horror.

Conclusion: confronting the iconography of terror with horror?

DeLillo's *Falling Man* is an iconoclastic moment. It confronts the ideology of substance and human permanence/resilience represented by the icon of terror with a deconstructive vision and narrative about the human body and life in a seemingly endless aftermath of terror/terrorism, war, and prevention performed through everyday security politics. DeLillo's *Falling Man* does not really antagonize the icon of 'Fallen Man' – the body who is blown by the bomb or the planes, falls down, but may rise again and sometimes even 'makes it across the line.' Rather, in its form and performance, Falling Man's act parodies this icon of terror. Eventually, it decenters it too by revealing that the visual representation of terror has no core, no essential substance, no identity, and perhaps no body. What sustains and maintains the appearance of the body captured by the icon of 'Fallen Man' is a loose and fragile agglomeration of body parts that, when terror's violence hits, are likely to 'buckle' under the pressure, collapse the unity/integrity of the human body, and eventually may become undistinguishable from non-human matter. What 'Fallen Man' as an icon of terror must never reveal, then, is the fragility or accidentality that is the configuration, form, or idea of the body as one or as whole, as a so-called human unity, or as an image of embodied continuity, integrity, or completeness. Yet this is precisely what DeLillo's Falling Man's performance shows us: the appearance of the unity of the human body, and human life, is always propped up and maintained by an arrangement of very autonomous, frail, and vulnerable body parts, a plurality of precarious bits that we are faced with during or as a result of the terror event.

What is not acceptable for the human body and that, in their own (but often complicit) ways, terror and security strive to occlude is the incongruity or incommensurability of the vulnerable body, the looseness or disconnectedness of the body's parts, and sometimes the horrifying rawness of exposed and mangled flesh that not even 'our' politics and policies of security can prevent (in fact, 'our' security politics and policies, by continuing their association or play with terror, perversely add to such vulnerability or rawness). Even in the moment of terror, the reunited, recomposed, or indeed resecuritized body must never give way to the sight of the disconnected and scattered body parts. Security's body of terror ('Fallen Man' as the icon of terror) cannot become a body of horror, that is to say a frozen, paralyzed, or immoveable body that is already in excess of its so-called human unity, integrity, or completeness. And yet, one must also wonder why, if this is the case, if occluding the sight of the body of horror has become humanity's categorical imperative, so many of 'our' contemporary images and sights of terror (starting with the image of 'Fallen Man' at the Boston Marathon bombing) seem to refuse to do away with a certain fascination with the horrifyingly disjointed or dismembered body parts that cause human bodies (just like material structures) to collapse and force human lives to vanish in a cloud of dust, debris, and other remains of things and objects.

Notes

1. See Globe Staff, '102 hours in pursuit of Marathon suspects,' *Boston Globe*, 28 April 2013. Online at: http://www.bostonglobe.com/metro/2013/04/28/bombreconstruct/VbSZhzHm35yR88EVmVdbDM/story.html.
2. See, for example, 'Boston Marathon bombings victim: it reminded me of 9/11,' *The Telegraph*, 21 October 2013. Online at: http://www.telegraph.co.uk/news/worldnews/northamerica/usa/10020061/Boston-Marathon-bombings-victim-it-reminded-me-of-911.html. See also 'Boston Marathon terror attack,' *CNN online*, 22 April 2013. Online at: http://www.cnn.com/interactive/2013/04/us/boston-marathon-terror-attack/.

3. See, for example, Matilda Battersby, 'Image of terror: 78-year-old runner knocked over by second Boston Marathon blast,' *The Independent*, 16 April 2013, Online at: http://www.independent.co.uk/news/world/americas/image-of-terror-78yearold-runner-knocked-over-by-second-boston-marathon-blast-8574515.html. See, also, Marc Tracy, 'The fallen man: marathons push ordinary people to be extraordinary. One photo from Monday's bombing made that clear,' 15 April 2015, *New Republic*. Online at: http://www.newrepublic.com/article/112927/boston-marathon-bombing-fallen-man-photo.

4. Judith Butler, *Frames of War: When Is Life Grievable?* (London: Verso, 2009).

5. See Jacques Rancière, *The Future of the Image* (London: Verso, 2007).

6. Julia Kristeva, *The Severed Head: Capital Visions* (New York: Columbia University Press, 2012), pp. 48–51.

7. Ibid., p. 51.

8. Ibid., p. 52.

9. Ibid., p. 55.

10. George W. Bush, 'Address to the Nation on the Terrorist Attacks,' 11 September 2001. Online at: The American Presidency Project, http://www.presidency.ucsb.edu/ws/?pid=58057#axzz2iJMceZ4F.

11. Adriana Cavarero, *Horrorism: Naming Contemporary Violence* (New York: Columbia University Press, 2009), pp. 4–5.

12. Ibid., p. 4.

13. See, for example, Achille Mbembe, 'Necropolitics,' *Public Culture*, Vol. 15, No. 1 (2003), pp. 11–40; Jenny Edkins, Veronique Pin-Fat, and Michael Shapiro (eds), *Sovereign Lives: Power in Global Politics* (London: Routledge, 2004); Elizabeth Dauphinee and Cristina Masters (eds), *The Logics of Biopower and the War on Terror: Living, Dying, Surviving* (London: Palgrave, 2006); Michael Dillon, 'Governing terror: the state of emergency of biopolitical emergence,' *International Political Sociology*, Vol. 1, No. 1 (2007), pp. 7–28; Butler, *Frames of War*; Julian Reid, *The Biopolitics of the War on Terror: Life Struggles, Liberal Modernity and the Defence of Logistical Societies* (Manchester: Manchester University Press, 2009); François Debrix and Mark Lacy (eds), *The Geopolitics of American Insecurity: Terror, Power and Foreign Policy* (London: Routledge, 2009); Luis Lobo-Guerrero, *Insuring Security: Biopolitics, Security and Risk* (London: Routledge, 2012); Brad Evans, *Liberal Terror* (Cambridge: Polity, 2013).

14. See François Debrix and Alexander Barder, *Beyond Biopolitics: Theory, Violence, and Horror in World Politics* (London: Routledge, 2012).

15. Elizabeth Povinelli, *Economies of Abandonment: Social Belonging and Endurance in Late Liberalism* (Durham, NC: Duke University Press, 2011), pp. 106–7.

16. Ibid., p. 106.

17. I draw this distinction between *zo* and *bios* from Agamben. See Giorgio Agamben, *Homo Sacer: Sovereign Power and Bare Life* (Stanford, CA: Stanford University Press, 1998).

18. Povinelli, *Economies of Abandonment*, p. 106.

19. Don DeLillo, *Falling Man* (New York: Picador, 2007).

20. As Nancy may put it. For Nancy, the 'inoperative community' is marked by the 'wasting away of liberty, of speech, or of simple happiness.' See Jean-Luc Nancy, *The Inoperative Community* (Minneapolis, MN: University of Minnesota Press, 1991), p. 1. Might we read DeLillo's *Falling Man* as a Nancyan fable about the rendering impossible or unworkable of the late-modern community?

21. DeLillo, *Falling Man*, pp. 159–64.

22. Ibid., pp. 164–8.

PART 8

Conclusion

14

CONCLUSION

Beyond terrorism?

Priya Dixit and Jacob L. Stump

Books on terrorism are produced at the rate of one every six hours. And yet terrorism scholars have acknowledged that the amount of research that goes into producing these books is minimal. Schmid and Jongman write, 'There are probably few areas in social science literature in which so much is written on the basis of so little research' (1988: 177). In addition to a lack of systematic research, there is also a lack of information summarizing and evaluating the current state of research in terrorism studies. Ranstorp claims, 'Far too few books, chapters, or journal articles actually exist taking stock in a unifying sense of the terrorism studies field to account for what we know; how we know what we know, and what research questions we ought to focus on in terms of individual and collective research efforts' (2009: 14). On the whole, there is a lack of 'evidence-based research' and of primary sources more generally (Ranstorp 2009: 17). There is also an excessive focus on al-Qaeda and related issues since 9/11 but also 'a paucity of work on the history of terrorism and theoretical/conceptual aspects' (Ranstorp 2009: 23). Furthermore, many scholars do not wish to be associated with 'terrorism studies' because of what they view as a lack of rigorous research standards (Gunning 2007: 380–1).

Recent books on critical terrorism studies have called for an increase in systematic research on terrorism and, especially, a focus on interpretive, critical methods. For instance, while a new book on terrorism comes out roughly every six hours, only three books evaluating the state of the field and its future directions have been published in the last ten years (Dolnik 2011). A brief survey of some of the major catalogues on terrorism studies indicates a lack of scholarship on research methods in general and critical methods in particular. *Conducting Terrorism Field Research: A Guide* (Routledge, 2013) edited by Adam Dolnik is one of the few research methods books on terrorism and, even then, it focuses on fieldwork methods and the challenges and opportunities in doing fieldwork. For anyone contemplating doing fieldwork, it is an excellent source with chapters ranging from discussions on why fieldwork is needed, how to interview elites, and the challenges and dangers of interviewing 'illicit non-state actors.' This is combined with case-related examples from Argentina, Northern Ireland, Southeast Asia, the Middle East, and Palestine/ Israel. Discussions of interviewing (and being in the presence of someone about whom you are going to write) are illuminating and useful.

And yet there is something missing here. Something unacknowledged. Almost all of the essays in Dolnik's collection are written by scholars from the Global North, who have the institutional and financial (and 'reputational') backing to be able to justify why they are doing what they want to do. They are often written by scholars who are not 'of' the area they are writing about and so can enter and leave more easily than someone who might be working in a local university and thus face a more immediate danger when talking with those considered 'terrorist.' There needs to be a deeper acknowledgement that not everyone has the resources to conduct fieldwork, especially if that person is a student or located in a part of the world in which research overseas is not easy. This calls for a greater recognition that scholars from and located in the Global South are unlikely to find it easy proposing and conducting fieldwork in the Global North.

This is something that our book, by presenting a series of different ways of doing critical, interpretive research, hopes to direct attention towards. This is not to say that we have provided a comprehensive overview of the many ways in which critical scholarship can proceed. No, what we have done here is to provide a range of ways of doing critical research that includes but also goes beyond fieldwork. We hope that the essays here inspire critical terrorism researchers to seek out more research by authors working outside conventional and traditional perspectives, and especially to seek out scholars from both the Global North and Global South as a means of learning from and engaging with alternative perspectives. Someone located in a university in the Global South may not be able to research radicalization in the United Kingdom or 'lone wolf terrorism' in the United States easily. They can, however, look at how such 'terrorism' and the figure of the 'lone wolf terrorist' or the 'radicalized Muslim' is produced in media, official documents, popular texts and everyday conversations (e.g. looking at tweets and social media) of people in the UK or the US. As such, the collection of essays we include here provides resources for scholars who may otherwise be unable to conduct critical scholarship as well as to those who are interested in learning more about the types of research that critical terrorism scholars are doing.

Many of the authors here have made it clear that they pursued critical (broadly defined) methods when they found their research puzzles could not be explored by conventional methods. This indicates that, while there is a proliferation of scholarship on terrorism, there is far less information on how to ask questions about meanings, representations and identities; how to shift focus away from the state to other levels; how to discuss historical connections and disconnections and how to focus attention on the knowledge-producing aspects of terrorism scholarship. One of the goals of this book was to provide readers with a sense of the wide array of pluralistic research methods that exist to study political violence termed 'terrorism' and also to indicate how a diverse range of scholars have used these different critical methods in their own works. These chapters are illustrations of how a particular research methodology has been adopted by scholars studying terrorism, broadly understood.

Directions for critical terrorism research

Some future directions for utilizing critical research methods in terrorism studies are discussed in the following sections.

Talking to 'terrorists' ... but also counter-terrorists

As examples in this book show, one of the growing areas of research is in ethnographic research of 'terrorists.' Joseba Zulaika and William Douglass's *Terror and Taboo* remains exemplary in this but scholars such as Harmonie Toros, Jeroen Gunning, John Horgan, Charlotte Heath-Kelly, Sophie-Anne Hemmingsen, among others, have also conducted fieldwork among so-called 'terrorists.' Yamuna Sangarasivam and Caitlin Ryan's chapters here are based on fieldwork in areas affected by both 'terrorists' and the 'counter-terrorist' state (Sri Lankan and Israel-Palestine). However, there remains potential for further research not just on 'talking to terrorists' but also 'talking to (counter-)terrorists'. Government officials, policy-makers, and especially security personnel who actually conduct operations in the name of 'terrorism' can be sources for how and why they act in the way(s) they do. Kerry B. Fosher investigated some of these processes, for example. She participated in and observed the construction of homeland security in Boston in the weeks and months following the events on 11 September 2001 in New York City (2009). In the process, the researcher may be able to interrogate the concepts and ideas of the security personnel and policy-makers themselves. The intimacy in interviews and in the fieldwork process might lead to a questioning and self-reflexivity on both sides. At the same time, by asking counter-terrorism officials to justify their actions and to explain them, their worldviews and how they make sense of 'terrorism' can be explicated and perhaps even challenged as part of the fieldwork and interview process.

Another possible avenue for research is to note how 'terrorism' and 'terrorists' have been made sense of outside of the 'usual places,' which tend to be the UK, the US and other English-speaking countries. Toros' work in the Philippines, Sangarasivam's in Sri Lanka and Heath-Kelly's in Italy are a start but there remain avenues for research even within the United States and its allies. States in the Middle East and their labeling of 'terrorism,' militia groups in the United States and their actions against the state, and so on are all avenues for asking how and why 'terrorism' is (and is not) used by the public, by government officials, by the media, etc. to make sense of particular events and actions.

Popular culture and world politics: speaking differently

The chapters by Weber and Debrix discuss the visual aspects of 'terror' and 'terrorism' but in different ways. Debrix focuses on photographs of the aftermath of what has been labeled 'terrorism' (the Boston bombing) and Weber outlines the challenges and benefits of producing popular culture artefacts as a critical scholar. Critical terrorism scholars have thus not just analyzed fiction and TV shows, films (and other forms of popular culture) but are now beginning to produce popular culture artefacts themselves. Jackson, in his chapter, describes his 2014 book *Confessions of a Terrorist* in which the discussion between a 'terrorist' and his interrogator is the central narrative. By writing the book, Jackson claims he is able to say things and express ideas that would otherwise be difficult to present in an academic journal article or a book manuscript.

Cynthia Weber makes a similar claim when discussing why she makes films – that films give her a way to engage with the audience that would otherwise be difficult, if not impossible. She also explains how films have affective qualities and engage the viewer on an emotional level, thus shifting and perhaps rearranging the self-other relationship from one in which the 'other' – the 'terrorist' – is always a dangerous threat to one where there is empathy between the film-maker, the viewers, and the subject ('terrorist' or otherwise). Future critical research could also produce visuals – films, photographs, perhaps even TV shows, etc. Other outputs could be written documents such as literature or genre fiction. Songs and poetry might be other media for engaging with the question of 'terrorism.'

Both Jackson and Weber direct attention to transdisciplinary research on terrorism, which draws from sociology, film studies, cultural studies, and creative expressions. The question of where such work might 'fit into' traditional international relations or security studies might be raised, but this assumes critical terrorism research has to remain within restrictive boundaries. Instead, the kind of research that Jackson and Weber have done indicates the possibility of going beyond disciplinary boundaries which restrict the type of output that is permissible with regard to research on terrorism. In other words, novels, songs, plays, and films about terrorism and about relations of communities to 'terrorists' are ways in which critical scholars can transverse various disciplines and produce a different form of research product.

Analyzing social networks: connections and ties, not individual entities

The development of new tools has provided a growing resource for critical scholars to use in exploring new and different research questions. Analyzing social networks offers the possibility of investigating, for example, Western citizens who go to fight in the Middle East and North Africa. What are (some of) the social ties that make such outcomes possible (friendship/alliances/religious/etc.)? What social ties have been weakened such that a feeling of belonging in 'the West' is not present (community/friendship/etc.)? Here, the research question is not: how have they been radicalized/turned into a jihadist/etc.? Instead, it is to ask which connections between particular individuals (or events or institutions) are strong or weak such that the outcome of the person leaving a social welfare state that has fairly good civil rights for its citizens to go to fight in a foreign country where they often have never been before becomes commonsensical?

A social network-based analysis examines relationships and ties rather than individuals. The overall structure of the network thus formed and the positions of 'nodes' (individuals, institutions, etc.) within the network become important rather than the dispositions of particular communities or individuals. For such analysis, open source data, including those from social media, can be used. Another possible data source would be the interviews that are collected in fieldwork or statements by 'terrorists' and others.

Aesthetics of terror(ism)

One of the key areas for the development of research methods in CTS is studying modes and practices of visual representations. For example, visuality is centralized in how 'insurgents' and 'targets' are determined by the United States and its allies and in eliminating them. The change from 'safe' individuals to threats and targets occurs partly due to visualization tools – surveillance technologies, cameras, and individuals viewing movements of other individuals on television screens. Visualization is also key in determining where unarmed aerial vehicles (drones) kill those deemed to be dangerous and in ensuring that death has occurred.

Visualization is not just centralized in determining who is targeted for killing, it also forms a key identity marker for those deemed different (and thus dangerous) within liberal democratic states such as the United States. Recent revelations about the New York Police Department spying on US Muslims (ACLU n.d.) is worth recalling here. Critical research could draw historical continuities with past practices that discriminated against people of color. Another possible avenue for visualization-related research is to study how those who visualize and kill others – e.g. drone operators, engineers who design drones, etc. – feel about and understand their actions. Research on how 'terrorism' and 'terrorists' have been visualized and portrayed in official and popular sites is another possibility. In much of these, the techniques and practices of visualizing – looking – can be studied. How are particular subjects visualized? Who is not visualized? What techniques of visualization operate in the process of looking at others and constituting them as 'dangerous'? What meanings of events and actions are promoted within specific ways of looking? Such questions become centralized when using visual methods.

Aesthetics can also include studying spaces and built environments. For example, critical scholars such as Heath-Kelly have examined memorials to terrorism. Jack Santino, in *Signs of War and Peace*, examines memorializations of violence in Northern Ireland. An awareness of and theorization of space also means discussing which spaces are visible and talked/written about and which are not. Discussing marginality, Brown writes (quoting bell hooks) that marginality is a site of radical possibility. This potential for something different and for creating a different set of relations with those considered 'terrorist' can be further researched.

Emotions and embodiment

Research on emotions and bodily representations is another avenue that is still lacking in CTS. How do people feel horror? Terror? Insecurity? What are the possible effects of emotions on counter-terrorism officials or insurgents or 'jihadists' or the general public? Related to this is the question of how the body of an individual can be theorized as it relates to or is engaged in acts of violence. Debrix writes: 'Bringing the human back into the picture in the form of a body that is shown to be vulnerable to insecurity and terror is no guarantee that humanity is recognized or, at least, sought after in "our" most common representations of terror and "our" responses to it.' In short, the way in which (some) bodies are portrayed and made visible and others ignored and made invisible are aspects of the study of terrorism that can be further pursued. Weber also pays attention to emotions and how film-making and films are used to communicate emotions, both of the people who are on film and of the film-maker herself. She claims: 'These issues of the ethics of looking as well as the creation of an "intimate space" when filming individuals and their stories are issues that become relevant in the production of visual images.' Tied into emotions are thus questions of intimacy and connecting with the research participants, issues that many of our authors foreground.

Worlding terror

The question of 'worlding' also becomes important when considering what the future of terrorism studies might involve. Worlding directs attention to the generative potential of meaning-making practices while reminding us that what is known now may change in the future. Studying the various understandings and historical developments of 'terrorism,' one can critique conventional understandings of terrorism and counter-terrorism but also how these current meanings are raced and gendered. The usefulness of terrorism in maintaining imperial relations of power is one aspect of research that Sangarasivam discusses: 'Terrorism is of cultural value to empire. As a place where imperial sentiments of nationalism and patriotism are nurtured and galvanized, terrorism is of cultural value for creating and maintaining a cohesive and unified national identity …' This is something worth recalling as critical research on terrorism expands.

Future research can examine and outline how 'worlding' occurs differently, depending on one's standpoint for researching 'terrorism.' The process of constructing different worlds is a concern of Spencer who writes, 'Thereby the chapter shows that metaphors do not only describe reality but they actively take part in the construction of the world as we see it, think of it and ultimately react to it.' For him, language and how it is used makes up the world as we know it. Hence, language – written and spoken – becomes important to analyze. Joseph emphasizes how a study of particular texts is not just about those texts but 'the crucial point then is that the question of how to read documents is intimately connected to the question of how to conceptualise the wider social context.' Maher and Thomson provide a timely reminder that terrorism is not studied in isolation; instead, it is part of a social system in which other aspects of the system are also relevant and inter-connected: 'Capitalism should not be understood myopically: it is not simply an economic system, but constitutes a whole way of being and acting. Capitalism is thus a political, economic and social force that shapes and continually interacts with certain outcomes, including terrorism.'

This process of worlding is also a concern for Toros who advocates 'speaking with' research participants and seeing what used to be called 'research subjects' as 'co-participants' in research. She acknowledges there is a power asymmetry between the researcher and the research population but calls for 'acknowledging the micro-level details and being aware of the process of talking, listening, hearing.' This bodily engagement – all the senses are involved in this research – becomes part of how future researchers can centralize a constant awareness of themselves and others in the context of doing research.

The chapters provided here are starting points to conducting research which, previously, would have been difficult to do. The way these chapters are written shows how it is not always possible to speak and write about research. In the words of one of the authors:

> Something important had happened which would escape me forever if I didn't sit, relax, and let it return in a verbalised and processed form. I couldn't 'find words' for several hours. Something striking had happened which I couldn't express. Why did language desert me so suddenly? (Heath-Kelly this volume)

In explaining this, Heath-Kelly directs attention not just to a lack of methodological diversity in terrorism studies but also to the continued silences – of issues of race, of analysis of class, of studying the effects of colonialism, of interrogating gendered structures of power, of asking questions about why is there so little primary research on terrorism – that still exist in terrorism studies. This book is a small step in the attempt to open up these conversations and provide some tools for future researchers to continue making critical terrorism studies more pluralist.

The future of critical scholarship can also go 'beyond terrorism' as it studies political violence or non-violence more generally, and goes beyond the state to a study of the everyday experiences of people who live in situations of violence. There is need for further research that examines insecurities and violences and how they are present in the daily lives of peoples, such that the experiences of 'terrorism' and the embodiment of 'terrorism' can be studied. Ryan (this volume) alludes to this:

> From my conversations with Palestinian women, and my travels through checkpoints and demonstrations and kitchens and women's groups, I came to understand how violent responses to the occupation are but a small element in the tapestry of women's resistance, and that focusing only on these small elements of violence would only contribute to the association of 'Palestinian' with 'terrorist.'

Let us end by a reminder that 'terrorism' – its meanings and how it is understood – changes over time. Jackson (this volume) makes this clear:

> These questions suggested that there was a great deal more to 'terrorism' than simply acts of political violence committed by small groups of dissidents – acts which could be objectively identified, measured and analyzed using empirical methods. Rather, they suggested that terrorism was a much broader and more complex cultural-political discourse made up of a series of narratives, metaphors, predicates, labels, assumptions and discursive formations. Moreover, it was a discourse that changed and shifted over time and place.

The authors in this book claimed space for doing research on terrorism, differently. They have found languages to ask questions that would ordinarily be silenced in terrorism studies and picked up tools that often remain unused in scholarship on terrorism. While carving spaces for change is a praiseworthy aim and we need to keep working at this, it is also essential to remember that there should also be a commitment to interrogating and dismantling existing modes of thinking, writing, representing, and communicating terrorism which mainly privileges a 'Western' masculinized view of the world. The chapters in this book are a start towards that goal.

References

American Civil Liberties Union (ACLU) (n.d.) *Factsheet: The NYPD Muslim Surveillance Program*. Available online at: https://www.aclu.org/national-security/factsheet-nypd-muslim-surveillance-program (accessed 12 April 2015).

Dolnik, A. (2011) 'Conducting field research on terrorism: a brief primer,' *Perspectives on Terrorism*, 5 (2). Available at: http://www.terrorismanalysts.com/pt/index.php/pot/article/view/dolnik-conducting-field-research/html.

Dolnik, A. (ed.) (2013) *Conducting Terrorism Field Research: A Guide*. New York: Routledge.

Fosher, K. (2009) 'Yes, both, absolutely: a commentary on anthropological engagement with military and intelligence organizations,' in J. D. Kelly, B. Jauregui, S. T. Mitchell, and J. Walton (eds), *Anthropology and Global Counterinsurgency*. Chicago: University of Chicago Press.

Gunning, J. (2007) 'A case for critical terrorism studies?' *Government and Opposition*, 42 (3): 363–93.

Jackson, R. (2014) *Confessions of a Terrorist*. London: Zed books.

Ranstorp, M. (2009) 'Mapping terrorism studies after 9/11: an academic field of old problems and new prospects,' in R. Jackson, J. Gunning, and M. B. Smyth (eds), *Critical Terrorism Studies: A New Research Agenda*. New York: Routledge.

Santino, J. (2004) *Signs of War and Peace*. Basingstoke and New York: Palgrave Macmillan.

Schmid, A. and Jongman, A. (1988) *Political Terrorism*. New Brunswick, NJ: Transaction Publishers.

Zulaika, J. and Douglass, W. (1996) *Terror and Taboo: The Follies, Fables, and Faces of Terrorism*. London and New York: Routledge.

INDEX